MARY NORWAK'S
Guide to
Home Freezing

MARY NORWAK'S
Guide to
Home Freezing

WARD LOCK LIMITED·LONDON

Acknowledgements

The author and publishers would like to thank the following firms and institutions who have provided pictures for this book:

Bacofoil Ltd (opp. page 25); British Egg Information Service (part of the Eggs Authority) (opp. page 184); Cadbury Typhoo Food Advisory Service (opp. page 185); Electrolux Ltd (betw. pages 24–25); I.A.Z. International (UK) Ltd (opp. page 24); Lakeland Plastics (Windermere) Ltd (polythene bags – betw. pages 24–25); Pasta Information Centre (opp. page 121); Thorpac p.l.c. (foil and plastic containers – betw. pages 24–25).

Text © Ward Lock Limited 1982
Illustrations © Orbis-Verlag für Publizistik 1982

First published in Great Britain in 1982
by Ward Lock Limited, 82 Gower Street,
London WC1E 6EQ, a Pentos Company.

Line drawings by Sue Sharples
Text set in 11/13 Times Roman by
E.B. Photosetting Ltd., Speke, Liverpool.

Printed and bound in Spain by
Editorial Fher, Bilbao

British Library Cataloguing in Publication Data

Norwak, Mary
  Mary Norwak's guide to home freezing.
  1. Home freezers—Amateurs' manuals
  I. Title
  641.4'53   TX610

  ISBN 0-7063-6194-6

Contents

Introduction

The advantages of home freezing, bulk buying and batch cooking are now appreciated by more and more people, both town and country dwellers. An efficient home-freezing system can save money through economic purchasing of seasonal or commercially frozen raw materials, and can also save shopping and cooking time. Many women now work outside the home, and there is tremendous growth in the field of leisure activities and adult education, so that many families rarely eat together in the traditional way. A freezer in the home can simplify the problem of trying to shop at odd hours, can make it worthwhile to batch-cook at weekends, and can enable different members of a family to heat and eat dishes at their convenience, rather than relying on unhealthy snacks or expensive grills.

The well-run freezer can serve a dual purpose, combining the long-term storage of bulk raw materials from garden, farm or market, and commercially frozen foods, with the short-term storage of cooked dishes and leftovers which are meant to be used up quickly.

The information in the first three chapters of this book will help the new freezer owner to select and buy a cabinet of most value to his or herself and to buy and prepare food in the most economical way – a factor of invaluable use also to the experienced freezer owner, as are the quick reference notes in the fourth chapter on methods of freezing.

Most favourite, everyday recipes can be used for the freezer without adaptation, but the final chapter gives you over 250 recipes for family use and for entertaining.

Notes

It is important to follow *either* the metric *or* the imperial measures when using the recipes in this book.

Each dish will serve 4–6 people, according to appetite.

1 The Freezer

BUYING A FREEZER – FACTORS TO CONSIDER

A food freezer is a major kitchen appliance, and many factors must be considered when making a choice. Do not make decisions in a hurry, but compare types and prices, and assess the space available, the amount and type of food a family consumes, and whether there is a lot of entertaining, or a number of people at home all day.

AVAILABLE SPACE

If a freezer is to be kept in the kitchen, this may affect the size chosen. A larger cabinet can generally be kept in a garage or outhouse, and the greater initial cost will be repaid by a greater capacity for bulk storage. The space available will also affect the design of cabinet chosen. An upright freezer is suitable for the kitchen, but might be unnecessarily expensive for use in an outside building. A rectangular chest cabinet is usually best stored outside, but a square chest shape can often be fitted into a large larder, kitchen or indoor store-room.

CAPACITY

The size of a freezer is indicated in litres/cubic feet and it is important to check the storage capacity. This will affect not only the amount of food which can be stored, but also the amount of fresh food which can be frozen down at any one time.

Storage capacity is the maximum storage space of a freezer. This is calculated by multiplying each litre/cubic foot by 28.3/30 to give the storage capacity in kg/lb per litre/cubic foot. This will be somewhat reduced by awkwardly shaped packages, by bad packing, and by the size of the fast-freezing compartment which may be in frequent use and which cannot then be used regularly for storing already frozen food.

Freezing capacity is normally one-tenth of the total storage capacity. This indicates the amount of fresh food which can safely be fast-frozen in a 24-hour period.

SIZE

The newest cabinets have thinner walls so that freezers now have a greater storage capacity for their size. It is generally recommended that 56.5 litres/2 cubic feet capacity should be allowed for food for each member of the family, with 56.5 litres/2 cubic feet additional space (ie a three-person family should buy a 226.5 litres/8 cubic feet cabinet). In practice, this recommended size is rather low if full advantage is to be taken of buying bulky items like meat, or of using the garden or oven to capacity. A larger size may also be needed if a number of members of the family work so that there is little time for everyday shopping and cooking and food must be bought and prepared in bulk. If the family entertains a lot, a large freezer is also extremely useful for bulk purchases and for food cooked ahead.

STAR MARKINGS

Most refrigerators have a frozen food storage compartment with a star marking, which indicates the recommended storage life of already frozen foods as follows:

Star Marking	Temperature	Maximum Recommended Life of bought frozen food and ice cream
* (one star)	−6°C/21°F or below	frozen food – 1 week ice cream – 1 day
** (two star)	−12°C/10°F or below	frozen food – 1 month ice cream – 1 week
*** (three star)	−18°C/0°F	frozen food – 3 months ice cream – 1 month

A food freezer or compartment of a household refrigerator which is suitable for freezing a stated weight of fresh food daily, has the following marking:

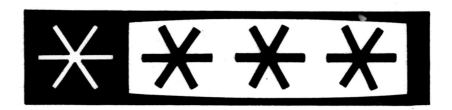

This symbol incorporates both the three star storage mark and a large differently coloured six-pointed star. Whenever it is used, the manufacturers must state the weight of food which can be frozen daily. If a freezer is overloaded with a weight of fresh food much heavier than that recommended by the manufacturer, the refrigerating system cannot extract the additional heat fast enough to prevent the temperature inside the freezer rising. This could be for a lengthy period, and there is a consequent loss and a shortening of high quality storage life of food already frozen.

A food freezer is capable of operating at −18°C/0°F and is additionally able to freeze unfrozen food to −18°C/0°F without significantly affecting the storage life of the frozen food already being stored. It can also store frozen food for many months.

TEMPERATURE GUIDE TO FREEZING

°C	°F	Temperature in refrigerator/freezer	Storage time for frozen food in freezer
16	60		
10	50		
4	40	main storage space of refrigerator	a day or so
0	32	water freezes	up to 2–3 days
−6	21	ice making compartment of refrigerator	up to 1 week (one star*)
−12	10	frozen food compartment of refrigerator	up to 1 month (two star**)
−18	0	normal temperature in home freezer	up to 3 months (three star***)
−23	−10		
−29	−20	level at which home freezer should operate with fresh load	long term storage of commercially frozen foods
−34	−30		
−40	−40		

CHOICE OF MODEL

CHEST FREEZER

This type of freezer is particularly useful for placing in a garage or outhouse. A chest is excellent for bulk storage, but should be fitted with dividers and baskets to make organization easier. A short or fat person may have difficulty in using a chest cabinet, and may find baskets heavy and awkward to lift. See that a chest freezer has a self-balancing lid and a magnetic lid seal.

Fast-freezing Compartment

Most chest freezers have a fast-freezing compartment, divided from the main cabinet by a panel. The fast-freezing switch cuts out thermostatic control so that the motor runs continuously. Heat is removed from the fresh food as quickly as possible, and already-stored foods do not rise in temperature. Sometimes the fast-freezing switch is connected to a light which will show when the motor is running continuously and the fast-freezing compartment is in action.

If a freezer does not have a fast-freeze compartment, food can be frozen against the back, sides or base of the freezer, since these are the coldest parts of the cabinet.

UPRIGHT FREEZER

The upright freezer is generally more attractive in a kitchen, and has the advantage of easy access and quicker checks on food supplies. Upright freezers have their weight concentrated in a small area, and it is wise to see that floors will take this weight. It used to be said that there was a greater loss of cold air from the opening of an upright rather than a chest freezer, but this is in fact negligible. Look for high capacity shelves in doors and a good door seal. Check whether a short person can reach the back of upper shelves without difficulty. Look for useful extras like interior lights and warning systems, and for special freezer shelves for fast freezing.

REFRIGERATOR-FREEZER

Specially designed kitchens and small areas can be fitted with combination refrigerator-freezers. Sometimes a small freezer is fitted on top of a large refrigerator; this is most suitable for freezing small packages. Very popular are the half-and-half models, with equal-sized refrigerator and freezer; the refrigerator is now often above the freezer, making for easier use. Sometimes the two cabinets can be installed side-by-side if this is more convenient. The trend is now towards larger freezers with smaller refrigerators.

CONSERVATOR

This kind of 'freezer' has been widely bought but it is only a storage cabinet for food which has been already frozen, and cannot be adjusted to sufficiently low temperatures for home freezing of food. A conservator is only useful in addition to a freezer for storing bulk animal food.

RUNNING COSTS

Running costs will be affected by the size of the freezer cabinet and its design. They will also be affected by the warmth of the room in which the freezer stands, the number of times the cabinet is opened daily, and the length of time it is kept open. The amount of fresh food being frozen can also affect running costs and the temperature of the food when it is put inside the freezer. It is more economical to run a well-packed freezer as the packages provide insulation. Current is wasted if used to chill air in large empty spaces.

Running costs are also affected by basic electricity charges. As a rough guide, a 170 litre/6 cubic feet freezer uses .3kW per 28.3 litres/cubic feet per 24 hours. 339.5 litres/12 cubic feet uses .25kW per 28.3 litres/cubic feet in the same time; 501 litres/18 cubic feet uses .2kW per 28.3 litres/cubic feet in the same time.

SERVICE AGREEMENTS

Some suppliers offer a service agreement with each freezer, which involves an annual payment. In practice, there is little to go wrong with a freezer, and the cost of an annual fee may outweigh the cost of a possible repair. If you do decide to sign a service agreement, make sure exactly what is covered, as it is possible the the fee may only cover the cost of labour and not the spare parts or vice versa.

INSTALLATION

See that somebody is at home to supervise the installation of the freezer, as it is important that it is positioned correctly.

POSITIONING THE FREEZER

1 Find a dry, cool and airy place.
2 Avoid a damp place, an unventilated cupboard, direct sunlight (eg a sun room), excessive warmth (eg next to a cooker, boiler or radiator).
3 Choose the cool part of the kitchen, a large airy larder, a dry garage or outhouse, a utility room, spare room or passage.
4 Put the freezer near a table, and near good natural or artificial light, for ease of packing and unpacking.
5 Put it in a position away from a wall.
6 Raise it on wooden blocks or bricks if locating it in a garage or outhouse so that there is an airspace beneath the floor of the cabinet.

7 If a garage or outhouse is dusty or damp, cover the cabinet with a sheet of polythene so that damage does not occur.

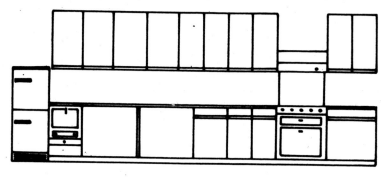

Siting a freezer

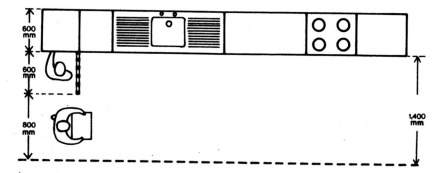

PREPARING THE FREEZER

1 Check with the manufacturer's booklet that the controls have been correctly set by the supplier and tested.
2 Wash it inside with plain warm water, and dry thoroughly.
3 Set the control knob to the recommended temperature for everyday use.
4 Switch on the freezer and leave it for 12 hours before filling so that the cabinet is thoroughly chilled.
5 Cover the plug and switch with a strip of adhesive tape. This will prevent children switching off the supply, and the casual unintentional use of the same plug for other domestic appliances.

MAINTENANCE

DEFROSTING

Defrost once or twice a year, when frost is about 0.5cm/¼ inch thick and food stocks are low.

Before defrosting

Put on fast-freeze switch the day before defrosting so that food packages are very cold. If there is no fast-freeze compartment, turn down the freezer to its coldest temperature.

During defrosting

1 Take out food packages, wrap them in cold newspaper and/or blankets and keep in a cold place.
2 Turn off freezer and disconnect from electricity supply.
3 Put newspapers or towels on the floor of the freezer.
4 Scrape down frost with a plastic or wooden spatula, *not* metal, sharp tools or wire brushes.
5 Cold water can be used to speed melting ice. *Do not use hot water, heaters or lamps.*
6 Leave cabinet open, and mop up moisture with clean cloths.

After defrosting

1 Wash the cabinet inside with warm water and a little bicarbonate of soda (15ml/1 tablespoon soda to 1.2 litres/2 pints water).
2 Rinse with clean water and dry thoroughly. *Do not use soap, detergent or caustic cleaners.*
3 Switch control to coldest setting and run the freezer for 30 minutes.
4 Repack freezer, checking packages for damage. Arrange items to be used up quickly at the top or front.
5 After 3 hours, return control to normal setting.

DO NOT FREEZE ANY FRESH FOOD FOR 24 HOURS AFTER DEFROSTING

CLEANING

Keep the freezer covered with a thick sheet of polythene to protect the cabinet if it is in an outside building. Wash the outside occasionally with warm soapy water, and polish with an enamel surface polish.

PROBLEM AREAS

POWER FAILURE CHECKLIST

1 Check if the switch has been turned off by mistake.
2 Check fuses.
3 Check if power failure is general and if the Electricity Board has been informed.

4 Do not touch the freezer motor.
5 Do not open the lid or door.
6 Leave the door or lid closed for 2 hours after supply is restored.
7 When power is restored, check the condition of food. It should last in good condition for 24 hours if the cabinet is well-insulated and full of food.
8 Quickly use up food which has thawed. Meat, fruit, pastry and vegetables may be cooked for re-freezing.

Note If your electricity supply and fuses are in order, call your freezer maintenance service immediately.

GOING ON HOLIDAY

Leave the freezer switched on during short holidays, and stock up with useful items like bread and cooked dishes for the return home. During a long break away from home, with the mains switch turned off, empty the freezer, clean the cabinet and leave the lid or door open.

MOVING HOUSE

For a one-day move, run down the food stocks as low as possible. Put on the fast-freeze switch 24 hours beforehand so that the food is very cold. See that the removal firm will handle the cabinet and contents, and that they will load the freezer last and unload it first. Check that a plug is ready to receive the freezer at once, and that the electricity supply is switched on. If the move will take a long time, use up the food stock, and clean the cabinet before transferring it to the new home.

Note If a freezer is empty and open, it can be a danger to children who may climb inside and shut the door or lid without being able to open it again. It is important that such a freezer should be stored in a room or garage with a door which can be locked and the key removed.

INSURING THE FREEZER

An insurance policy will cover the food in the freezer against various kinds of loss, but not against the accidental switching off of the machine, nor against the failure of power through industrial action. *Read the conditions of the policy carefully.* Such a policy is invaluable as it ensures against the loss of money spent on raw materials, packaging and time spent in preparation.

2 The Food

FOODS TO AVOID FREEZING

Nearly all foods freeze well, but there are a few items to avoid completely, or to freeze only with great care. A few other foods cannot be frozen to eat raw, but can be used for cooking.

Here is a list of foods which are unsuitable for freezing:

Hard-boiled eggs (including Scotch eggs, eggs in pies and in sandwiches)

Soured cream and single cream (less than 40% butterfat) which separate

Custards (including tarts). The custard mixture of eggs and milk can be frozen uncooked but there is little point in this

Soft meringue toppings

Mayonnaise and salad dressings

Milk puddings

Royal icing and frosting without fat

Salad vegetables with a high water content, eg lettuce, watercress, radishes

Old boiled potatoes (potatoes can be frozen mashed, roasted, baked or as chips)

Stuffed poultry (the storage life of stuffing is very short, compared with poultry)

Food with a high proportion of gelatine

Whole eggs in shells which will crack (eggs can be frozen in packages).

FOODS TO FREEZE WITH CARE

Onions, garlic, spices and herbs. They sometimes get a musty flavour in cooked dishes in the freezer, and quantities should be reduced in such dishes as casseroles, and adjusted during reheating. Careful packing will help to prevent these strong flavours spreading to other food, and a short storage life is recommended.

Rice, spaghetti and potatoes should only be frozen without liquid. They become mushy in liquid and should not be frozen in soups or stews.

Sauces and gravy are best thickened by reduction, or with tomato or vegetable purée. If flour is used, it must be reheated with great care, preferably in a double saucepan, to avoid separation. Cornflour can be used but gives a glutinous quality. Egg and cream thickening should be added after freezing.

Bananas, apples, pears, whole melons and avocados cannot be successfully frozen whole to eat raw. They can be prepared in various ways for freezer storage (although pears are never very satisfactory). Bananas are not worth while as they are in season at a reasonable price throughout the year.

Cabbage cannot be frozen successfully to eat raw, and is not worth freezing as it occupies valuable freezer space. Red cabbage may be useful to keep frozen, as it has a short season and is never very plentiful.

Celery and chicory cannot be frozen to eat raw. They are useful to freeze in liquid to serve as vegetables. Celery can be used in stews or soup.

Tomatoes cannot be frozen to eat raw, but are invaluable in the freezer to use for soups, stews and sauces, or to freeze as purée or juice.

Milk must be homogenized and packed in waxed cartons.

BULK BUYING AND COOKING

BULK BUYING

Most people assume that buying in bulk will lead to a considerable saving in the family budget. Savings depend however on the number of people in the family, on shopping and eating habits and the accessibility of shops, Freezer owners find in fact that they save on such hidden factors as public transport fares, or petrol and parking charges for cars, and also on a great deal of shopping time (which represents money). They also find that, despite their overall shopping bills often remaining the same, they tend to live better, since the price of better cuts of meat or out-of-season vegetables is balanced by freezing cheaper meat or home produce.

It is a mistake to buy in bulk with price as the only consideration. This can result in poor quality food. For instance, a cheap bag of prawns will probably have come from warmer waters and be tasteless compared with cold-water prawns from Greenland or Norway which are initially more expensive. In fact, the customer usually gets exactly what he pays for, and quality rarely combines with cheapness. When choosing a source of supply for buying food in bulk, therefore, it is worth considering the quality of the food, the service offered and the amount of food to be bought at one time.

As stated earlier on, it is also important to know the storage capacity of the freezer, and to judge how much space will be taken up by bulk purchases, since a lot depends on the packaging and the shape of the food packages stored.

Some consideration must also be given to high quality storage life. There is little point in buying a large pack of fish fingers for instance, if the family cannot eat these up within 3 months, as quality, flavour and texture deteriorate when the recommended storage life is exceeded.

How to Buy in Bulk

Before making out bulk orders, check how the family money is spent and where the greatest savings can be made. Some bulk purchases, such as meat, save money. Other purchases, such as bread, save time. Some families hate spending time on shopping or cooking; so these factors should be considered when choosing the types to buy in bulk.

Test small quantities of food before placing a large order. It is expensive, in the long run, if a bulk order of meat pies turns out to be unpopular with the family after one has been eaten. The remaining pies will take up valuable freezer space, and may put the whole family off this type of frozen food for ever; little is lost by trying an individual item first.

See that bulk food is properly packed for long-term storage. Food originally prepared for commercial and rapid use may come simply packed in cardboard boxes or a polythene bag. A 3.2kg/7 lb slab of pastry or 4.5kg/10 lb minced meat clinging together in an enormous lump will be almost useless under home conditions. Be prepared to re-pack large purchases in usable quantities as soon as the food is purchased. Check also whether it will be more convenient and cheaper in the long run to buy a bulk quantity of individual or family-size portions rather than enormous packs which are difficult to handle and store.

Transporting Food from Shop to Home

It is important to insulate food well after purchasing. Pack tightly in an insulated bag to obtain maximum value.

Ready-made insulated bags are available, but these can be improvised by the use of newspapers or blankets.

If buying frozen food in a supermarket or other general store, pack the frozen food last so that it can be unpacked and stored first.

Where to Buy in Bulk

Delivery Services Some frozen food manufacturers and some freezer centres deliver in bulk to the door. This is a convenient way of ordering food since it can be transferred straight from the refrigerated van to storage, and it is particularly useful in country areas. A minimum order is normally stipulated, and it is worth preparing a bulk order with friends to make the delivery a worth-while business. Sample small quantities of items which have not been bought before, and check delivery lists carefully to see that the order has been properly filled.

Frozen Food Centres These are found in many towns, and are useful for buying a wide variety of foods in both family and commercial pack sizes. They are useful places for trying new items before placing bulk orders, and the customer has the advantage of seeing and comparing the types of food. Try to choose a centre which is near a good parking space, and from which food can be taken home quickly. It is better to stick to reputable shops where the turnover is quick and the storage conditions are good. Some centres buy mainly on price, and quality may be poor. Try to find the best shopping day for freezer centres when they take their main deliveries. It is not always a good idea to shop at a freezer centre on a Friday or Saturday, when most other people are shopping; stocks of popular items may be low, so that a planned list cannot be completely filled and valuable shopping time is wasted. Check also on highly seasonal items, particularly fruit. Popular fruits such as redcurrants and raspberries tend to be in short supply after a while, so if the family likes them, stock up in the summer when first supplies come in since these fruits have a long storage life.

Specialist Producers Meat, in particular, is sold by specialist producers, either frozen or prepared for freezing. Such firms operate delivery services or express postal services, or food can be collected. The quality is usually high.

Local Shops, Markets and Farms Local shops and markets can usually supply fruit by the case and vegetables by the sack at reduced rates, as can local growers. A check should be kept on quality, as food may remain in shops for some days before sale. It is not a good idea to buy in this way if time is short, as there is a lot of labour involved in preparing a sack of vegetables for the freezer. Farmers often supply vegetables, fruit, meat or poultry, and fruit or vegetables are often very cheap if picked by the customer. Fish and shellfish are worth buying direct from the boat or from a seaside shop which has daily supplies. Home-baked bread, cakes and pies can often be obtained from local shops, W.I. stalls, etc, and some housewives undertake bulk cooking for the freezer.

What to Buy in Bulk

Bread and Cakes

Considerable time is saved by buying baked goods in bulk. This is an opportunity to buy crusty loaves; bread made from special flours; rolls and baps; sliced loaves for sandwiches and toast; buns; crumpets; malt and fruit loaves and cakes.

Convenience Foods

Food which has been prepared to save cooking and serving time is useful for quick meals, and particularly for in-between meals such as high tea for children which may not be required for the whole family. There are considerable savings in bulk packs of hamburgers, fish fingers, fish cakes, sausages and thin cuts of meat and fish. Check the different kinds of variations in flavour and texture to see which are most popular with the family.

Prepared Dishes

Prepared pies, casseroles, puddings and gourmet dishes are useful for families which have little time for cooking. They should be bought in sizes most convenient for family use or for entertaining. Party dishes which need elaborate ingredients or lengthy cooking time are also useful. It is a good idea to buy small sizes first to see if they are acceptable.

Fruit and Vegetables

Farm or market produce can be home-frozen but takes time for preparation. It may be more useful to buy commercially frozen fruit and vegetables in large packs. Particularly useful are such items as chips, mushrooms, green and red peppers, onions and mixed casserole vegetables. These are all in constant use in the kitchen, but are not always on hand in an accessible shop; nor are they particularly easy to prepare for freezing at home. Small quantities for recipe use can be shaken out of loose-packed commercial bags.

Ice Cream

Ice cream in bulk containers is useful for a family with children. The quality soon deteriorates, however, if a container is frequently opened and 'scooped', and the product has a relatively short high quality storage life, so it may be more practical to buy bulk supplies of smaller packs, or of individual ices such as lollies and chocolate bars which are easy to serve and have a longer storage life.

Poultry

Whole birds and poultry pieces are very useful for adding variety to family menus, and prices are usually reasonable. They are very useful for converting into cooked dishes for the freezer for both family use and entertaining. Some farms and shops prepare free-range birds in quantity for home freezing; others supply commercially frozen poultry in bulk. It is best to pack giblets and livers separately in bulk for the freezer as they do not store well inside birds, and are useful on their own for many recipes.

Meat

Meat is usually the most expensive item in the family budget, and is one of the most useful raw materials to buy in bulk. Bulk meat needs careful buying, and it is worth studying the problems before making an expensive purchase.

It is usually most practical to buy enough meat for the family's needs for 3 months, which is a reasonable turnover time and about the cheapest length of time to store the meat, allowing for the running costs of a freezer. It is a great mistake to purchase a quarter of beef, a pig and a lamb all at the same time since this overloads the freezer at the expense of other items. Pork, in particular, may deteriorate if kept beyond the recommended high quality storage life period. It is better to combine with one or two other families to get the advantage of bulk purchase with a variety of types of meat and different cuts.

Whole carcasses are ideal for those who will cook and eat cheaper cuts. Otherwise these will be wasted, and the roasting and grilling cuts will prove more expensive in the end. If a family only likes the better cuts, it is better to make a bulk purchase of these or to buy a good variety pack of different meats. There will not be much financial saving, but there will be shopping convenience and no wastage. In bulk carcass buying, there may be considerable wastage in bones and suet; prices must be checked carefully to ensure the actual price of the meat used is not in excess of that quoted by the supplier.

Many experts do not recommend the home freezing of meat at all. This is because meat must be frozen very quickly to retain its high quality, and commercial blast-freezing techniques give better results. If you do freeze meat at home, it is important to set the freezer correctly and only to freeze the recommended quantities at one time, and to label meat very carefully with the name of the cut and its possible uses. It is often better to choose the meat and have it frozen by the supplier. This does not apply, of course, to home-killed meat or home-caught game and fish.

When buying meat, choose good quality, and see that it has been properly hung. See also that a list is made of all the cuts in the order and their possible uses, and also that they are packed in usable quantities. Get the meat properly prepared in the form in which it is wanted, either joints, steaks, casserole meat or mince.

These specific points on our four principal meats are worth noting:

Beef is a really bulky purchase. A forequarter will account for about 45kg/100 lb and a hindquarter is even larger. The forequarter is more manageable, but consists mainly of slow-cooking cuts. Boned joints take up far less space in the freezer. The bones will account for about one-quarter of a bulk purchase, but can be made into concentrated stock for freezing (the butcher should be asked to saw them in reasonable pieces for the saucepan). Suet can be used for a wide variety of puddings, and can also be rendered down for fat. Check whether bones and suet are included in the overall price and if they will be delivered with the meat. Have the slow-cooking meat cut into slices and/or cubes for easy use, and ask for plenty of lean mince in 450g/1 lb packs which are very useful. Try to convert some of the cuts straight into pies or casseroles when they are delivered; this will save freezer space and provide some useful meals for quick use.

Veal is not very often available in bulk, and is not very successful in the freezer, since it tends to lose flavour in storage conditions. If veal is bought, see that it is carefully divided into prepared boned roasting joints, escalopes and chops, and pie veal, etc.

Lamb is worth buying. A small lean one will weigh 11.25–13.5kg/ 25–30 lb with little waste. Decide if you want chops in roasting joints or divided. If the cheaper chops and breast of lamb are not liked, it may be better value simply to buy roasting joints and bags of chops.

Pork has a shorter storage life than other meats and should not be purchased in over-large quantities. Half a pig will weigh about 22.5kg/50 lb and consists mostly of roasting and frying joints. The head and trotters may be included, but freezer space should not be wasted on them. They are better used at once in brawn or a dish which requires meat jelly.

BULK COOKING

It can be all too easy to become a slave to the freezer, endlessly shopping and cooking to keep the white box topped up. It is important to take advantage of the fact that this is the only way of safely preserving cooked dishes. Cooking should be organized ahead so that two or three ready meals are always 'in hand' in the freezer. The great thing is to avoid inflicting the same kind of food on the family for weeks ahead, so new bulk purchases should be slightly different from the one recently made, and the cooked dishes used to vary those already in hand.

One of the greatest advantages of bulk cooking is that quantities of raw materials, such as bulk-bought meat, can be converted into cooked dishes as soon as they have been bought, saving considerable space. Stewing steak, for instance, can be made into casseroles and pies; mince can be converted into individual pies and cottage pies; chicken pieces can be used with a whole variety of sauces; offal can be made into casseroles and pâtés.

For most people, it is best to double or treble quantities of such dishes as casseroles, using one immediately and saving the other portions for future use with added seasonings. Batch-baking is also sensible, to take full advantage of oven heat. It takes little more effort to make two cakes instead of one, 50 scones instead of ten. The same goes for pâtés, ice creams etc.

The Right Equipment

It pays to have the right-sized equipment and one or two labour-saving machines to use in conjunction with the freezer. Normal household equipment may not be suitable for bulk cooking.

Large saucepans are useful not only for making stock, but for blanching vegetables and preparing fruit and meat. A large flat pan is useful for cooking ingredients in fat at the first stage of many recipes.

Large casseroles are another essential. At least one 3.6–4.8 litres/6–8 pints size is needed for bulk cooking, or a large double roaster.

A pressure cooker speeds up the cooking of meat and poultry in particular. It can also double as an ordinary large pan.

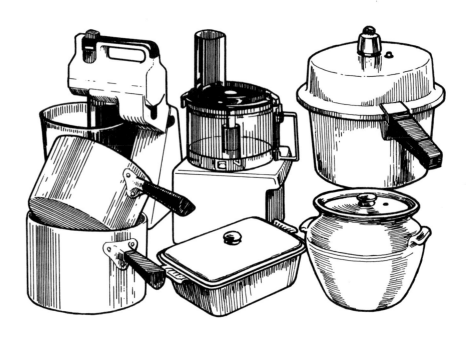

An electric mixer with attachments is invaluable in cooking for the freezer. The mixer itself is useful for making all types of cakes, and for beating ice cream and whipping up puddings. The blender attachment, or an independent blender, is useful for soups, purées and sauces. A mincer attachment aids the making of mince and sausages from bulk-bought meat, and speeds up pâté-making. A slicing attachment is handy for preparing vegetables, and a dough hook is useful for yeast doughs for bread, buns and pizzas.

A food processor is another most useful piece of equipment – as an alternative, or in addition to an electric mixer.

An adequate oven is necessary to take batch-baking, etc. If a new one is being purchased, see that there is plenty of oven space, and if possible buy a cooker with a fan-assisted oven. This ensures that heat is circulated and a steady baking temperature is maintained throughout the oven. Cooks who have an Aga or similar cooker with two ovens are fortunate, as different types of dishes can be cooked at the same time.

What to Cook for Freezing

Before cooking foods for freezing, it is wise to assess which items are worth freezer space. Briefly, these are:

1 Dishes which need long cooking or long and tedious preparation
2 Dishes made from seasonal foods
3 Dishes which can be made in large quantities with little more work (ie three cakes instead of one; double or treble casseroles)
4 Dishes for special occasions, such as parties or holidays
5 Convenience foods for invalids, small children, unexpected illness.

3 Preparation for Freezing

FOODS AND HIGH QUALITY STORAGE LIFE

One of the secrets of successful freezing is the maintenance of a regular turnover, so that frozen food keeps perfect texture, colour and flavour. It is a waste of valuable freezer space to keep food for longer than the recommended storage life in which it will retain its high quality.

Raw materials keep longer than anything which has been cooked, and for cooked dishes a turnover of 1–2 months is recommended. The factors which can affect and shorten storage life are:

1 The wrong packaging material which allows moisture to escape from food.
2 Bad packing which allows air to enter spaces in food packages.
3 Excess fat in both raw and cooked foods which becomes rancid under freezer conditions.
4 Salt, spices, herbs, onions and garlic which can cause off-flavours.

The high quality storage life of individual foods is given in the relevant sections of the chapter on Methods of Freezing (see pages 38–107).

PLANNING THE CONTENTS OF THE FREEZER

Freeze food which the family enjoys and which is eaten frequently. This means assessing the type of meals most commonly eaten, whether pastry, cakes and sandwiches are an important part of the diet and whether money is often spent on roasting or grilling meat.

Keep a month's or year's budget in mind, and see if more money can be saved by freezing slow-cooked dishes of economy cuts of meat, by home-baking bread and cakes, or by growing fruit and vegetables. See what proportion of each type of food will save money if stored in the freezer, or will save time if more important.

A chest freezer with a self-balancing lid and separating baskets are important features when choosing a model

A combination refrigerator-freezer is particularly useful where space is limited

Foil dishes serve many purposes and enable food to be cooked, frozen and reheated in the same container

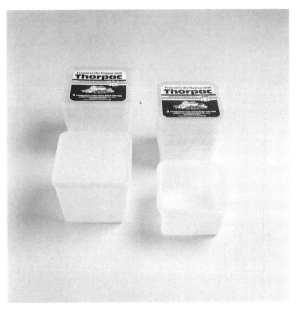

Rigid plastic containers with close-fitting airtight lids stack easily and are a practical way of freezing soups and stews

Polythene bags can be used to freeze a large variety of foods. Different coloured bags aid identification

Cooked pancakes should be cooled, then layered separately before being wrapped and frozen

Aim for variety in meal planning. The advantage of a freezer is that it can store a lot of foods with a short seasonal life or which are not easily obtainable in local shops.

Follow the seasons when choosing fruit, vegetables, meat, poultry, game and fish to freeze in bulk. Plan the garden to yield good crops of food you like, but also look for seasonal bargains in shops and markets.

ORGANIZING FREEZER SPACE

Pack food as neatly as possible, using square containers, or forming bags or sheet-wrapped items into squares (see pages 29–32). Label packages carefully.

Arrange food in categories, and arrange each type of food in date order so that items are not left in the freezer beyond their high quality storage life. Food to be used first must be most accessible.

Keep an inventory so that there is a constant check on items in the freezer, when they should be eaten up, and when new supplies are needed.

Keep the food in use and do not use the freezer as a miser's hoard. Use it as a shop for supplying most of your daily needs and keep the 'stock' turning over, checking always on high quality storage life.

Have a basket or bag or shelf for all the odd items left from batches of food, eg the last iced cake, leftover stew, a spare pot of sauce, a few egg yolks, so that they are used up quickly.

Eliminate items which prove to be unpopular and do not waste next year's freezer space on them.

PACKING, LABELLING AND RECORDING

PACKAGING AND LABELLING MATERIALS

Food must be prevented from drying out as air penetrates the food and moisture leaves it. Food must be protected from cross-contamination of flavours and smells, and delicate foods must be protected from bruising or chipping.

Packaging is important to retain the quality of frozen food. Buy the minimum packaging necessary to begin with, but see that it is of good quality, and do not waste the money spent on good food by using inferior packaging.

On the other hand, it is not necessary to spend a lot of money on sophisticated or complicated packaging materials. Try the basic essentials first. Most people find they manage with a combination of rigid containers, polythene bags and sheet foil, but the choice will depend a great deal on the type of food most commonly packed, and how important it is to save freezer space by using easily stacked containers. The important thing to remember is that the aim of packaging is to eliminate air at the beginning of the freezing process, and to exclude air during storage.

Packaging which is suitable for freezing is specially marked. Look out for all types of packaging in stationers, chemists, super-markets and department stores, or buy by mail order.

Choosing Packaging

1 See that packaging does not allow air or moisture to penetrate (this is known as moisture-vapour-proof packaging).
2 Check that packaging is waterproof and cannot leak.
3 See that packaging is greaseproof, thereby avoiding rancid smells. These can also be caused by poorly cleaned or stored packaging, and by some materials which smell strongly.
4 Check that packaging is resistant to low temperatures for a long time. Some plastics become brittle, split and crack. Glass jars must also be tested before use (see page 28).

Choosing Suitable Packing Materials

Item	Rigid Containers	Foil Containers	Foil Sheeting	Polythene Bags or Sheeting
Fresh Meat			*	*
Fresh Poultry and Game			*	*
Fresh Fish			*	*
Cooked Meat and Fish Dishes	*	*	*	*
Fresh Vegetables	*			*
Fresh Fruit (unsweetened or dry sugar pack)	*			*
Fresh Fruit (syrup pack)	*			
Cheese			*	*
Eggs	*			
Soups and Sauces	*			
Bread, Cakes and Biscuits			*	*
Pastry and Pies		*	*	*
Puddings	*	*	*	*
Ice Cream	*			

Note Most food can be packed in alternative ways. An upright freezer with shelves enables food to be packed more easily without crushing, so that pies and cakes may be packed in bags, but need rigid packaging for storage in chest freezers. Consider the alternatives given in this chart if some types of packaging are not easily available.

Substitute Packaging

Whereas specially bought packaging has been tested under freezer conditions, substitute packaging must be tested before use as many everyday materials are not suitable for the freezer.

Packages from commercially frozen food, ice cream containers, and some grocery packs (eg cottage cheese cartons, margarine tubs) can be used for home freezing after being carefully cleaned and tested.

Rigid Containers

Plastic boxes with close-fitting lids can be used indefinitely, and are extremely useful for frozen items such as sandwiches or fruit for lunches which may be carried while thawing. They are also useful for items like stews which can be turned out into a saucepan for thawing, as the flexible sides can be lightly pressed to aid removal. For long-term storage, it is important that the boxes have perfectly fitting airtight lids. Choose square or rectangular containers which stack easily.

Polythene Sheets

These sheets are useful for wrapping joints, poultry and large pies, and pieces of sheeting may be used to divide meat, etc for easy thawing. The wrapping must be sealed with special freezer tape.

Polythene Bags

These bags are very cheap to use and simple to handle. They may be used for meat, poultry, fruit and vegetables, pies, cakes and sandwiches. Buy bags which are gusseted for easy packing. They may be sealed by heat or twist fastening. If the bags are subjected to frequent handling, they should be overwrapped to avoid punctures. If the contents are likely to contaminate other items with their smell and flavour, they should also be overwrapped. Coloured bags aid identification in the freezer.

Foil

Foil is an invaluable freezer packaging as it is clean, easy to handle, and with care can be re-used a number of times.

Sheet foil is specially made for freezer use and is good for wrapping awkward parcels as it can be moulded close to the food. It can also be used to make lids for other containers. Ordinary household foil can be used, but two thicknesses give the best protection.

Foil dishes, pie plates and pudding basins are useful for cooking food which can then be frozen in the same container, followed by reheating. These containers can be covered with a lid of sheet foil, or they can be packed in polythene sheeting or polythene bags.

Deep foil dishes are obtainable with specially treated cardboard lids to protect the food. These are useful for casseroles, cottage pies, meat balls in gravy, meat and poultry slices in gravy, and a variety of sweet puddings. The food can be prepared in the containers, then covered with the lids on which the name of the food can be written.

These containers can be re-used, but the lids are rarely usable a second time and can be replaced by sheet foil. These containers can be round, square or rectangular and range from individual sizes through family sizes to very large containers for party dishes.

Gusseted bags made from foil or from foil-paper laminate, are easy to fill and store, and are particularly suitable for such items as cheese since they prevent cross-contamination of smells.

Glass Jars

Screw top preserving jars, bottles and honey jars may be used for freezing if they have been tested first for resistance to low temperatures. To do this, put an empty jar into a plastic bag and put into the freezer overnight; if the jar breaks, the bag will hold the pieces. These jars are easy to use and economical in storage space, but 1–2.5cm/½–1 inch headspace must be allowed for expansion which might cause breakage. Jars are very useful for soups and stews, but be careful not to use those with 'shoulders' which make thawing difficult if the items are needed in a hurry. Ovenglass can be used for the freezer, though this is an expensive way of packing, since the utensils are then out of use in the kitchen; they cannot be taken straight from the freezer to oven unless they are of the special type advertised for this purpose.

Fastening Materials

Packages may be sealed with twist-ties, with freezer tape, or by heat-sealing. Rubber bands will deteriorate in cold conditions and should not be used for securing bags, while ordinary sealing tape will curl and pull off packages.

Labelling Materials

Special labels are made for freezer use, with gum which is resistant to low temperatures. Ordinary gummed labels will curl and drop off at low temperatures, while tie-on labels may tear off during storage. Twist-ties with attached labels are available. In transparent packages, ordinary paper labels may be placed *inside* the pack, but they may be difficult to read if frosting occurs. Alternately, write directly on the freezer wrap. Labels must be written in wax crayon, felt pen or Chinagraph pencil; ordinary ink is not suitable as it fades.

FREEZER ACCESSORIES

Baskets can be used which hang across a cabinet freezer and slide along the top. Baskets can also be used on the floor of the cabinet but are heavy to lift when full.

Bags of brightly coloured nylon mesh used for shopping are useful for the floor of the freezer cabinet. They can be filled with bag-wrapped food and are easy to lift.

Polythene Bags in bright colours, and of a large size like laundry bags, are also useful for holding a number of small items in a chest freezer. Use the colours for easy identification.

Dividers are useful in the bottom of chest freezers where heavy items are stored. These provide a useful and easily moved division to separate meat, fruit, vegetables and fish.

Heat Sealing Unit is a machine for welding polythene, which is useful for making large quantities of bags, and for heat-sealing bag tops.

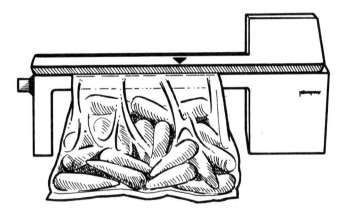

Recording Equipment can be a very simple plastic shopping list and felt pen which is easily wiped clean. Card index systems, logbooks and freezer diaries are also available, or an exercise book can be used.

PACKING FOR THE FREEZER

Preparation

Before beginning the freezing process, collect together all the packaging materials including sealing equipment and labels. Prepare all food immediately after picking or buying, and in the way in which it will be most useful when it is taken from the freezer. This means that meat should be cut and trimmed, poultry trussed, fish cleaned and gutted, fruit and vegetables cleaned, trimmed and cut if necessary. Work with only small amounts of food at a time, and use clean equipment in a cool atmosphere. Do not leave food lying around in the kitchen where it can be contaminated by dust or insects, or where it will not cool quickly. Prepare and completely cool cooked foods before packing.

Padding and Separating

Before packing small pieces of meat, fish or cake layers, separate them with foil, polythene or transparent film. Pad the bones of meat or poultry with twists of paper or foil.

Open Freezing

Most food stored in a single pack will become solid when frozen. To keep small items of food separate, such as strawberries, peas, small fish or meat balls, freeze them unwrapped on small trays, baking sheets or large lids from rigid containers. When the food is hard, pack in rigid containers or bags, seal and label. This means that the food can be shaken out in small quantities from the pack, and it also helps to keep food such as strawberries in good shape.

Iced cakes and delicate pies are also best open-frozen before packing so that they are not smudged or crushed. They can then be packed in crushproof boxes or in bags, or wrapped in foil.

Cube and Brick Freezing

Rigid containers need not be wasted on liquids. Small quantities of sauces, syrups, baby foods and herbs can be frozen in ice cube trays. When the cubes are frozen, they should be removed from the tray and placed in a polythene bag for storage. For easy separation they can be wrapped in twists of foil, or can be sprayed with soda water before packing in bags. One cube will be a useful portion for many recipes.

Larger quantities of liquid such as soup or purée can be frozen in brick shapes. This is most easily done by pouring the liquid into a loaf tin or rigid container. When it has frozen into a solid 'brick', remove from the container, and wrap in foil or polythene for storage.

Shape Freezing

Another way to save using expensive containers, is to freeze items in shaped foil or polythene in one of two ways:

1 Put a polythene bag into an empty sugar box. Fill with the food, which may be fresh vegetables or fruit, or liquid such as stew. Seal the bag and freeze the food. After freezing, remove from the box and stack the neat square shapes. Empty fruit punnets can also be used to shape small square packages.

2 If a favourite casserole dish is needed over and over again and cannot be spared for the freezer, use it to shape the food which is going to be reheated in it. Line the dish with foil and pour in the stew. Fold over the foil to make a package, and seal. After freezing, remove the package from the casserole and store it. When the stew is needed, unwrap and return it to the casserole for heating and serving.

Note Remember to test the casserole dish beforehand for resistance to freezing temperatures.

Container Packing

Moisture will expand during freezing, so headspace must be left between the surface of the food and the seal of the container. This is usually 2.5cm/1 inch space above the food, but if containers are narrow, allow 1.5–2.5cm/¾–1 inch headspace.

1 Fill containers carefully to avoid soiling the rims if liquid food is being packed. Use a funnel or scoop to aid packing.
2 Eliminate air pockets by plunging a knife into the contents once or twice.
3 Leave headspace above the food. Fruit packed in syrup will rise to the surface and discolour, so a crumpled piece of foil or transparent film should be placed into the headspace to weigh the food down.
4 Press on the container lid firmly. If it does not have a patent seal, finish with freezer tape.

Bag Packing

Use bags which are strong and of a heavy gauge designed for the freezer. Bags with gussets are easier to pack.

1 Fill bags carefully, making sure food goes into the corners, and using a funnel or scoop to avoid soiling the edges of the bags. Put bags into sugar boxes, rigid containers or fruit punnets so that they freeze into a neat square shape.
2 Take out air (see page 33).
3 Close the bag (see page 33).
4 For extra security and neatness, use a gooseneck closing. Bend the long end of the bag back to the wire twist, making a second turn of the fastener.

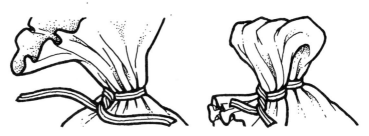

Sheet Wrapping

Foil or polythene sheeting can be used for wrapping. This can be used in two ways:

Chemist's Wrap   Put the food in the centre of the sheet of wrapping material. Bring the two sides of the sheet together above the food and fold them neatly downwards over the food. Bring the wrapping as close to the food as possible, pressing out the air. Seal the fold of the wrapping, then fold the ends in like a parcel, making them close and tight and excluding air. Seal all folds.

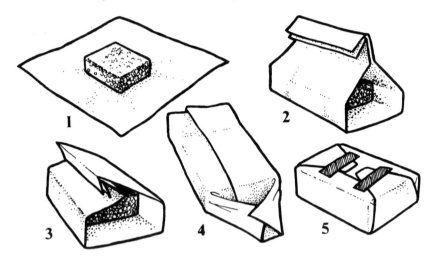

Butcher's Wrap   Put the food diagonally on the sheet of wrapping material. Bring in the opposite corners and seal them. Bring in a third corner and then fold over the last corner. Seal all openings. This pack is slightly less bulky than the chemist's wrap, and is more easily used for slightly irregular packages such as bone-in meat.

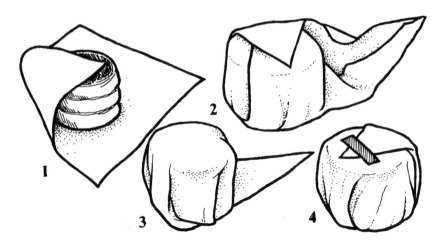

Excluding Air

It is most important to exclude air and to remove air pockets in packages. This may be done by pressing the package with the hands, by sucking out air with a straw or special pump, or by exerting water pressure on the package placed in a bowl of water. Air pockets in rigid containers can be released by plunging a knife into the contents two or three times.

Sealing

All packages must be sealed by one of three methods:

Taping Special freezer-proof tape must be used, and should be on containers with lids, and on sheet-wrapped items. Be sure that all folds are taped.

Heat Polythene bags may be sealed by a heat sealing unit (see page 29), but a domestic iron can be used successfully if a piece of paper is put between the iron and the polythene to be fused. Heat-sealing gives a neat package which can be stored easily.

Twist-tying After extracting air from a polythene bag, a plastic-covered fastener should be twisted round the end of the bag, the top of the bag turned down over this twist and the fastener twisted again round the bunched neck of the bag (see page 31).

Labelling

All items in a freezer should be clearly labelled with contents, weight or number of portions, date of freezing, and any special thawing, heating or seasoning instructions.

RECORDING

Record the type of food frozen, the number and size of packages, and the date of freezing for all items in the freezer. The length of high quality storage life should be noted if possible, and it is a good idea to note how many packages have been removed. Some people also like to record the position occupied in the freezer, but this may be difficult to maintain.

CONTENTS	NO. AND SIZE OF PACKAGES	DATE OF FREEZING	STORAGE LIFE	USED
Raspberries	5 x 450g/1 lb	Aug 81	12 months	IIII
Rump steak	3 x 1.8 kg/2 lbs	Jan 82	12 months	I

PACKING CHECKLIST

1 See that the packaging chosen is suitable for the food.
2 See that the packaging is clean and dust free, and that re-used packaging is carefully washed and dried.
3 Only use food which is clean and in peak condition.
4 Pack food without pressure to see that it avoids damage and distortion.
5 Pack only in usable portions, varying packages to suit family needs, eg single servings, family meals or parties.
6 Eliminate air spaces from packages, except for 1cm/½ inch headspace for expansion in foods with a high water content, since water expands on freezing.

FREEZING CHECKLIST

1 Turn down freezer to 'Coldest' or put on fast-freeze switch at least 2 hours before food will be ready to process.
2 Select packaging and equipment in various sizes, sealing and labelling equipment.
3 Prepare food quickly and cleanly.
4 Cool food *quickly*.
5 Open freeze fruit, vegetables and iced cakes if preferred.
6 Pack, seal and label carefully.
7 Arrange packs in coldest part of freezer or in fast-freeze compartment, avoiding a solid block of containers. (Do not add more than one-tenth of the entire freezer capacity at one time for freezing down, as this slows up the freezing process.)
8 While freezing is in progress, keep the packages away from other frozen food already in the cabinet.
9 Freeze packages till solid, remove to storage area, and re-adjust freezer temperature or fast-freeze switch to the 'normal storage' position.

ORGANIZING FOOD IN THE FREEZER

It is important to keep a check on items in the freezer, and to avoid a waste of valuable freezer space. It is much easier to do this if the space is correctly planned and the food is arranged systematically.

For an upright freezer with shelves, label rigid containers on the *front*, and face labels forward so that they are quickly identified.

For a chest freezer, label containers on *lids* so that they can be chosen easily.

Make space in the freezer log book for a 'position record' unless this is variable.

COLOUR IDENTIFICATION

Coloured lids, labels and bags are available in a wide range of colours to suit every need. A colour can be used to identify one type of food (eg red tops for fruit containers), or to sub-divide a food category (eg red for raspberries; green for gooseberries). Large coloured bags can be used for collecting together all items in one food category. Coloured labels are the quickest and cheapest aid to identification.

SPACE SAVING

The freezer is easier to organize if food is packed in neat shapes. Square or rectangular containers are easier to pack than cylindrical ones or tubs. Bags can be formed into square shapes during freezing (see page 30). Awkward packages such as joints of meat are best collected together in baskets or large bags. Fragile cakes and pies are best packed in rigid square containers or cake boxes.

ARRANGING THE CABINET

Upright and chest cabinets need slightly different packing plans according to the space available.

Upright freezers are easy to pack and keep tidy. Use the lowest shelf or compartment for meat and fish, and above this, have a compartment for vegetables and one for fruit. Vegetables and fruit can be combined on a shelf if space is limited, but will then need careful labelling or colour identification. Use upper shelves for convenience foods (eg fish fingers), and for cooked savoury dishes, cakes, puddings and desserts. These can be sub-divided if space is available, or combined but with easy identification. Door shelves are best used for short storage of small packs of sauces, dairy produce and pastry goods, and for single packs which are to be used up quickly.

Chest freezers are less easy to organize, but have more space for bulk items. Use the bottom of the freezer for meat and fish, vegetables, and bulk ice cream containers, in the proportion of space needed. Use baskets for fruit and for cooked dishes. Keep a basket, or part of one, for small packs of sauces, syrups etc, and for food packages which are to be used quickly. The fast-freeze compartment may be used for storage, but should not contain frozen food when fresh food is being frozen down.

WHEN THINGS GO WRONG

If food is correctly prepared for freezing, results should be good, and food should have a fine flavour and colour, and a good texture. Sometimes however, an item proves disappointing, and it is worth checking what is wrong to prevent the problem recurring. Freezer space, food and packaging are expensive, so it is important to aim at perfect results.

Badly chosen packaging, incorrect packing and freezing are the most common faults which cause deterioration of frozen food. A freezer is a box of cold dry air and when a package is put into the freezer, a battle ensues between that cold dry air and any moisture and heat in the package. The cold air attempts to draw out the warmth and moisture of the food. The warmth must be withdrawn, but moisture must be retained, and this can only be achieved by moisture-vapour-proof packaging and fast freezing.

Dehydration
Dehydration is the removal of moisture and juices from food, usually after a long period of storage. Meat is particularly subject to this problem, giving a tough, dry and tasteless result. It can only be avoided by careful wrapping in moisture-vapour-proof packaging.

Oxidation
Oxidation is a process whereby oxygen moves inwards from air to food, so that food must be protected by the correct wrappings. Oxidation causes the mingling of oxygen with food fat cells, which react to form chemicals which give meat and fish a bad taste and smell, and fatty foods become rancid.

Freezer Burn
Dehydration causes discoloured greyish-brown areas on the surface of food when it is removed from the freezer. It is only avoided by correct packaging materials, wrapping and sealing.

Rancidity
This is the effect of oxidation or absorption of oxygen into fat cells, and is recognized by the unpleasant flavour and smell of the food affected. Fried foods suffer from this problem, and are not generally recommended for freezer storage. Salt accelerates the reaction which causes rancidity and should not be added to minced meat or sausages before freezing; salt butter will have a shorter freezer life than fresh butter.

Pork is particularly subject to rancidity, since it contains not only thick layers of fat but also a greater number of tiny fat cells than other meat, so that its freezer life is shorter. Fat fish has similar problems.

Cross-Flavouring
Strongly flavoured foods may affect other items in storage with their smell or flavour and should be carefully overwrapped.

Flabbiness
Fruit and vegetables which are flabby and limp may be of the wrong variety for freezing, or be overblanched. In general however, depending on cell structure, slow freezing of fruit and vegetables will result in flabbiness.

Ice Crystals
Too great headspace on top of liquid foods such as soup may cause a layer of ice crystals to form which will affect storage and flavour. This is not too serious in liquids which will be heated or thawed, as the liquid melts back into its original form and can be shaken or stirred back into emulsion.

However, meat, fish, vegetables and fruit can be affected by ice crystals if slow freezing has taken place. Moisture in the food cells forms ice which will expand if slow-frozen, and, in occupying more space, these crystals will puncture and destroy surrounding tissues. This breaking down of tissues allows juices, particularly in meat, to escape, taking with them flavour. Fast freezing is essential for all foods.

4 Methods of Freezing

Note These are general guidelines. Always follow the manufacturer's instructions for your particular freezer.

FISH AND SHELLFISH

If you intend to freeze fish at home make certain that the fish is absolutely fresh and that you have the proper facilities for freezing and storage. Unless you can obtain really *fresh* supplies it is better to rely on commercially frozen fish which has been processed with special equipment at very low temperatures.

Note Do not attempt to freeze fish in a domestic refrigerator, even one with a three-star compartment. Do not attempt to freeze fish in a conservator with a fixed temperature of around zero. This is intended for storage of commercially frozen produce only.

It is essential to know the history of the fish you plan to freeze. Ideally it should be caught and frozen on the same day, and certainly within 24 hours. Likely sources of supply are sea or river fish caught by family anglers, or for those who live near the sea, a local inshore fisherman who sells direct. In any case the fish should be kept iced or refrigerated during any short journey home and whilst being prepared for the freezer. Generally speaking, the best results come from freezing fish raw, and fish in season and, therefore, in prime condition.

Thin pieces of food freeze fastest so it is best to divide fish into fillets, cutlets or portions, and to freeze these in *shallow* packages. Small fish such as mackerel, trout, mullet or herring can be frozen whole. For special occasions and short-term storage a fish such as a salmon can be frozen whole in a home freezer provided it is not more than 5cm/2 inches thick and that no more than one fish is frozen at a time.

In the case of shellfish the importance of freshness is paramount. Oysters and mussels offered for sale in Great Britain must have been cleansed and purified in salt water according to Public Health Authority Regulations. Some varieties of shellfish are better cooked before freezing.

For recommended methods of preparation and freezing of specific fish, see pages 40–43.

PACKAGING FOR FISH

The cold air in the freezer has an intensely drying effect from which the fish must be protected. The simplest method is by wrapping *closely* in a suitable material so that as much air as possible is excluded.

The most useful packaging materials for fish are:

Heavy Gauge Polythene sealed with special adhesive sealing tape suitable for freezer use.

Heavy Duty Aluminium Foil with the joins and ends pressed firmly together so that no further sealing is required. Thin foils are not recommended unless used double, or overwrapped.

Shallow Foil Dishes into which the fish fits closely without leaving large air spaces. Cover and seal with sheet foil or polythene. Also useful for cooked fish dishes.

Individual Plastic or Waxed Containers such as those used for cream or yoghurt. These are useful for small quantities of shellfish or fish pâté.

Separators for several fillets or portions packaged together. They are easier to separate for cooking if a small piece of thin plastic film is placed between the pieces.

Stiffeners such as a thin piece of white card cut to shape which will give rigidity to a package.

ICE GLAZING

A natural and simple method of protecting fish from the drying effects of the freezer is by encasing it in a layer of ice. This is a useful method when no suitable packaging materials are available. The fish needs to be handled very carefully throughout, however, since ice is brittle and liable to crack, and, unless overwrapped, ice glazing alone cannot be recommended for other than very short-term storage.

To glaze, place the prepared but unwrapped fish or fish fillets separately in the freezer (previously set at 'Fast Freeze' or 'Coldest') and leave until frozen solid. Remove and dip in cold fresh water; a thin film of ice will form over the entire fish. Immediately return to the freezer. Repeat about three times at 30 minute intervals.

STORING FROZEN FISH

Fish is stored commercially at −30°C (−20°F, or 52 degrees of frost on the Fahrenheit scale). The average storage temperature operating in a home freezer, conservator, or three star domestic refrigerator is only −18°C/0°F, so do not attempt to keep fish for long periods. It will not go bad, but it will lose its 'fresh caught' flavour and texture, and oily fish in particular may develop rancid flavours. Remember to date-label packages clearly so that you can see at a glance how long they have been in store.

THAWING FROZEN FISH

Unless you are dealing with a large whole fish or large portions for deep fat frying there is no need to thaw fish prior to cooking. Simply separate the small white fish or fillets and cook from the frozen or partially frozen state. When thawing is necessary, allow 5 to 6 hours per 450g/lb in a cold place or domestic refrigerator and from 3 to 4 hours at room temperature. For speedy thawing of whole fish, about 1 hour submerged in cold water will do the trick, but this type of thawing is apt to result in some loss of flavour and texture and is not generally recommended. Once thawed, fish should be used promptly.

COOKING FROZEN FISH

Use any of the methods normally used for wet fish but allow a rather longer time at a lower temperature. The actual time will vary according to the thickness of the fish and to the degree of thaw when cooking commences. When the flakes separate easily in the centre of the fish you know it is cooked right through. Take care not to overcook and thus loose the succulence and flavour which correct freezing and storing will have preserved.

Note To make it easy to separate the fillets, consumer packs of commercially frozen fish are interleaved with plastic film dividers. For the benefit of freezer owners, a similar system applies to bulk packs (known as 'shatter packs' in the trade) and these or individually loose frozen fillets packed in bags are the ones to look for when shopping at frozen food centres. From either pack you can take the exact number of fillets needed for cooking at any one time and leave the rest in the freezer.

FREEZING SPECIFIC FISH

White Fish (eg cod, plaice, sole, whiting)
Clean. Fillet or cut in steaks if liked, or leave whole. Separate pieces of fish with double thickness of clingfilm. Wrap in freezer paper, or put in box or bag. Be sure air is excluded, or fish will be dry and tasteless. Wrap to form flat packages. Seal, label, date and freeze quickly.

Note If small fish are being frozen whole, pack individually, or side by side in a single layer of 2–4 fish, with separators between.

To serve
Thaw large fish in unopened container in refrigerator. Cook small pieces of fish whole frozen.
High Quality Storage Life 3 months

Fatty Fish (eg haddock, halibut, mackerel, salmon, trout, turbot)

Clean. Fillet or cut in steaks if liked, or leave whole. Separate pieces of fish with double thickness of clingfilm. Wrap in freezer paper, or put in box or bag. Be sure air is excluded, or fish will be dry and tasteless. Keep pack shallow. Seal, label, date and freeze quickly. Large fish may be prepared in solid ice pack. Do not use brine pack.
Note If freezing a large fish whole, freeze only one fish at a time.

To serve
Thaw large fish in unopened container in refrigerator. Cook small pieces of fish while frozen.
High Quality Storage Life 2 months

Smoked Fish (eg bloaters, eel, haddock, kippers, mackerel, salmon, sprats, trout)

Pack raw or cooked fish in layers with clingfilm between. Keep pack shallow.
Note Do not freeze smoked fish which has already been frozen for distribution purposes and then thawed for sale.

To serve
To eat cold, thaw in refrigerator. Haddock and kippers may be cooked while frozen.
High Quality Storage Life 2 months

Crab

Crab must be absolutely fresh, and freshly boiled and cooled before freezing.

For best results, closely wrap whole cooked crab in heavy gauge polythene or foil. Alternatively, remove cooked crabmeat from the shell and pack brown and white meat in separate small containers, or arrange meats as for serving in a well scrubbed crab shell, cover with greaseproof paper and overwrap closely with polythene or foil. Seal, label, date and freeze.

To serve
Thaw 6–8 hours in refrigerator.
High Quality Storage Life 1 month

Lobster

Like crab, lobster must also be absolutely fresh, and freshly boiled and cooled before freezing.

For best results, closely wrap whole cooked lobster in heavy gauge polythene or foil. Seal, label, date and freeze. Alternatively split shell in half lengthways, remove tail and claw meat, cut into neat pieces and pack in a polythene bag or suitable container. Seal, label, date and freeze.

To serve
Thaw 6–8 hours in refrigerator.
High Quality Storage Life   1 month

Norway Lobsters (Scampi or Dublin Bay Prawns)

These must be very fresh and give best results when frozen raw in unshelled tails.

Soon after catching, twist off the head and carapace with legs and claws attached. Wash the tails and pack tightly into suitable containers or heavy gauge polythene bags. Seal, label, date and freeze.

To cook
Lower the frozen tails into boiling salted water and when the water regains boiling point, simmer for 4–6 minutes depending on size. Cool and serve.
High Quality Storage Life   1 month

Shrimps and Prawns

They must be very fresh. They may be frozen raw or cooked but are generally considered better when cooked before freezing.

Remove heads but leave tails in shell. Wash in salted water, drain well, pack into suitable containers or polythene bags. Seal, label, date and freeze.

To cook
Simply drop into boiling slightly salted water and when the water regains boiling point, simmer for 2–4 minutes.
Cooked
Wash thoroughly in fresh cold water. Boil in lightly salted water until the fish just turn 'pink', ie from 2–4 minutes. Cool in this liquid, drain and 'pack'. When cold, pack closely into suitable cartons, cover and seal, label, date and freeze.
High Quality Storage Life   1 month

Scallops and Queens

Freeze the same day as taken from the water. They may be frozen raw or as a cooked scallop dish. Scallops tend to develop an oily taste under freezer conditions. Scrub outside of shells thoroughly.

Place in a hot oven for several minutes but remove immediately the shells open. Discard the black fringe around the scallop. Wash the fish thoroughly in salted water. Cut the fish with orange roe attached away from the shell, rinse and drain. Pack into suitable containers, cover and seal. Label, date and freeze.

To serve
Thaw scallops in refrigerator overnight, then cook as fresh scallops. Alternatively, put frozen into hot water or sauce, and cook.
High Quality Storage Life   1 month

Oysters
Freeze same day as taken from water. They are usually frozen raw. Wash outside of shell thoroughly. Open (or ask fishmonger to do this for you) over a muslin lined strainer to catch juice in bowl beneath. Wash oysters in salted water (15ml/1 tablespoon salt to 600ml/1 pint cold water). Drain, and pack in suitable containers with strained juices. Cover and seal. Label, date and freeze.

To serve raw
Leave in unopened package in refrigerator until just thawed – about 6–8 hours.
To serve cooked
Add frozen to hot soup or sauce to thaw and cook at the same time. Do not boil or overcook; they will be cooked in 4–6 minutes.
High Quality Storage Life   1 month

Mussels
Scrub very thoroughly and remove any fibrous matter sticking out from the shell. Put in a large saucepan and cover with a damp cloth. Put over medium heat about 3 minutes until they open. Cool in the pan. Remove from shells and pack in boxes, covering with their own juice. Seal, label, date and freeze.

To serve
Thaw in container in refrigerator and cook. Use as fresh fish.
High Quality Storage Life   1 month

POULTRY

Birds to be frozen should be in perfect condition. They should be starved for 24 hours before killing, then hung and bled well. When the bird is plucked, it is important to avoid skin damage; if scalding, beware of over-scalding which may increase the chance of freezer burn. The bird should be cooled in a refrigerator or cold larder for 12 hours, drawn and completely cleaned.

PACKING

When packing pieces, it is not always ideal to pack a complete bird in each package; it may be more useful ultimately if all drumsticks are packaged together, all breasts or all wings, according to the way in which the flesh will be cooked.

Giblets have only a storage life of 2 months, so unless a whole bird is to be used within that time, it is not advisable to pack them inside the bird. Giblets should be cleaned, washed, dried and chilled, then wrapped in moisture-vapour-proof paper or a bag, excluding air. Frozen in batches, they can be used for soups, stews or pies. Livers should be treated in the same way, and packaged in batches for use in omelets, risotto or pâtés.

Bones of poultry joints should be padded with paper or foil to avoid tearing the freezer wrappings. Joints should be divided by two layers of clingfilm. Bones of young birds may turn brown in storage, but this does not affect flavour or quality.

Stuffings

It is not advisable to stuff a bird before freezing as the storage life of stuffing is only about 1 month. It is better to package stuffing separately.

THAWING FROZEN POULTRY

Uncooked poultry must thaw completely before cooking. Thawing in the refrigerator will allow slow, even thawing; thawing at room temperature will be twice as fast but the product will be much less satisfactory. A 1.8–2.3kg/4–5 lb chicken will thaw overnight in a refrigerator and will take 6 hours at room temperature. A turkey weighing 4kg/9 lb will take 36 hours; as much as 3 days should be allowed for a very large bird. A thawed bird can be stored for up to 24 hours in a refrigerator, but no more.

All poultry should be thawed in the unopened freezer wrappings.

FREEZING SPECIFIC POULTRY

Chicken

After cleaning, truss a whole bird, bone it or cut into joints, then chill for 12 hours before packing in a polythene bag and removing the air. Pack the giblets separately.
High Quality Storage Life 12 months

Duck

Ducks for freezing should be young with pliable breastbones and flexible beaks. Young ducklings may be frozen between 6 and 12 weeks, but older ducks between 1.35–3.2 kg/3–7 lb weight are suitable. Pluck them while still warm. The oil glands of ducks must be removed before freezing. Chill the birds well, and pack in polythene bags.

Duck must be completely thawed before cooking. For a delicious bird which is not greasy, but has a crisp skin and full-flavoured meat, roast it with 1cm/½ inch water and with salt on the breast but no extra fat, turning the bird half-way through cooking to brown the breast.

High Quality Storage Life (pre-cooked)   6 months

Guinea-Fowl

Guinea-fowl can be reared like chickens, and they taste rather like pheasant. For freezing, prepare them like chickens. When cooking, baste guinea-fowl often as they can be rather dry.

High Quality Storage Life (pre-cooked)   12 months

Goose

A goose for the freezer should be young and tender and not more than 5.4kg/12 lb weight. It may be hung up to 5 days before freezing. The oil glands must be removed.

On average, a goose loses half its weight in waste and cooking, so a 5.4kg/12 lb bird would come down to about 2.7kg/6 lb at the table. It needs more cooking for its size than turkey or chicken, and care must be taken to crisp the outside fat without drying the meat. Cook the bird on a rack in a large tin, and 20 minutes after beginning cooking, prick the skin with a fork to allow fat to drain out. Drain off some of the fat during cooking, and baste the bird two or three times. Start the bird at 230°C/450°F/Gas 8 for 30 minutes, then reduce heat to 200°C/400°F/Gas 6 and allow 20 minutes per 450g/lb plus 20 minutes. The skin will be crisper if flour is rubbed over it before cooking begins.

High Quality Storage Life (pre-cooked)   6 months

Turkey

Prepare in the same way as a chicken for freezing. Turkey legs are useful freezer items for small family meals. A frozen turkey will take a long time to thaw (up to 3 days for a large bird), but it must be thawed in the unopened bag in a cold place.

For best results when roasting turkey, place it on a rack in a greased roasting tin, brush with melted butter, sprinkle with salt and cover with a square of aluminium foil. Place in an oven preheated to 160°C/325°F/Gas 3. Remove the foil 45 minutes before cooking time is completed, baste and return to the oven to brown all over.

Cook turkey slowly at the recommended times given below. (Calculate the cooking time beforehand from the labelled weight.)

Labelled weight	Unstuffed or neck stuffed at 160°C/325°F/Gas 3	Main Cavity Stuffed Cook for 20 minutes at 200°C/400°F/Gas 6 then reduce heat to 180°C/350°F/ Gas 4 and allow –
2.3–2.7 kg/5–6 lb	2½–3 hours	2½–3 hours
2.7–3.6 kg/6–8 lb	3–3½ hours	3–3¾ hours
3.6–4.5 kg/8–10 lb	3½–4 hours	3¾–4½ hours
4.5–5.4 kg/10–12 lb	4–4½ hours	4½–5 hours
5.4–13.5 kg/12–30 lb	20 mins per 450g/lb +20 mins	+20 mins per 450g/lb +20 mins

If the turkey is to be eaten cold, cool quickly and keep in a cold place or refrigerator.

High Quality Storage Life (pre-cooked)   12 months

GAME

Freeze raw birds or animals which are young and well shot. Old or badly shot game is usually best converted immediately into made-up dishes such as casseroles.

All game intended for freezing should be hung to its required state *before* freezing, as hanging after thawing will result in the flesh going bad.

All game should be kept cool between shooting and freezing. It should be thawed in its sealed freezer package; thawing in a refrigerator is more uniform, but of course takes longer. In a refrigerator, allow 5 hours per 450g/lb thawing time; at room temperature, allow 2 hours per 450g/lb. Start cooking as soon as game is thawed and still cold, to prevent loss of juices.

FREEZING SPECIFIC GAME

Grouse

Young birds have pointed wings and rounded spurs; one young bird will be enough for two people, and an older bird may do for three people.

Remove shot and clean wounds, keep cool and hang to taste. Pluck, draw and truss as for poultry, padding the bones. Pack in a polythene bag, removing air, and freeze.

Grouse is best roasted unless very old or badly shot. For roasting, the bird should be seasoned inside and out with pepper and salt, and a piece of butter put inside with a piece of bacon over the breast. Roast at 200°C/400°F/Gas 6 for 25 minutes, basting frequently during cooking. A piece of toasted or fried bread can be placed under the bird after 15 minutes' cooking, so that the liquid from the bird drains into it, and this is included in the serving. The toast may be spread with a little of the cooked grouse liver mashed in a little stock.

High Quality Storage Life (pre-cooked)   6 months

Partridge

First year birds have the first flight feather pointed at the tip, not rounded. The grey partridge is most delicious after only 3–4 days hanging, but the redlegged variety needs 6–7 days. One bird will serve two people. Remove shot and clean wounds, keep cool and hang to taste. Pluck, draw and truss as for poultry, padding the bones. Pack in polythene bag, removing air, and freeze.

Roast a partridge with bacon on the breast, basting with butter, at 180°C/350°F/Gas 4 for 25 minutes, and avoid overcooking. Split in two to serve.

High Quality Storage Life (pre-cooked)   6 months

Pheasant

A young cock bird has round spurs in the first year, short pointed ones in the second year and sharp long ones when older. A young hen has soft feet and light feathers, while the older one has hard feet and dark feathers; hens are smaller, but less dry and more tender with good flavour. A pheasant is best hung for about 7 days in normal temperatures. One good bird should be enough for four people. Remove shot and clean wounds, keep cool and hang to taste. Pluck, draw and truss as for poultry, padding the bones. Pack in polythene bag, removing air, and freeze.

Roast a pheasant at 200°C/400°F/Gas 6 for 45 minutes, with bacon on the breast and a seasoning inside and out of salt and pepper. Baste the bird with a little butter, and add a little red wine to the pan during roasting.

High Quality Storage Life (pre-cooked)   6 months

Plover, Quail, Snipe, Woodcock

These birds should be prepared for the freezer in the same way as other feathered game, but should not be drawn.

High Quality Storage Life   6 months

Pigeon

Remove the shot and clean wounds. Pluck and pack as other feathered game, packing in twos and threes. The birds need not be hung but are best hung head downwards for an hour immediately after killing so that they bleed freely and the flesh will be paler. Only young fat pigeons should be roasted, with some fat bacon, but the fat should not be too hot as it toughens the flesh and destroys the flavour. Older birds are close and dry and are better used for pies or casseroles. Allow one pigeon for two people, or one each for hearty appetites.

High Quality Storage Life (pre-cooked)   6 months

Hare

A young hare can generally be recognized by white pointed teeth and fresh-looking fur. Older hares have cracked brown teeth and are scruffy-looking. A hare is enough for about 10 people and makes excellent casseroles and pâtés for the freezer. Clean the shot wounds and behead and clean as soon as possible, collecting the hare's blood in a carton if this is needed for cooking. Hang in a cool place: for some people 24 hours is enough, but a longer hanging will soften the 'strings' in this fast-moving animal, and some people will leave a hare from 10–14 days. Skin the animal and clean and wipe the joints. Wrap each joint separately before packing in bags, and only pack in usable quantities. Pack the blood in a carton, and freeze separately.

High Quality Storage Life   6 months

Rabbit

Clean the shot wounds, and hang for 24 hours in a cool place, then skin and divide into joints, packing as for hare. A good rabbit should feed six people.

High Quality Storage Life   6 months

Venison

This is useful meat to store in the freezer as the texture and flavour seem to improve in cold storage, and the rich 'meaty' flavour is very good for all sorts of pies and casseroles. As it can take up a lot of space, it is best to keep the best roasting joints for freezing (ie leg and saddle). Convert the other pieces into meat loaves, pies, pâté and minced meat dishes for freezing, and use the bones and trimmings for stock.

When the animal has been shot, clean the wounds and keep the carcass cold until butchered; this is best done professionally. The animal should be beheaded, bled, skinned and cleaned, with the flesh wiped dry. It should be hung for at least 4 days, but in very cold weather can hang for up to 14 days, although the flavour becomes very strong after that. Pack joints carefully, removing all air. It is best if aged 5–6 days before freezing.

Venison is a very dry meat and must be carefully treated for roasting. It may be larded, or marinaded. To do this, mix 300ml/½

48

pint red wine, 300ml/½ pint vinegar, 1 large sliced onion, parsley, thyme and bay leaf and leave the venison in this for 24 hours while it thaws, turning the meat often. Use this marinade for gravy or casseroles.

Roast young or well-hung venison at 230°C/450°F/Gas 8 for 20 minutes per 450g/lb if meat is old or not well hung, and cook in a wrapping of foil, or in a self-basting roasting tin, with plenty of butter or bacon.

High Quality Storage Life (pre-cooked)   12 months

MEAT

Both raw and cooked meat usually store extremely well in the freezer. But it is important to choose high-quality raw meat for storage, whether fresh or frozen, since freezing does not improve poor meat in either texture or flavour (although tender meat may become a little more tender in storage).

Meat should be chosen with the family needs in mind. The better cuts are bound to be more popular, but bulk buying will be a false economy if the family does not eat the cheaper cuts at all. It is important that meat is properly hung (beef 8–12 days; lamb 5–7 days; pork and veal chilled only). Before buying meat in bulk, check the diagrams given on pages 52, 54, 55, 56 and 57, and the suggested uses for each part of the animal, and see if this will fit into the family eating plan.

It is also important not to overload the freezer with bulky quantities of meat at the expense of other items, and to keep a good regular turnover of supplies. One good compromise is to use the freezer for keeping special high quality cuts, or those which are not often obtainable, such as pork fillet, veal and fillet steak, together with a variety of cooked and prepared dishes made from the cheaper cuts which are useful when time is likely to be short for food preparation.

FAST FREEZING

Do not try to freeze more than 1.8kg/4 lb meat per 28.3 litres/cubic feet of freezer space, as meat must be frozen quickly. If there is a lot of meat to freeze, deal with offal first, then pork, veal and lamb, and finally beef. Keep the unfrozen meat in the refrigerator until it is ready to be processed. Fast freezing is essential to maintain the fine texture of meat. If it is slow-frozen, it will coarsen, and will lose juices during thawing, resulting in loss of flavour and nutritive value.

PACKING

Wrapping for meat must be strong, so that oxygen does not enter the bags, affecting the fat and causing rancidity. Pad bones to prevent damage and be sure to exclude air completely from the wrapping so that it stays close to the meat and drying out is prevented. Overwrapping prevents damage to packaging.

Joints

Trim off surplus fat, and bone and roll if possible to save space. Pad any sharp bones. Wipe the meat and pack in polythene bag or sheeting, or foil. Remove all air and freeze quickly.
High Quality Storage Life   12 months (beef); 9 months (lamb and veal); 6 months (pork)

Steaks and Chops

Package in usable quantities, separating pieces of meat with clingfilm or foil. Pack in polythene bag or sheeting, or foil. Remove all air and freeze quickly.
High Quality Storage Life   6–12 months (depending on meat)

Cubed Meat

Package in usable quantities. Trim fat and cube meat. Press tightly into bags or boxes, removing air. Freeze quickly.
High Quality Storage Life   2 months

Minced Meat

Package good quality mince without fat. Press tightly into bags or boxes, and do not add salt. Mince may be shaped into patties, separated with clingfilm or foil, and packed into bags or boxes. Freeze quickly.
High Quality Storage Life   2 months

Hearts, Kidneys, Sweetbreads, Tongue

Wash and dry well. Remove blood vessels and pipes. Wrap in clingfilm or polythene and pack in bags or boxes. Off-flavours can develop if offal is not packed with care.
High Quality Storage Life   2 months

Tripe

Cut in 2.5cm/1 inch squares and pack tightly in bags or boxes, removing air and freezing quickly.
High Quality Storage Life   2 months

Liver

Package whole or in slices, separating slices with clingfilm or polythene. Exclude air and freeze quickly.
High Quality Storage Life   2 months

Sausages and Sausage-meat

Leave out salt in preparation. Pack in small quantities. Wrap tightly in polythene or foil.
High Quality Storage Life 1 month

Galantines and Meat Loaves

Galantines and meat loaves are easily stored if prepared in loaf tins for cooking, then turned out, wrapped and frozen. Meat loaves may be frozen uncooked, and this is most easily achieved if the mixture is packed into loaf tins lined with foil, the foil then being formed into a parcel and put into the freezer; the frozen meat can be transferred to its original tin for baking. For quick serving, meat loaves and galantines may be packed in slices. Pack slices with a piece of clingfilm or greaseproof paper between each, reform each shape and pack for freezing. Slices can be separated while still frozen, and thawed quickly on absorbent paper.
High Quality Storage Life 2 months

THAWING FROZEN MEAT

Frozen meat may be cooked thawed or unthawed, but partial or complete thawing helps retain juiciness, and this is the best method to follow. Thin cuts of meat and minced meat may toughen if cooked from the frozen state. Offal must always be completely thawed. Meat is best thawed in its wrapping, and preferably in a refrigerator, since slow even thawing is required. Allow 5 hours per 450g/lb in a refrigerator and 2 hours per 450g/lb at room temperature. When thawing offal, sausages and mince, allow 1½ hours at room temperature or 3 hours in a refrigerator.

COOKING FROZEN MEAT

Meat which has been frozen may be roasted, braised, grilled, fried or stewed in the same way as fresh meat. In any roasting process, however, it is best to use a slow oven method (for beef, use 150°C/300°F/Gas 2 and also for lamb; for pork, use 180°C/350°F/Gas 4). Frozen chops and steaks will cook well if put into a thick frying pan just rubbed with fat and cooked very gently for the first 5 minutes on each side, then browned more quickly.

COOKING JOINTS WHILE FROZEN

Boiling joints should not be cooked while still frozen or the flavour will be poor and weight will be lost.

Pot-roasting joints may be cooked while frozen. All cut surfaces must be sealed in hot fat to prevent excessive loss of juices.

Boneless joints should not be cooked from the frozen state, as the bone is needed to ensure good conduction of the heat.

Roasting Frozen Joints

A meat thermometer must be used, which indicates when the meat is cooked to the required degree of 'doneness'.

1 Put the joint in a roasting bag and loosely seal with twist-tie, then put in a shallow roasting tin.
2 In a roasting bag, cook the joint at 180°C/350°F/Gas 4. Without a roasting bag, seal the joint in a hot oven at 230°C/325°F/Gas 8 for 20 minutes, then continue cooking at 160°C/325°F/Gas 3 for 60 minutes per 450g/lb.

    Cooking times at 180°C/350°F/Gas 4

    Beef (under 1.8kg/4 lb weight)   30 minutes per 450g/lb + 30 minutes
    Beef (over 1.8kg/4 lb weight)   35 minutes per 450g/lb + 35 minutes
    Lamb (under 1.8kg/4 lb weight)   35 minutes per 450g/lb + 35 minutes
    Pork (over 1.8kg/4 lb weight)   45 minutes per 450kg/lb + 45 minutes
    Note Small pork joints should not be cooked by this method.

3 About 15 minutes before the end of the estimated cooking time, plunge the thermometer into the middle of the joint and check the reading. Read the temperature every 10 minutes until the joint is cooked as liked.

FREEZING SPECIFIC MEATS

Beef

Look for beef with a fresh, slightly moist appearance. The lean of roasting joints should be smooth and velvety in texture, surrounded by a layer of creamy-white fat which is firm and dry. The flesh should have small flecks of fat, known as 'marbling' which will ensure that the meat is tender when cooked.

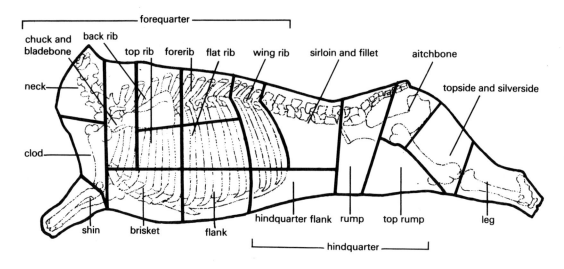

52

The Better Cuts
Ribs   A good roast on or off the bone. Can be braised or pot-roasted. May be sold as Foreribs, Back Ribs, Top Ribs, Wing Ribs.

Sirloin   A tender cut with good flavour, for roasting on or off the bone. The top part of sirloin can be cut into Entrecôte Steaks, Porterhouse Steaks, Sirloin Steaks or T-Bone Steaks. The undercut of the sirloin is the *Fillet*, a very tender steak to be roasted in the piece as Châteaubriand, or used as Fillet Steaks or Tournedos.

Rump   A popular cut for steaks which are suitable for grilling or frying.

Topside   A lean joint suitable for slow or medium roasting with some extra fat. It can also be used for braising or pot-roasting. *Top Rump* is a similar cut, suitable for pot-roasting, braising and stewing.

The Economy Cuts
Neck and Clod   This meat needs long slow cooking and can be used for stewing and braising. It makes very good beef stock.

Chuck   Very good steak for braising and stewing if cooked slowly. This is a lean cut and is also good in pies and puddings. If the meat is cut very thinly, with all muscle fibre and excess fat trimmed, it can be used as frying steak when beaten out thinly first.

Shin   This is very lean but needs long slow cooking. It can be used for stews, but is excellent for stock, gravy and soup.

Brisket   Use for pot-roasting, braising or slow-roasting.

Flank   This is a fairly lean cut, but needs long moist cooking such as braising, stewing or pot-roasting. If rolled, it can be roasted very slowly, but is better pot-roasted or braised.

Silverside   The joint can be slow-roasted or pot-roasted. Steaks can be cut from the joint to cook in the oven.

Leg   This is a very economical cut, very lean and with a good flavour. It should be given long slow cooking and used for stews or stock.

Lamb and Mutton
Look for lamb with fine-grained lean of a bright colour. The fat should be crisp and white; it should not be brittle. The better cuts have a moderate layer of fat covering the lean. This in turn should be covered by a thin, paper-like skin which is pliable to the touch.

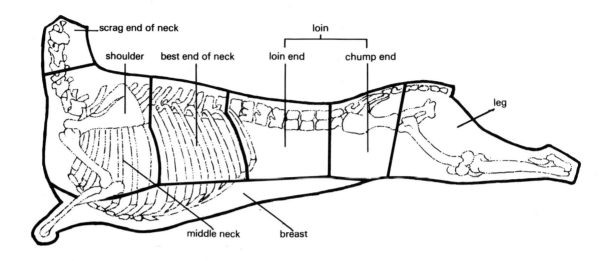

The Better Cuts
Shoulder   A good joint roasted on the bone, or boned and rolled. The joint can be cut into Blade End and Knuckle End and roasted or braised. The meat can also be cut in cubes to be used for kebabs.

Loin   This can be roasted or braised whole, or can be boned and rolled for roasting. A Double Loin or Saddle is a large roasting joint suitable for entertaining. The loin can be cut into chops for grilling or frying.

Leg   An excellent roasting joint which can be divided into Fillet End, and Shank or Knuckle End. The Fillet can be used like a steak, or cut into cubes for kebabs.

The Economy Cuts
Scrag End   Good for stews and soups.

Middle Neck   Use for stew, or boil as a small joint with root vegetables.

Best End   Use in the piece for roasting, or bone and roll for roasting or braising. Can be cut up into cutlets.

Breast   A rather fatty cut which can be boned and rolled round a fatless stuffing and then roasted. Can also be used to make stews and stock.

Veal
Look for veal which is pale pink in colour. It is a lean meat, and often needs to be cooked with a moist stuffing or sauce to offset any dryness. The bones are very soft and may easily be cut with a well-sharpened knife.

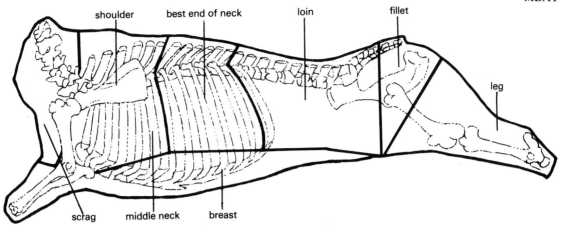

The Better Cuts

Leg A large joint which may be roasted on the bone, or boned and rolled. The hind knuckle or shin may be removed at the knee joint and used with the bone for some dishes, or as stewing veal.

Fillet An expensive cut which may be roasted, or cut into escalopes.

Loin This may be roasted on the bone, or boned and stuffed before roasting. The loin may be cut into chops, then grilled, fried or casseroled.

The Economy Cuts

Best end of neck May be roasted or braised in one piece. Sometimes cut into cutlets.

Breast A good piece of meat to bone, stuff and roast.

Shoulder An economical joint often roasted on the bone, or boned and rolled.

Middle neck Usually sold in cutlets for braising or stewing, or may be boned for stewing veal.

Scrag A bony piece of meat which may be used for stewing.

Pork

Look for pork which is smooth, firm and dry, with a good pink colour and a fine grain. The fat should be firm and creamy-white and the flesh should be 'marbled' with fat to ensure tenderness when cooked. Leave the skin on if crisp crackling is liked.

The Better Cuts

Loin Use this for roasting on the bone, or boned and rolled. It can be cut into loin or chump chops which are large and meaty and suitable for grilling, frying or baking. The Fillet or Tenderloin is a long narrow tender piece of meat from under the loin which can be roasted, or cut in thin slices for frying. This is not to be confused with the fillet end of the leg.

Leg   Another roasting joint on the bone, or boned and rolled. The joint can be divided into Fillet End and Knuckle End. Slices of fillet can be fried or grilled.

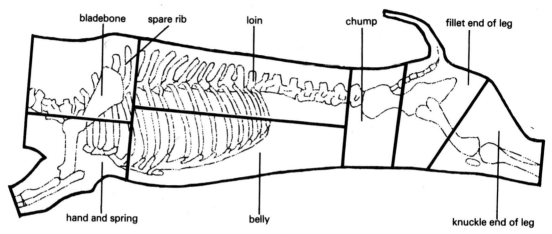

The Economy Cuts
Blade and Spare Rib or Chine   The Blade is a roasting joint which can be prepared with or without the bone. The Spare Rib joint can be roasted whole or cut into cutlets for grilling or frying.

Hand and Spring   This is the foreleg, which can be roasted on the bone, or boned and rolled. It can also be used for casseroles and kebabs.

Belly   This can be roasted on the bone, or boned and rolled. Slices are good for grilling or frying, or for casseroles. The mixture of lean and fat in this cut is useful for pâté and meat loaf.

Bacon
Collar   A good boiling joint, and the leftovers are useful for a variety of dishes.

Forehock   Best boned and rolled for a roasting or boiling joint.

Back   Good as rashers, but thick 'chops' make a substantial meal.

Streaky   Useful fat-and-lean rashers for including in many cooked dishes and for wrapping round pâtés. Can be boiled in the piece.

Gammon Leg   An attractive joint for boiling and slicing.

Gammon Steaks   Pieces cut from the prime gammon which are lean and excellent for grilling or frying.

56

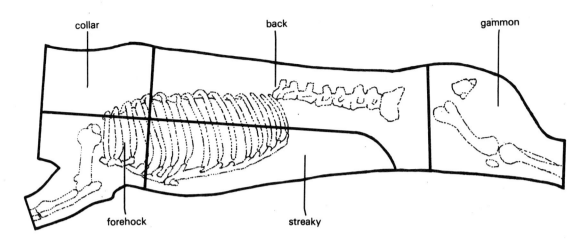

collar   back   gammon

forehock   streaky

High Quality Storage Life for Bacon

Bacon joints wrapped as recommended

Smoked bacon	up to 8 weeks
Unsmoked bacon	up to 5 weeks
Vacuum packed bacon joints	up to 10 weeks
Vacuum packed rashers or steaks	up to 10 weeks
Foil-wrapped rashers, chops or steaks, smoked	2–4 weeks only

Buying Bacon For Freezing

Freshness of the bacon is the first step to successful freezing. Inform your retailer so that he can meet this requirement. Try and get the bacon the day that he gets delivery from his supplier.

Determine the storage period in relation to freshness, and reduce the recommended period if you have any doubts.

The quicker bacon is frozen through, the better it will be. It is therefore inadvisable to freeze pieces weighing more than 2.3kg/5 lb.

Smoked bacon can be stored for longer than unsmoked bacon.

Preparing Bacon For Freezing

Freshly cut bacon joints

Determine the size of joint to be required for each meal and cut to this size. Wrap each piece in foil, allowing ample coverage. Exclude as much air as possible. Place each parcel of bacon into a polythene bag. The thicker the bag the better. Again exclude as much air as possible. Then clip or tie the bag immediately. Label, date and freeze.

Bacon rashers, chops and steaks

It may be necessary to freeze these small pieces of bacon but

57

storage time is much less than for joints, ie from 2 to 4 weeks. This is because so much of the meat and fat surface has been exposed to air with risk of rancidity developing. It is more practical to buy vacuum packed bacon which can be stored in a refrigerator for the same periods. 225g/½ lb packets which can be thawed and eaten promptly are recommended. Follow packing instructions for bacon joints.

Freezing Vacuum Packed Bacon

Vacuum packing of bacon is the ideal preparation for storage in the freezer because air has been withdrawn from the packet. Vacuum packing is a commercial process and cannot be undertaken at home.

A lot of vacuum packed bacon is so marked, but as it can be confused with other types of wrapping it is advisable to check this with your retailer if in doubt.

To prepare these packets for the freezer, inspect each one to ensure the vacuum is not damaged, ie the bacon should not be loose in the packet. Wrap the packets in foil, then label.

Thawing Frozen Bacon

Joints

Allow bacon plenty of time to thaw slowly, preferably in a refrigerator. Bacon can be thawed at room temperature before cooking. The time required depends on the thickness of the piece and the temperature. The wrapping should be removed as soon as possible during thawing.

Bacon rashers and small pieces

May be thawed overnight in the refrigerator or dipped in hot water for a few minutes until soft. Dry on kitchen paper before cooking.

Vacuum packed joints

These should be thawed in the bag, in the refrigerator or at room temperature. Cook immediately, following instructions on packet. **Note** If time is short, joints may be thawed in running water. They should, however, be wrapped in a plastic bag to prevent them getting wet.

Cooking Frozen Bacon

All frozen bacon should be cooked immediately it has thawed. The usual cooking methods – boiling, grilling, frying and baking are suitable. Once cooked, the bacon will keep 1–2 days in a refrigerator.

Do not re-freeze after thawing either in the raw or cooked state.

DAIRY FOODS AND FATS

Dairy produce is subject to a seasonal fluctuation in price, so it is worth saving butter and eggs particularly when the price is lower than average. Good cheese and cream are not always available locally, but are worth buying in markets or speciality shops for future family use or for entertaining.

Eggs

Eggs are worth freezing in quantity, since they are subject to seasonal price variation. Leftover yolks and whites may also be frozen for future use. They must be very fresh and of top quality, and should be washed and broken into a dish before processing to check freshness. Eggs cannot be frozen in shells as the shells may crack and the yolks harden so that they cannot be amalgamated with the whites.

Hard-boiled eggs should not be frozen, either alone or in sandwich fillings, as they become leathery and unpalatable.

Pack eggs in small or large containers according to end use, and use waxed or rigid plastic containers or special waxed cups for individual eggs. Eggs can also be frozen in ice cube trays, each cube being wrapped in foil and a quantity of cubes then packaged in polythene bags for easy storage. Eggs can be frozen whole, or the yolks and whites frozen separately. Either salt or sugar should be added to prevent the yolks or whites thickening.

Whole eggs should be lightly blended with a fork without incorporating too much air, then 2.5ml/½ teaspoon salt or 7.5ml/½ tablespoon sugar added to 5 eggs, and the package labelled carefully for quantity and contents.

Whites need no pre-freezing treatment.

Yolks should be mixed lightly with a fork, adding 2.5ml/½ teaspoon salt or 7.5ml/½ tablespoon sugar to 6 yolks, and the package labelled carefully for quantity and contents.

Eggs should be thawed in the unopened container in a refrigerator, but can be thawed unopened at room temperature for 1½ hours if they are needed quickly. They should be used as fresh eggs, but quality deteriorates rapidly when frozen eggs are left to stand. Egg whites may be kept for 24 hours in a refrigerator after thawing.

Liquid measure   When eggs have been packed in quantity, it may be necessary to measure them for cooking with a spoon (see over).

Equivalents are as follows:

37.5ml/2½ tablespoons whole egg	=1 egg
22.5ml/1½ tablespoons egg white	=1 egg white
15ml/1 tablespoon egg yolk	=1 yolk

High Quality Storage Life   12 months

Milk

Pasteurized homogenized milk can be frozen if necessary in cartons, and stored for 1 month. Headspace must be allowed in containers, and these should be small enough for the milk to be used up at one time.

Cream

Cream freezes well if it contains 40 per cent butterfat. It can be used for puddings, ice cream, cereals or fruit. The texture can be heavy and grainy, and if used in hot coffee, oil will rise to the surface. Cream should be thawed at room temperature and lightly beaten with a fork to restore smoothness.

Cream for processing should be pasteurized and cooled rapidly, and packed in containers, leaving 2.5cm/1 inch headspace. Devonshire and Cornish creams are heat-treated in preparation. 15ml/1 tablespoon sugar to each 600ml/1 pint of cream will lengthen keeping time. Thick Jersey cream from shop, farm or market will freeze perfectly in the waxed containers in which it is purchased, without further treatment.

High Quality Storage Life   6 months

Whipped Cream

Whipped cream may be frozen as a garnish for puddings. It may be frozen in a container, or piped ready for use. Whip 600ml/1 pint cream with 50g/2 oz icing sugar until just stiff, and pipe rosettes on to foil covered cardboard. Open freeze for 2 hours. Working quickly, transfer to polythene bags and return to the freezer for storage. To use, put rosettes on to puddings and leave to stand for 10 minutes at room temperature to thaw.

High Quality Storage Life   6 months

Cheese

Most types of cheese can be frozen, but the most satisfactory are the hard types like Cheddar. Cheese should be frozen in small quantities, sufficient for one or two days' supply (ie 225g/8 oz or less) as it dries more quickly after having been frozen, and large cheeses should be divided and repackaged. Slices should be divided by double clingfilm before wrapping in foil or freezer paper. Grated cheese can be packaged in small containers or polythene bags. All cheeses must be carefully wrapped and sealed

to prevent drying out and cross-contamination. They are best thawed in packaging in the refrigerator, but will take 1½ to 2 hours at room temperature if required.
High Quality Storage Life   3 months

Cream Cheese does not freeze well and tends to fall apart on thawing. It can be frozen if blended with double cream for use later as a cocktail dip, when it will be combined with mayonnaise after thawing, and smoothness can be restored. *Cottage Cheese* made from pasteurized milk can be stored if frozen quickly to avoid water separation on thawing.
High Quality Storage Life   3 months

Special Cheeses such as Brie, Camembert, Port Salut, Stilton, Danish Blue, Gruyère, Mozzarella, Emmenthal, Parmesan, Derby and Roquefort freeze well. Blue cheeses are inclined to crumble when thawed, and are best used for salads or toppings for other dishes. This type of cheese is best matured for the individual palate before freezing so that it will be at the peak of perfection when thawed.
High Quality Storage Life   2 months

Butter

Butter can be frozen in its original wrappings if still firm and put into polythene bags for easy storage. Unsalted butter will keep for 6 months, salted butter for 3 months. When thawing, only take enough fat from the freezer to be used up within a week. It is best to thaw butter at room temperature overnight.

Butter Balls   Decorative balls of butter can be prepared and frozen in advance. Make butter balls or curls and freeze on trays wrapped in polythene.

Flavoured Butters   Flavoured butters such as those made with brandy, parsley and other herbs, mustard or horseradish, can easily be frozen. The butter should be creamed and blended with the flavouring, then formed into a long roll. It should then be wrapped in foil and packed in a polythene bag. To serve, cut in slices while still frozen.

Margarine

Block margarine may be frozen in its original wrapping if still firm and overwrapped with foil or polythene. It will keep for 6 months. When thawing, only take enough fat from the freezer to be used up within a week; thawing is best at room temperature overnight.

Suet

When a meat carcass is purchased, a quantity of suet is often included. Some of this can be shredded and used to make steamed puddings for the freezer. The remaining suet is best made into a rich fat for general baking, which can be stored in the refrigerator or freezer.

To make this, chop or mince the suet while fresh and put it in a covered bowl in the refrigerator for 24 hours. Put this suet into a thick pan over a low heat and stir frequently as the fat begins to run. When the fat is clear and smooth and the bits of unmelted fibre are crisp and brown, strain through butter muslin and measure the fat. Add half the weight of vegetable salad oil, and chill the mixture quickly, stirring occasionally as it hardens, then pack into 600ml/1 pint containers. 450g/1 lb of chopped suet, rendered, and half its weight in oil will yield about 1.5 litres/2½ pints of cooking fat.
High Quality Storage Life   3 months
Note This rich fat is particularly good for meat pies; a little less than ordinary cooking fat should be used for baking.

VEGETABLES

Nearly all vegetables freeze well, but they must be carefully selected from garden or shop, and must be prepared correctly. Vegetables cannot be frozen to eat raw afterwards, eg in salads, and crisp green salad and radishes cannot be frozen at all because of their high water content. A few vegetables need special care in preparation, ie tomatoes, celery, onions. These are very satisfactory to use in dishes after freezing, but cannot be used in salads.

All vegetables must be young, tender and very fresh. If buying in bulk from farm or market, check that the vegetables are freshly picked. Sacks of produce are often bruised and tired, and the quantity involved is overwhelming to prepare for the freezer. The most useful items to buy are imported vegetables such as peppers and aubergines which cannot always be bought fresh but are useful for many recipes.

Vegetables for freezing from the garden must be freshly picked. It is better to process a few kg/lbs each day when preparing vegetables for family meals than wait until there is a glut of overgrown, overripe produce.

PREPARATION

1 Check that the freezer can cope with the amount of vegetables you want to freeze. 1.35kg/3 lb of fresh food to each 28.3 litres/cubic foot of freezer space every 6 hours is the usual allowance but this should be checked with the manufacturer's instructions.

2 Adjust fast-freeze switch where available at least 6 hours before beginning freezing. Alternatively, see that packages are frozen next to the floor and sides of the freezer.

3 Prepare large quantities of ice for chilling the cooling water. Even a large bowl or bucket of chilled water warms up quickly when there is a large quantity of vegetables to cool.

4 Wash vegetables in cold water and grade them for size. Prepare and freeze them quickly as indicated below.

5 Make sure all packaging is ready, and there is plenty of boiling water for blanching.

BLANCHING

It is absolutely vital to blanch vegetables (ie subject them to heat treatment) for a short time before freezing, to retard enzyme action. This action will cause loss of colour, flavour and nutritive value.

It has been said that blanching is not necessary and that vegetables can be stored for 3 months without harm without this processing. This has been disproved after extensive tests at Long Ashton Research Station, and those who prefer fresh-tasting, colourful vegetables should continue to blanch.

Water Blanching

This is the most commonly used way of preparing vegetables. Timing must be checked carefully as under-blanching results in loss of nutritive value and colour change. Over-blanching results in loss of flavour and crisp texture.

1 Use a large pan holding at least 4.8 litres/8 pints water, with a lid.

2 Use a blanching basket, wire salad basket, chip basket or muslin bag which will hold 4.5kg/1 lb vegetables comfortably.

3 Bring the water in the pan to the boil, adding lemon juice if required.

4 Plunge in the basket of vegetables, cover and bring quickly to the boil again.

5 Time blanching from the second when the water is boiling again. Individual blanching times are given on pages 65–72 for each vegetable.

6 Remove vegetables immediately blanching time is complete and plunge them into plenty of ice-cold water. A large bucketful should be used.

7 Cool completely. This should take approximately as long as the blanching time, and vegetables must be cooled to the centre. If not cooled, they will continue cooking and become mushy.

8 Drain very thoroughly before open freezing or packing.

9 Boil water again before blanching another batch of vegetables.

Steam Blanching

This method is seldom used although it retains minerals and vitamins better than water blanching. Leafy vegetables such as spinach will stick together if steam blanched.

1 Use a large steamer with a lid.
2 Put the prepared vegetables into a basket or bag, and put in the steamer. Cover the steamer.
3 Time blanching from when the steam escapes from the lid. This will take half as long again as water blanching (eg 2 minutes water blanching equals 3 minutes steam blanching).
4 Cool and freeze as for water blanching.

OPEN FREEZING

After blanching, peas, beans, sprouts and other small vegetables can be frozen on trays without covering, then packed in usable quantities and stored. This enables them to remain separate during freezing so that they can be quickly shaken out of a package for cooking.

PACKAGING FOR VEGETABLES

Vegetables may be conviently packaged in bags or rigid containers, depending on freezer space available. Delicate vegetables such as asparagus are best packed in rigid containers to avoid damage. Vegetables with a strong smell, eg onions, sprouts, are best overwrapped so that their smell does not affect other food in the freezer.

COOKING FROZEN VEGETABLES

Most vegetables are best cooked straight from the freezer, except broccoli and spinach which are better for partial thawing. Corn on the cob needs complete thawing, and tomatoes skin themselves if thawed before cooking. Thawed vegetables must be cooked at once. Since vegetables have been partly cooked during blanching, and since temperature changes during freezer storage have tenderized them, they must not be over-cooked for serving. They will cook in one-third to one-half the time allowed for fresh vegetables. Cook them in very little water, usually about 150ml/¼ pint to 450g/1 lb vegetables. Make sure the water is boiling, cover the vegetables with a lid and bring the water to the boil again. Simmer for the required time.

Frozen vegetables may also be steamed, cooked in a double saucepan, baked or fried, and will have an excellent flavour cooked in any of these ways.

Baking

Put vegetables in a greased casserole, separating them as much as possible. Put in a knob of butter, salt and pepper, cover tightly, and bake at 180°C/350°F/Gas 4 for 30 minutes. This is a useful method for an auto-timed cooker.

Frying

Use a heavy frying pan with 25g/1 oz melted butter to 450g/1 lb vegetables. Put in the vegetables, cover tightly and cook gently until tender.

FREEZING SPECIFIC VEGETABLES

Artichokes (Globe)

(a) Remove outer leaves. Wash, trim stalks and remove 'chokes'. Blanch in 4.8 litres/8 pints water with 15ml/1 tablespoon lemon juice for 7 minutes. Cool and drain upside-down. Pack in boxes.
(b) Remove all green leaves and 'chokes'. Blanch artichoke hearts for 5 minutes.

To serve
(a) Cook in boiling water for 5 minutes.
(b) Use as fresh artichokes for special dishes.
High Quality Storage Life   (a) 12 months (b) 12 months

Artichokes (Jerusalem)

Peel and cut in slices. Soften in a little butter, and simmer in chicken stock. Rub through a sieve and pack in boxes.

To serve
Use as a basis for soup with milk or cream and seasoning.
High Quality Storage Life   3 months

Asparagus

Wash and remove woody portions and scales. Grade for size and cut in 15cm/6 inch lengths. Blanch 2 minutes (small spears); 3 minutes (medium spears); 4 minutes (large spears). Cool and drain. Pack in boxes.

To serve
Cook 5 minutes in boiling water.
High Quality Storage Life   9 months

Aubergines

Use mature, tender, medium-sized vegetables.
(a) Peel and cut in 2.5cm/1 inch slices. Blanch 4 minutes, chill and drain. Pack in layers separated by paper in boxes.

(b) Coat slices in thin batter, or egg and breadcrumbs. Deep fry, drain and cool. Pack in layers in boxes.

To serve
(a) Cook 5 minutes in boiling water.
(b) Heat in a slow oven or part thaw and deep fry.
High Quality Storage Life (a) 12 months (b) 2 months

Beans (Broad)

Use small young beans. Shell and blanch for 1½ minutes. Pack in bags or boxes.

To serve
Cook 8 minutes in boiling water.
High Quality Storage Life 12 months

Beans (French)

Top and tail. Leave small beans whole; cut larger ones into 2.5cm/1 inch pieces. Blanch 3 minutes (whole beans); 2 minutes (cut beans). Cool and pack in bags.

To serve
Cook 7 minutes in boiling water (whole beans); 5 minutes (cut beans).
High Quality Storage Life 12 months

Beans (Runner)

Cut in pieces and blanch 2 minutes. Do not shred. Cool and pack.

To serve
Cook 7 minutes in boiling water.
High Quality Storage Life 12 months

Beetroot

Use very young beetroot, under 7.5cm/3 inches across. Cook in boiling water until tender. Rub off skins and pack in boxes, either whole or cut in slices.

To serve
Thaw 2 hours in container in refrigerator. Drain and add dressing.
High Quality Storage Life 6 months

Broccoli

Use green, compact heads with tender stalks 2.5cm/1 inch thick or less. Trim stalks and remove outer leaves. Wash well and soak in salt water for 30 minutes (10ml/2 teaspoons salt to 4.8 litres/8 pints water). Wash in fresh water, and cut into sprigs. Blanch 3 minutes (thin stems); 4 minutes (5 minutes thick stems). Pack into boxes or bags, alternating heads.

To serve
Cook 8 minutes in boiling water.
High Quality Storage Life   12 months

Brussels Sprouts

Grade small compact heads. Clean and wash well. Blanch 3 minutes (small); 4 minutes (medium). Cool and pack in bags or boxes. Overwrap.

To serve
Cook 8 minutes in boiling water.
High Quality Storage Life   12 months

Cabbage (Green and Red)

Use crisp young cabbage. Wash and shred finely. Blanch 1½ minutes. Pack in bags.

To serve
Cook 8 minutes in boiling water. Do not use raw.
High Quality Storage Life   6 months

Carrots

Use very young carrots. Wash and scrape. Blanch 3 minutes for small whole carrots, sliced or diced carrots. Pack in bags or boxes.

To serve
Cook 8 minutes in boiling water.
High Quality Storage Life   12 months

Cauliflower

Use firm compact heads with close white flowers. Wash and break into sprigs. Blanch 3 minutes in 4.8 litres/8 pints water with 15ml/1 tablespoon lemon juice. Cool and pack in lined boxes or bags.

To serve
Cook 10 minutes in boiling water.
High Quality Storage Life   6 months

Celery

(a) Use crisp young stalks. Scrub well and string. Cut in 2.5cm/1 inch lengths and blanch 2 minutes. Cool, drain and pack in bags.
(b) Prepare as above, but pack in boxes with water used for blanching, leaving 1cm/½ inch headspace.

To serve
Use as a vegetable, or for stews or soups, using liquid if available. Do not use raw.
High Quality Storage Life   6 months

Chestnuts

Boil unshelled chestnuts. Drain; peel off shells. Pack in boxes or bags.

To serve
Cook in boiling water or milk, according to recipe.
High Quality Storage Life   6 months

Chicory

Wash well and remove outer leaves. Blanch 3 minutes and cool in cooking liquid. Pack in the blanching liquid in boxes, leaving 1 cm/½ inch headspace.

To serve
Put into a covered dish in the oven in blanching liquid and heat at 180°C/350°F/Gas 4 for 40 minutes. Drain and serve with butter.
High Quality Storage Life   6 months

Corn on the Cob

(a) Use fresh tender corn. Remove leaves and threads and grade cobs for size. Blanch 4 minutes (small cobs); 6 minutes (medium cobs); 8 minutes (large cobs). Cool and dry. Pack individually in foil or freezer paper. Freeze and pack in bags.
(b) Blanch cobs and scrape off kernels. Pack in boxes, leaving 1 cm/½ inch headspace.

To serve
(a) Thaw before cooking. Put cobs in cold water, bring to a fast boil and simmer 5 minutes.
(b) Thaw in wrappings in refrigerator. Cook 10 minutes in boiling water.
High Quality Storage Life   12 months

Cucumber

Cut in thin slices and pack in boxes. Cover with equal quantities white vinegar and water, seasoned with 2.5ml/½ teaspoon sugar and 5ml/1 teaspoon black pepper to 600ml/1 pint liquid.

To serve
Thaw in container in refrigerator. Drain and season with salt.
High Quality Storage Life   2 months

Fennel

Use crisp young stalks. Scrub well. Blanch 3 minutes. Cool and pack in blanching water in boxes.

To serve
Simmer 30 minutes in blanching water or stock. Slip hard cores from roots when cooked.
High Quality Storage Life   6 months

Herbs (mint, parsley and chives)

(a) Wash and pack sprigs in bags.

(b) Chop finely and pack into ice cube trays. Transfer frozen cubes to bags for storage.

To serve

Thaw at room temperature if using for sandwich fillings. Add cubes to sauces, soups or stews. Do not use for garnish as they become limp.

High Quality Storage Life   6 months

Kale

Use young, tender kale. Remove dry or tough leaves. Strip leaves from stems and blanch 1 minute. Cool and drain. Chop leaves for convenient packing. Pack into bags.

To serve

Cook 8 minutes in boiling water.

High Quality Storage Life   6 months

Kohlrabi

Use young and tender, not too large, and mild-flavoured. Trim, wash and peel. Small ones may be frozen whole, but large ones should be diced. Blanch 3 minutes (whole); 2 minutes (diced). Cool and pack in bags or boxes.

To serve

Cook 10 minutes in boiling water.

High Quality Storage Life   12 months

Leeks

Trim off roots and green stems. Wash very well and remove dirty outer layers. Cut either finely or coarsely into even lengths. Blanch finely cut leeks for 1½ minutes, coarsely cut leeks for 3 minutes. Cool thoroughly and drain, or pack in blanching liquid.

To serve

Cook drained leeks until tender in salted water, and serve with butter or sauce, or make into a purée, or add to a soup or stew. Leeks packed in blanching liquid can be used to make soup.

High Quality Storage Life   12 months

Marrow

(a) Cut young marrows or courgettes in 1 cm/½ inch slices without peeling. Blanch 3 minutes and pack in boxes, leaving 1 cm/½ inch headspace.

(b) Peel and seed large marrows. Cook until soft, mash and pack in boxes.

To serve
(a) Fry in oil, and season well.
(b) Reheat in double boiler with butter and seasoning.
High Quality Storage Life 2 months

Mushrooms

(a) Wipe but do not peel. Cut large mushrooms in slices. Stalks may be frozen separately. Blanch 1½ minutes in 3.6 litres/6 pints water with 15ml/1 tablespoon lemon juice. Pack cups down in boxes, leaving 3cm/1½ inches headspace.
(b) Grade and cook in butter for 5 minutes. Allow 90ml/6 tablespoons butter to 450g/1 lb mushrooms. Cool quickly, take off excess fat, and pack in boxes.

To serve
(a) Thaw in container in refrigerator, and cook in butter.
(b) Add while frozen to soups, stews or other dishes.
High Quality Storage Life (a) 3 months (b) 2 months

Onions

(a) Peel, chop and pack in small boxes. Overwrap.
(b) Cut in slices and wrap in foil or freezer paper, dividing layers with paper. Overwrap.
(c) Chop or slice, blanch 2 minutes. Cool and drain. Pack in boxes. Overwrap.
(d) Leave tiny onions whole. Blanch 4 minutes. Pack in boxes. Overwrap.

To serve
Thaw raw onions in refrigerator. Add to salads while frosty. Add frozen onions to dishes according to recipe.
High Quality Storage Life 2 months

Parsnips

Use young parsnips. Trim and peel. Cut into narrow strips or dice. Blanch 2 minutes. Pack in bags or boxes.

To serve
Cook 15 minutes in boiling water.
High Quality Storage Life 12 months

Peas (Green)

Use young sweet peas. Shell. Blanch 1 minute, shaking basket to distribute heat. Cool and drain. Pack in boxes or bags.

To serve
Cook 7 minutes in boiling water.
High Quality Storage Life 12 months

Peas (Edible Pods)
Use flat tender pods. Wash well. Remove ends and strings. Blanch ½ minute in small quantities.

To serve
Cook 7 minutes in boiling water.
High Quality Storage Life 12 months

Peppers (Green and Red)
(a) Wash well. Remove seeds and membranes. Blanch 2 minutes (slices); 3 minutes (halves). Pack in boxes or bags.
(b) Grill on high heat until skin is charred. Plunge into cold water and rub off skins. Remove caps and seeds. Pack tightly in boxes in salt solution (15ml/1 tablespoon salt to 600ml/1 pint water), leaving 2.5cm/1 inch headspace.

To serve
(a) Thaw 1½ hours at room temperature.
(b) Thaw in liquid and drain. Dress with oil and seasoning.
High Quality Storage Life 12 months

Potatoes
(a) Scrape and wash new potatoes. Blanch 4 minutes. Cool and pack in bags.
(b) Slightly undercook new potatoes. Drain, toss in butter, cool and pack in bags.
(c) Mash potatoes with butter and hot milk. Pack in boxes or bags.
(d) Form potatoes into croquettes or Duchesse Potatoes. Cook, cool and pack in boxes.
(e) Fry chips in clean fat for 4 minutes. Do not brown. Cool and pack in bags.

To serve
(a) Cook 15 minutes in boiling water.
(b) Plunge bag in boiling water. Remove from heat and leave 10 minutes.
(c) Reheat in double boiler.
(d) Thaw 2 hours. Heat at 180°C/350°F/Gas 4 for 20 minutes.
(e) Fry in deep fat.
High Quality Storage Life (a) 12 months (b)–(e) 3 months

Pumpkin
Peel and seed. Cook until soft. Mash and pack in boxes.

To serve
(a) Reheat in double boiler with butter and seasoning.
(b) Thaw 2 hours at room temperature and use as a pie filling.
High Quality Storage Life 6 months

Spinach

Use young tender spinach. Remove stems. Wash very well. Blanch 2 minutes, shaking basket so that the leaves separate. Cool and press out moisture. Pack in boxes or bags.

To serve
Melt a little butter and cook frozen spinach 7 minutes.
High Quality Storage Life   12 months

Tomatoes

(a) Wipe tomatoes and remove stems. Grade and pack in small quantities in bags.
(b) Skin and core tomatoes. Simmer in own juice for 5 minutes until soft. Sieve, cool and pack in boxes.
(c) Core tomatoes and cut in quarters. Simmer with lid on for 10 minutes. Put through muslin. Cool juice and pack in boxes, leaving 2.5cm/1 inch headspace.

To serve
(a) Thaw 2 hours at room temperature (skins slip off when thawed). Grill, or use in recipes. Do not use raw.
(b) Thaw 2 hours at room temperature. Use for soups or stews.
(c) Thaw in refrigerator. Serve frosty. Add seasoning.
High Quality Storage Life   12 months

Turnips

(a) Use small, young mild turnips. Peel and cut in dice. Blanch 2½ minutes. Cool and pack in boxes.
(b) Cook turnips until tender. Drain and mash. Pack in boxes, leaving 1 cm/½ inch headspace.

To serve
(a) Cook 10 minutes in boiling water.
(b) Reheat in double boiler with butter and seasoning.
High Quality Storage Life   (a) 12 months (b) 3 months

Vegetables (mixed)

Prepare and blanch vegetables separately. Mix and pack in boxes.

To serve
Cook 7 minutes in boiling water.
High Quality Storage Life   12 months

FRUIT

All types of fruit can be frozen, but the best results are obtained from fully flavoured fruit such as berries. Blander fruit such as pears can be frozen but have little flavour. Only first quality fruit should be used which is ripe but not mushy. Underripe fruit will be tasteless and poorly coloured. Fruit should only be picked or purchased in manageable quantities which can be processed quickly.

Choose *garden fruit* which is fresh and of top quality. Berries, currants, rhubarb, plums, apples and cherries can all be frozen. If large quantities are available and time is short, some of the fruit can be packed unsweetened for later jam-making.

Choose *shop fruit* when it is plentiful and cheap. Melons, pineapples, apricots, grapes and peaches are all worth freezing, even in small quantities, to add to winter fruit salads. Citrus fruit freezes well, but is in season throughout the year, and is not worth processing unless it can be bought in bulk. Bananas are not worth freezing in quantity, as they process badly, and are in season throughout the year at a stable price.

PREPARATION

Most fruit can be prepared for the freezer in three or four different ways. It is worth freezing each fruit in at least two ways with a view to its final use, eg gooseberries will probably be eaten in pies, jam or fools, and are therefore best frozen raw and unsweetened as cooked purée. This will save a certain amount of freezer space, and will also encourage the use of the fruit which can be overwhelming and boring if it is always prepared in the same way.

Fruit can be prepared raw and unsweetened, with sugar or syrup, or made into purée, syrup or juice. It can also be prepared in the form of ices and cooked puddings. Mixed packs of summer fruits are useful for later use, eg strawberries, raspberries, red and black currants, dessert gooseberries and black cherries, and this means that only small quantities of each fruit are needed for freezing at one time. Two-fruit mixes such as grapes and pears, or pineapples and raspberries, are also useful.

Before packing, fruit should be well washed in ice-chilled water. This will prevent sogginess and loss of juice. Drain the fruit at once in enamel, aluminium, stainless steel or earthenware (copper, iron and galvanized ware produce off-flavours). Remove stems and stones gently where necessary, using the tips of the fingers. Do not squeeze.

Discoloration

Fruit which contains plenty of vitamin C does not discolour as much as apples, peaches and pears, which tend to darken quickly during preparation, freezer storage and thawing. If lemon juice or citric acid is added to these fruits it will help to prevent darkening.

Allow the juice of 1 lemon to 900ml/1½ pints liquid, or 5ml/1 teaspoon citric acid to each 450g/1 lb sugar in a dry pack.

Air reacts on the cells of fruit to produce darkening, so that fruit must always be prepared quickly once the skin or rind (which forms a natural protection) has been broken. Fruit also discolours quickly after thawing when exposed to the air, so it should be eaten immediately after thawing while a few ice crystals remain.

Fruit purée darkens quickly because large amounts of air are forced through the sieve during preparation, and should be used quickly after thawing. It is also better to store purée only from 4–8 months if high quality is to be maintained.

Preparation Methods

Use *Dry Unsweetened Pack* for fruit which will be used for pies, puddings and jams, or for those on sugar-free diets. This is good for berries and currants.

Use *Dry Sugar Pack* for fruit which can be eaten immediately on thawing. This method draws out the juices and therefore tends to make strawberries and raspberries slushy. Also, many people on diets prefer less sweetening than that normally recommended for freezing. Sugar does, however, help to retain a good colour in the fruit.

A *Syrup Pack* is good for non-juicy fruit and that which discolours easily, although it limits the end-use of the pack as the fruit cannot be easily converted into pies, puddings or ices. An *Unsweetened Wet Pack* can be prepared for those on a sugar-free diet, but there is little use of this method as dishes can more easily be prepared for eating from a dry unsweetened pack.

METHODS OF FREEZING

Open Freezing

Fruit can be packed straight into containers or bags for freezing, but it often sticks together. This spoils the shape of the fruit, and a pack will take longer to thaw when needed. If fruit is open-frozen, it will remain separate in the packs, and small quantities can be shaken out when needed.

No special equipment is necessary for open freezing. Use a tray, foil container, lid of a plastic box, or a baking sheet. Spread out the fruit on this and do not cover it. Freeze in the fast-freeze compartment, or in the coldest part of the freezer, and when the fruit is firm, pack in bags or boxes. This will take 1-2 hours, and the fruit will not be rock-hard, so it should be packed carefully. To get the best results from open-frozen fruit, spread it out again so that the shape of the fruit is retained. This is a particularly good method for strawberries or other fruit which crush easily.

Dry Unsweetened Pack

Wash fruit in ice-chilled water, drain well and open freeze if fruit is delicate. Pack into bags or rigid containers.

Dry Sugar Pack

1 Wash fruit in ice chilled water, drain well. Crush or slice if liked.
2 Pack in rigid containers in layers with sugar, using sugar as the top layer and leaving 1cm/½ inch headspace before closing.

or

Mix fruit and sugar with a spoon which will not stain, until the sugar has dissolved. Pack in bags or containers, leaving 1cm/½ inch headspace.

Syrup Pack

Prepare the syrup with white sugar and water. Brown sugar discolours the fruit; honey flavours the fruit strongly. Make up the syrup by dissolving the sugar in boiling water, and then chilling the syrup before using. The type of syrup varies from a mixture of 125g/4 oz sugar to 600ml/1 pint water (which gives a very light syrup) to 625g/25 oz sugar to 600ml/1 pint (a very heavy syrup). In general, a proportion of 275g/11 oz or 450g/1 lb sugar to 600ml/1 pint water is used, giving a medium syrup most suitable for the majority of fruit. Heavy syrup tends to make fruit flabby. Sometimes the syrup is referred to in a percentage:

Sugar	Water	Type of Syrup
125g/4 oz	600ml/1 pint	20% very light syrup
200g/7 oz	600ml/1 pint	30% light syrup
300g/11 oz	600ml/1 pint	40% medium syrup
450g/16 oz	600ml/1 pint	50% heavy syrup
625g/25 oz	600ml/1 pint	60% very heavy syrup

1 Prepare and chill syrup in recommended proportions of sugar and water. Add lemon juice for fruit which discolours easily. Add pure vanilla essence to improve flavour of bland fruit such as pears.
2 Wash and drain fruit. Slice if necessary and drop into water or lemon juice if recommended to prevent discoloration.
3 Pack fruit and syrup into rigid containers, leaving 1cm/½ inch headspace.
4 Fill this space with crumpled clingfilm, foil or transparent film to prevent fruit rising and discolouring.

Fruit Purée

Do not use overripe or bruised fruit. Sieve raw fruit such as raspberries or strawberries which mash easily. Sweeten to taste and pack into rigid containers in quantities which can be used for one meal or recipe. If fruit such as apples or damsons need cooking, use the minimum of liquid, and cook in a covered oven dish for best flavour. Sieve, cool and sweeten before packing.

Fruit Juice

Apple, redcurrant and citrus fruit juice can be frozen, but juices are only worth preparing if there is a glut of fruit.

Apple juice should be made in the proportion of 300ml/½ pint water to 900g/2 lb apples. Do not sweeten as fermentation sets in quickly.

Redcurrant juice should be made from juicy currants just covered in water. This is useful for jam-making later in the year.

Citrus fruit juice should be made from good quality heavy fruit, chilled before the juice is extracted. The juice can be strained or not, as preferred.

Apple or redcurrant juice should be strained through a jelly bag or cloth. All juice should be chilled before being put into the freezer. Freeze in small rigid containers, leaving 1cm/½ inch headspace. Juice can also be frozen in loaf tins or ice cube trays, and the frozen cubes then wrapped in foil or polythene for storage.

Fruit Syrup

Syrups are difficult to bottle and keep well, but they are very easily stored in the freezer, and are useful for drinks, sauces and flavouring for a variety of dishes. Blackcurrant syrup is particularly good, but raspberry is also excellent, or a mixture of raspberries and redcurrants. Use a standard recipe for preparing fruit syrup. Chill and freeze in small rigid containers, or in loaf tins or ice cube trays, wrapping the cubes for storage. One syrup cube gives an individual serving for sauces or drinks.

THAWING FRUIT

Fruit loses quality and flavour if it stands about after thawing, so only thaw the amount which is needed for one meal. Cooked left-over fruit will however keep for some days in a refrigerator.

Fruit which discolours badly is best thawed rapidly with a lid on the container, and unsweetened frozen fruit can be put at once into hot syrup to cook so that discoloration is avoided. Fruit can also be put straight into a pie while it is frozen.

Thaw fruit in unopened containers. Allow 6–8 hours thawing time in the refrigerator, or 2–4 hours at room temperature. These times can be speeded up if the container is placed in a bowl of cold water. Unsweetened packs take longer to thaw than sweetened ones; fruit in dry sugar thaws most quickly.

A lot of juice runs from fruit when thawed, so if the fruit is to be used for pies or cake fillings, add a little thickening such as cornflour, arrowroot or flake tapioca, or drain off any excess juice to use as syrup or sauce.

FREEZING SPECIFIC FRUITS

Apples
Peel, core and drop in cold water. Cut in twelfths or sixteenths. Pack in bags or boxes.
(a) Dry sugar pack (225g/8 oz sugar to 900g/2 lb fruit).
(b) 40% syrup pack.
(c) Sweetened purée.

To serve
(a) and (b) Use for pies and puddings.
(c) Use for sauce, fools and ices.
High Quality Storage Life   (a) and (b) 12 months (c) 4 months

Apricots
(a) Peeled and halved in dry sugar pack (125g/4 oz to 450g/1 lb fruit) or 40% syrup pack.
(b) Peeled and sliced in 40% syrup pack.
(c) Sweetened purée (very ripe fruit).

To serve
(a) Thaw 3½ hours at room temperature.
(b) Use for sauce and ices.
High Quality Storage Life   (a) and (b) 12 months (c) 4 months

Avocado Pears
(a) Rub halves in lemon juice, wrap in foil and pack in polythene bags.
(b) Dip slices in lemon juice and freeze in boxes.
(c) Mash pulp with lemon juice (15ml/1 tablespoon to 1 avocado) and pack in small containers.

To serve
(a) Thaw 2½ hours to 3 hours at room temperature and use at once.
(b) Season pulp with onion, garlic or herbs.
High Quality Storage Life   2 months

Bananas
Mash with sugar and lemon juice (225g/8 oz sugar to 45ml/3 tablespoons lemon juice to 3 breakfastcups banana pulp). Pack in small containers.

To serve
Thaw 6 hours in unopened container in refrigerator. Use in sandwiches or cakes.
High Quality Storage Life   1 month

Blackberries

Wash dark ripe berries and dry well.
(a) Fast-freeze unsweetened berries on trays and pack in bags.
(b) Dry sugar pack (225g/8 oz sugar to 900g/2 lb fruit).
(c) Sweetened purée (raw or cooked fruit).

To serve
Thaw 3 hours at room temperature. Use raw, cooked or in pies and puddings.
High Quality Storage Life   (a) and (b) 12 months (c) 4 months

Blueberries

Wash in chilled water and drain thoroughly. Crush fruit slightly as skins toughen on freezing.
(a) Fast-freeze unsweetened berries on trays and pack in bags.
(b) Dry sugar pack (125g/4 oz sugar to 4 cups crushed berries).
(c) 50% syrup pack.

To serve
Use raw, cooked or in pies and puddings.
High Quality Storage Life   12 months

Cherries

Put in chilled water for 1 hour; remove stones. Pack in glass or plastic containers, as cherry juice remains liquid and leaks through waxed containers.
(a) Dry sugar pack (225g/8 oz sugar to 900g/2 lb stoned cherries).
(b) 40% syrup pack for sweet cherries.
(c) 50% or 60% syrup pack for sour cherries.

To serve
Thaw 3 hours at room temperature. Serve cold, or use for pies.
High Quality Storage Life   12 months

Coconut

Grate or shred, moisten with coconut milk, and pack into bags or boxes; 125g/4 oz sugar to 4 breakfastcups shredded coconut may be added if liked.

To serve
Thaw 2 hours at room temperature. Drain off milk. Use for fruit salads, icings or curries.
High Quality Storage Life   2 months

Cranberries

Wash firm glossy berries and drain.

(a) Dry unsweetened pack.

(b) Sweetened purée.

To serve

Cook in water and sugar while still frozen. Can be thawed 3½ hours at room temperature.

High Quality Storage Life   (a) 12 months (b) 4 months

Currants (Black, Red and White)

Prepare black, red or white currants by the same methods. Strip fruit from stems with a fork, wash in chilled water and dry gently. Currants can be fast-frozen on trays and the stalks stripped off before packing. This makes the job easier.

(a) Dry unsweetened pack.

(b) Dry sugar pack (225g/8 oz sugar to 450g/1 lb currants).

(c) 40% syrup pack.

(d) Sweetened purée (particularly blackcurrants).

To serve

(a) and (b) Thaw 45 minutes at room temperature. Use for jam, pies and puddings.

(c) and (d) Use as sauce, or for drinks, ices or puddings.

High Quality Storage Life   (a) (b) (c) 12 months (d) 4 months

Damsons

Wash in chilled water; cut in half and remove stones.

(a) 50% syrup pack.

(b) Sweetened purée.

To serve

Thaw at room temperature for 2½ hours. Use cold, or for pies or puddings.

High Quality Storage Life   (a) 12 months (b) 4 months

Dates (Dried)

(a) Wrap block dates in foil or polythene bags.

(b) Remove stones from dessert dates; pack in bags or boxes.

To serve

Thaw 30 minutes at room temperature. Serve as dessert, or use for cakes or puddings.

High Quality Storage Life   12 months

Figs

Wash fresh sweet ripe figs in chilled water; remove stems. Do not bruise.

(a) Peeled or unpeeled in dry unsweetened pack.
(b) 30% syrup pack for peeled figs.
(c) Wrap dried dessert figs in foil or polythene bags.

To serve
Thaw for 1½ hours at room temperature. Eat raw or cooked in syrup.
High Quality Storage Life   12 months

Gooseberries
Wash in chilled water and dry. For pies, freeze fully ripe fruit; for jam, fruit may be slightly underripe.
(a) Dry unsweetened pack.
(b) 40% syrup pack.
(c) Sweetened purée.

To serve
(a) and (b) Thaw for 2½ hours at room temperature.
Fruit may be put into pies or cooked while still frozen.
(c) Thaw 2½ hours at room temperature and use for fools, mousses or ices.
High Quality Storage Life   (a) and (b) 12 months (c) 4 months

Grapefruit
Peel; remove pith; cut into segments.
(a) Dry sugar pack (225g/8 oz sugar to 2 breakfastcups segments).
(b) 50% syrup pack.

To serve
Thaw 2½ hours at room temperature.
High Quality Storage Life   12 months

Grapes
Pack seedless varieties whole. Skin, seed other types. Pack in 30% syrup.

To serve
Thaw 2½ hours at room temperature.
High Quality Storage Life   12 months

Greengages
Wash in chilled water and dry. Cut in half and remove stones. Pack in 40% syrup.

To serve
Thaw 2½ hours at room temperature.
High Quality Storage Life   12 months

Guavas
(a) Wash fruit, cook in a little water, and purée. Pineapple juice gives better flavour than water.
(b) Peel, halve and cook until tender, then pack in 30% syrup.

To serve
Thaw 1½ hours at room temperature.
High Quality Storage Life   12 months

Kumquats
(a) Wrap whole fruit in foil.
(b) 50% syrup pack.

To serve
Thaw 2 hours at room temperature.
High Quality Storage Life   (a) 2 months (b) 12 months

Lemons and Limes
Peel fruit, cut in slices, and pack in 20% syrup.

To serve
Thaw 1 hour at room temperature.
High Quality Storage Life   12 months

Loganberries
Wash berries and dry well.
(a) Fast freeze unsweetened berries on trays and pack in bags.
(b) Dry sugar pack (225g/8 oz sugar to 900g/2 lb fruit).
(c) 50% syrup pack.
(d) Sweetened purée (cooked fruit).

To serve
Thaw 3 hours at room temperature. Use for ices and mousses.
High Quality Storage Life   12 months

Mangoes
Peel ripe fruit, and pack in slices in 50% syrup. Add 15ml/1 tablespoon lemon juice to 1.2 litres/2 pints syrup.

To serve
Thaw 1½ hours at room temperature.
High Quality Storage Life   12 months

Melons
Cut into cubes or balls. Toss in lemon juice and pack in 30% syrup.

To serve
Thaw unopened in refrigerator. Serve while still frosty.
High Quality Storage Life   12 months

Nectarines

Wipe fruit, and peel or not as desired. Cut in halves or slices and brush with lemon juice.

(a) 40% syrup pack.

(b) Sweetened purée (fresh fruit) with 15ml/1 tablespoonful lemon juice to each 450g/1 lb fruit.

To serve
Thaw 3 hours in refrigerator.
High Quality Storage Life   (a) 12 months (b) 4 months

Oranges

Peel and divide into sections or cut into slices.

(a) Dry sugar pack (225g/8 oz sugar to 3 breakfastcups sections or slices).

(b) 30% syrup.

(c) Pack slices in slightly sweetened fresh orange juice.

Note Navel oranges become bitter in the freezer. Seville oranges may be frozen whole in their skins in polythene bags for marmalade.

To serve
Thaw 2½ hours at room temperature.
High Quality Storage Life   12 months

Peaches

Work quickly as fruit discolours. Peel, cut in halves or slices and brush with lemon juice.

(a) 40% syrup pack.

(b) Sweetened purée (fresh fruit) with 15ml/1 tablespoon lemon juice to each 450g/1 lb fruit.

To serve
Thaw 3 hours in refrigerator.
High Quality Storage Life   (a) 12 months (b) 4 months

Pears

Pears should be ripe, but not overripe. They discolour quickly and do not retain their delicate flavour in the freezer. Peel and quarter the fruit, remove cores, and dip pieces in lemon juice. Poach in 30% syrup for 1½ minutes, then drain and cool. Pack in cold 30% syrup.

To serve
Thaw 3 hours at room temperature.
High Quality Storage Life   12 months

Persimmons

(a) Wrap whole fruit in foil.

(b) Peel and freeze in 50% syrup, adding 10ml/1 dessertspoon lemon juice to 1.2 litres/2 pints syrup.
(c) Sweetened purée (fresh fruit).

To serve
Thaw 3 hours at room temperature. Use unpeeled raw fruit as soon as it has thawed, or it will darken.
High Quality Storage Life (a) 2 months (b) 12 months (c) 3 months

Pineapple
Use fully ripe fruit. Peel and cut into slices or chunks.
(a) Dry unsweetened pack, separated by clingfilm.
(b) Dry sugar pack (125g/4 oz sugar to 450g/1 lb fruit).
(c) 30% syrup pack.
(d) Crush fruit and mix 125g/4 oz sugar to 2 cups fruit.

To serve
Thaw 3 hours at room temperature.
High Quality Storage Life 12 months

Plums
Wash in chilled water and dry. Halve and store. Pack in 40% syrup.

To serve
Thaw 2½ hours at room temperature.
High Quality Storage Life 12 months

Pomegranates
(a) Halve ripe fruit; scoop out juice sacs and pack in 50% syrup.
(b) Extract juice and sweeten to taste. Freeze in ice cube trays, and wrap frozen cubes in foil for storage.

To serve
Thaw 3 hours at room temperature.
High Quality Storage Life 12 months

Quinces
Peel, core and slice. Simmer in boiling 20% syrup for 20 minutes. Cool and pack in cold 20% syrup.

To serve
Thaw 3 hours at room temperature.
High Quality Storage Life 12 months

Raspberries
(a) Dry unsweetened pack.

(b) Dry sugar pack (125g/4 oz sugar to 450g/1 lb fruit).
(c) 30% syrup.
(d) Sweetened purée (fresh fruit).

To serve
Thaw 3 hours at room temperature.
High Quality Storage Life   (a) (b) (c) 12 months (d) 4 months

Rhubarb

Wash sticks in cold running water, and trim to the required length.
(a) Blanch sticks 1 minute, then wrap in foil or polythene.
(b) 40% syrup pack.
(c) Sweetened purée (cooked fruit).

To serve
Thaw 3 hours at room temperature. Raw fruit can be cooked while still frozen.
High Quality Storage Life   (a) and (b) 12 months (c) 4 months

Strawberries

Use ripe, mature and firm fruit. Pick over fruit, removing the hulls.
(a) Grade for size in dry unsweetened pack.
(b) Dry sugar pack (125g/4 oz sugar to 450g/1 lb fruit). Fruit may be sliced or lightly crushed.
(c) 40% syrup for whole or sliced fruit.
(d) Sweetened purée (fresh fruit).

To serve
Thaw 1½ hours at room temperature.
High Quality Storage Life   (a) (b) (c) 12 months (d) 4 months

PUDDINGS AND ICES

PUDDINGS

A selection of puddings which can be served straight from the freezer or reheated is an invaluable aid in planning meals. Gelatine sweets, cold soufflés and mousses, cheesecakes, and fruit in wine or liqueurs need no further cooking. Steamed suet and sponge puddings, baked sponge puddings, crumbles and pastry items can be prepared in bulk from time to time, and save preparation time before each meal; they also provide a useful way of freezing surplus fruit or other ingredients. The only types of pudding which do not freeze well are milk puddings and custards. Custard pies and trifles are available in commercial packs, but traditional home recipes are not suitable for freezing. Meringue toppings should also be avoided as they 'weep' and lose crispness after freezing.

Packing

Puddings are best prepared in dishes which can be taken straight from the freezer to the table, or which can be reheated in the oven before service. Foil pudding basins, pie plates and deep containers with lids are the most useful for this purpose.

FREEZING SPECIFIC PUDDINGS

Babas and Savarins

An enriched yeast dough incorporating eggs and sugar freezes well, and may be cooked in the form of a 'baba'. A variation is a 'savarin' made in a ring mould. A baba may be frozen with or without syrup poured over. The basic cake can be wrapped in foil or polythene, but is best placed in a rigid container if syrup has been used.

To serve
A baba should be thawed for 2–3 hours at room temperature without wrappings. If the cake has been frozen without syrup, the warm syrup may be poured over during thawing; additional syrup may be used even if the cake has been frozen ready for eating.
High Quality Storage Life 2 months

Baked and Steamed Puddings

These can be made from standard cake and pudding recipes, and are most easily made in foil containers which can be used for freezing and for heating. It is better not to put jam or syrup in the bottom of these puddings before cooking, as they become soggy on thawing, but dried fruit, fresh fruit and nuts may be added. Highly spiced puddings may develop off-flavours. Suet puddings containing fresh fruit may be frozen raw or cooked. It is more useful to cook them before freezing, since only a short time need then be allowed for reheating before serving. Puddings made from cake mixtures or the traditional sponge or suet puddings can also be frozen raw or cooked. Cake mixtures may be used to top such fruits as apples, plums, gooseberries and apricots; these are just as easily frozen raw since complete cooking time in the oven will be little longer than reheating time. This also applies to fruit puddings with a crumble topping.

To serve
Thaw baked puddings at room temperature for about 3 hours, then reheat at 180°C/350°F/Gas 4 for 1 hour. Steamed puddings can be reheated from frozen.
High Quality Storage Life 2 months

Cheesecake

A gelatine based cheesecake on a biscuit crumb base or a pastry based baked cheesecake are both suitable for freezing, and any standard recipe can be used. A cheesecake should be packed in foil after freezing, and then in a box to avoid crushing.

To serve
Thaw in refrigerator for about 8 hours.
High Quality Storage Life   1 month

Fruit Puddings

It is useful to use some fruit to make prepared puddings for the freezer. Fruit in syrup may be flavoured with wine or liqueurs and served without cooking; this is particularly useful for such fruits as pears and peaches which are difficult to freeze well in their raw state.

To serve
Reheat from frozen in a double boiler.
High Quality Storage Life   12 months

Gelatine Puddings

Many cold puddings such as jellies, mousses and soufflés involve the use of gelatine. When it is used for creamy mixtures to be frozen, gelatine is entirely successful, but clear jellies are not recommended for the freezer. The ice crystals formed in freezing break up the structure of the jelly, and while it retains its setting quality, the jelly becomes granular and uneven and loses clarity. The granular effect is masked in such puddings as cold soufflés.

All gelatine dishes should first be allowed to set in an ordinary refrigerator or cool place before freezing. Unmoulded puddings should be open frozen, then wrapped in foil or polythene for storage. Dishes prepared in moulds should, when set, be turned out in the usual way on to a tray or cakeboard, open frozen and then wrapped for storage.

Cream or decorations should not be put on before freezing.

To serve
Keep unmoulded puddings closely covered while thawing to prevent condensation forming and causing the jelly to liquefy. Return open frozen puddings to their mould and cover well before thawing.
High Quality Storage Life   2 months

Pancakes

Pancakes freeze very well, either plain or filled and covered with sauce. They should be cooled thoroughly before freezing, and large thin pancakes should be layered with clingfilm or greaseproof paper like a cake, then wrapped in foil or polythene.

To serve
Thaw block of pancakes in wrappings at room temperature, or separate before thawing. Heat in a low oven or on a plate over steam, covered with a cloth. They may be filled after thawing and before heating.
High Quality Storage Life   2 months
Note If they are filled and/or covered with sauce before freezing they will only store for 1 month.

Sponge Fruit Puddings
Sweetened fruit such as plums, gooseberries or apricots can be topped with sponge mixture and baked in a foil case before freezing. Cooking time almost equals thawing and reheating time, so it may be most practical to freeze these puddings uncooked.

To serve cooked puddings
Thaw at room temperature for 2 hours, then heat at 190°C/375°F/Gas 5 for 30 minutes.
To serve frozen puddings
Put into oven while still frozen and bake at 200°C/400°F/Gas 6 for 30 minutes, then at 190°C/375°F/Gas 5 for 30 minutes.
High Quality Storage Life   2 months

Sweet Sauces
A supply of sweet sauces such as fruit sauce or chocolate sauce can be usefully frozen for use with puddings or ices. These are best prepared and frozen in small containers.

To serve
Reheat, if necessary, in a double saucepan.
High Quality Storage Life 12 months (fruit sauces); 1 month (pudding sauces)

ICES

Home-made ice cream can be stored in the freezer for 3 months. Bought ice cream is best stored for up to 1 month. If large containers of bought ice cream are stored, and not repackaged into serving sizes before storage, use them sooner than this after opening. When portions have been taken out of a large container, a piece of foil over the unused portion helps retain flavour and texture.

Home-made ice cream for the freezer is best made with pure cream and gelatine or egg yolks. For immediate use, evaporated milk may be used, but the flavour is less good than cream (before using, the unopened tin of milk should be boiled for 10 minutes, cooled and left in a refrigerator overnight). A smooth commercial product cannot be produced from a home freezer. The ingredients are different and so is the equipment which gives a smooth ice cream. Sorbetières can be bought for freezers, however, which work on the principle of the old dasher-churn, giving a constant beating which produces a relatively smooth product.

All home-made ice cream should be frozen quickly, or it will be 'grainy'. The correct emulsifying agent will help to make a smooth product. Egg, gelatine, cream or sugar syrup will stop large ice crystals forming; gelatine gives a particularly smooth ice. Whipped egg whites give lightness. Freezing diminishes sweetness, but too much sugar will prevent freezing. The correct proportion is one part sugar to four parts liquid.

Preparation for Freezing Ice Cream

Whatever emulsifying agent is used, the preparation is similar. The mixture should be packed into trays and frozen until just solid about 1cm/½ inch from the edge. The mixture should then be beaten quickly in a chilled bowl, and then frozen again for a further hour. This 'freezing and beating' technique should be repeated for up to 3 hours. Some freezer owners save time by packing the ice cream into storage containers and freezing after the first beating, but results are less smooth, and it is preferable to complete the ice cream before packing for storage. To remove portions of ice cream from a large container, dip a scoop into boiling water before cutting into the ice cream.

Basic Ice Cream

Prepare standard recipe and freeze in trays. When completed, pack in rigid plastic boxes, filling air space with crumpled foil or clingfilm. Seal tightly.

To serve
Scoop out into dishes. Fill remaining airspace in container with crumpled foil or clingfilm.
High Quality Storage Life   3 months

Fresh Fruit Ices

Prepare standard recipe and freeze in trays. Add pieces of fresh fruit before final freezing. Pack in rigid plastic boxes, filling air space with crumpled foil or clingfilm. Seal tightly.

To serve
Scoop out into dishes. Fill remaining airspace in container with crumpled foil or clingfilm.
High Quality Storage Life   3 months

Moulds or Bombes

Use double-sided moulds, jelly moulds or pudding basins. Soften ice cream slightly and line the mould. Freeze for 1 hour, then put in the next layer of ice cream. Freeze again, then add another ice cream, or a filling of fruit and/or liqueur. Wrap in foil, seal and freeze.

Two-flavoured moulds can be made by lining the mould with one flavour and filling with another (chopped fruit or nuts may be added to the inner ice cream).

To serve
Turn out on chilled plate, using cloth wrung out in hot water. Wrap in foil and freeze 1 hour before serving.
High Quality Storage Life   3 months

Sorbets
(a) Pack in leakproof rigid plastic or waxed containers and seal tightly, as these water ices do not freeze completely hard during storage.
(b) Pack into clean orange or lemon skins and wrap in foil, sealing tightly.

To serve
(a) Scoop on to plates or fill fresh fruit skins.
(b) Remove foil and return to the freezer for 1 hour to frost the skins.
High Quality Storage Life   1 month

PASTRY

Shortcrust pastry and flaky pastry freeze equally well either cooked or uncooked, but a standard balanced recipe should be used for best results. Commercially frozen pastry is one of the most useful and successful freezer standbys. Pastry may be stored both unbaked and baked, but unbaked pastry has a better flavour and scent, and is crisper and flakier.

Unbaked Pastry
Pastry may be rolled, formed into a square, wrapped in greaseproof paper, then in foil or polythene for freezing. This pastry takes time to thaw, and may crumble when rolled.

To serve
Thaw slowly, then cook as fresh pastry and eat fresh-baked. Do not return to the freezer in cooked form.
High Quality Storage Life   4 months

Baked Pastry

Flan cases, patty cases and vol-au-vent cases are all useful if ready baked. For storage, it is best to keep them in the cases in which they are baked or in foil cases. Small cases may be packed in boxes in layers with paper between.

To serve
Baked cases should be thawed in wrappings at room temperature before filling. A hot filling may be used and the cases heated in a low oven.
Heat Quality Storage Life   6 months

Baked Pies

Pies may be baked in the normal way, then cooled quickly before freezing. A pie is best prepared and frozen in foil, but can be stored in a freezer-proof container. The container should then be put into the freezer paper or polythene for freezing.

To serve
Heat a cooked pie at 180°C/350°F/Gas 4 for 40–50 minutes for a double-crust pie, 30–35 minutes for a one-crust pie, depending on size. Alternatively, thaw in wrapping at room temperature and eat without reheating.
High Quality Storage Life   2 months

Unbaked Pies

Pies may be prepared with or without a bottom crust. Air vents in pastry should not be cut before freezing. To prevent sogginess, it is better to freeze unbaked pies before wrapping them.

To serve
Cut slits in top crust and bake unthawed as for fresh pies, allowing about 10 minutes longer than normal cooking time.
High Quality Storage Life   2 months

Flan Cases

Unfilled flan cases may be frozen baked or unbaked. Unbaked cases should be frozen in flan rings. Baked cases are fragile and are best packed in boxes to avoid crushing. Baked cases are the most useful to keep in the freezer since a meal can be produced more quickly with them.

To serve
Thaw in wrappings at room temperature before filling (about 1 hour should be enough). A hot filling may be used when the case is taken from the freezer and the whole flan heated in a slow oven.
High Quality Storage Life   2 months

Flans and Quiches

Filled flans with open tops are best completed and baked before freezing, whether they are savoury or sweet. They should be frozen without wrapping to avoid spoiling the surface, then wrapped in foil or polythene for storage, or packed in boxes to avoid damage. It is easier to bake and freeze these flans in foil cases, but this does not give much depth of filling, so that it is preferable to prepare them in flan rings.

The traditional Quiche Lorraine freezes well, and spinach, shellfish and mushroom flans are also good. Leftover meat, fish or vegetables may also be bound with a savoury sauce and frozen in a pastry case.

Custard fillings should be avoided, as should meringue toppings which toughen and dry during storage. A meringue topping can be added before serving.

To serve
Thaw flans in loose wrappings at room temperature for about 2 hours to serve cold, or reheat if required.
High Quality Storage Life 2 months

Mince Pies

The storage life of mince pies is limited in the freezer to 1 month, because mincemeat is highly spiced and spices tend to develop off-flavours when frozen. It is useful, however, to bake ahead even a week or two before Christmas. Pies may be baked and packed in cartons for freezing. If there is more space, pies may be frozen unbaked in their baking tins.

Fruit Fillings

If the surface of the bottom crust of fruit pies is brushed with egg white, it will prevent sogginess. Fruit pies may be made with cooked or uncooked fillings. Apples tend to brown if stored in a pie for more than 4 weeks, even if treated with lemon juice, and it is better to combine frozen pastry and frozen apples when making a pie.

If time is short, it is convenient to freeze ready-made fruit pie fillings, ready to fit into fresh pastry when needed, and this is a good way of freezing surplus fruit in a handy form. The mixture is best frozen in a sponge cake tin or an ovenglass pie plate lined with foil, then removed from the container and wrapped in foil for storage; the same container can then be used for making a pie at a later date.

A little cornflour or flaked tapioca gives a firm pie filling which cuts well and does not seep through the pastry.
High Quality Storage Life 2 months

CAKES, BISCUITS, BREADS AND SANDWICHES

CAKES

Cakes freeze extremely well both cooked and uncooked. When cooked, they taste fresher than when stored in tins. Filled and iced cakes may also be successfully frozen, saving time for parties and special occasions, since these cakes cannot be stored in tins.

Good fresh ingredients must be used for cakes which are to be frozen. Stale flour deteriorates quickly after freezing. Cakes made with butter have the best flavour, but margarine may be used for strongly flavoured cakes such as chocolate, and gives a good light texture. Eggs must be fresh and well-beaten since yolks and whites freeze at different speeds and this will affect the texture of the cake.

Synthetic flavourings develop off-flavours during freezing; this is particularly the case with vanilla, and vanilla pod or vanilla sugar should be used. Spiced foods also develop off-flavours, and spice cakes are best not frozen, although basic gingerbread is satisfactory for a short time. Chocolate, coffee and fruit-flavoured cakes freeze very well.

Cake Fillings and Icings

Cakes for freezing should not be filled with cream, jam or fruit. Cream may crumble after thawing, and jam or fruit will make a cake soggy. A butter filling and icing should be used, and any flavouring should be pure (eg vanilla extract or sugar rather than synthetic flavouring). Fillings and icings must be firm before a cake is wrapped and frozen; it is often preferable to open freeze without wrapping, before covering the cake for storage. It is better not to decorate iced cakes before freezing, as the decorations often absorb moisture during thawing and colour changes will affect the appearance of the cake.

Boiled icings and those made with cream or egg whites will crumble on thawing. Butter icings are best; these can also be prepared and packed in containers and frozen separately, then thawed and spread on either fresh or thawed frozen cakes. This does not appreciably save time, but it can be useful to freeze leftover icing.

Packing Cakes

Small cakes can be frozen in polythene bags in convenient quantities; small iced cakes are better packed in boxes to avoid crushing or smudging. Large quantities of small iced cakes can be frozen on baking trays unwrapped, then packed in layers in boxes with clingfilm or greaseproof paper between. Cakes to be cut in squares can be frozen in the baking tin or in a foil container, which can be covered with foil for storage. Alternatively, it can be put into a polythene bag and the cake cut when thawed.

Large cakes can be frozen in polythene bags or in heavy-duty foil. Iced cakes are better frozen before wrapping to avoid smudging (wrappings should be removed before thawing to allow moisture to escape). It is also possible to pack individual pieces of cake for lunch-boxes; these pieces may be frozen individually in bags or boxes, but it is easier to slice the whole cake in wedges before freezing, and to withdraw slices as they are needed without thawing the whole cake.

DIFFERENT TYPES OF CAKES

Choux Pastry

Choux pastry may be frozen for éclairs or cream puffs, or for savoury puffs. The raw mixture may be shaped on trays, frozen and then packed. It is, however, easier to cook the choux pastry and freeze the cases ready to be filled. Unfilled cases are best packed in rigid containers to avoid crushing; they can be filled while still frozen and the filling will help to thaw them. Filled choux pastry cases will go soggy in the freezer, filled with ice cream.

To serve
Thaw at room temperature for 1 hour before filling and icing. If filling beforehand, thaw for 10 minutes before serving.
High Quality Storage Life   1 month

Fruit Cakes

Rich fruit cakes may be stored in the freezer, but if space is limited, it is better to store them in tins. Dundee cakes, sultana cakes and other light fruit mixtures freeze very well, but are better unspiced.

To serve
Thaw in wrappings at room temperature.
High Quality Storage Life   4 months

Gingerbread

Cakes which are heavily flavoured with spices are not advised for the freezer, since they develop off-flavours. A basic gingerbread may, however, be frozen for a short period, and is useful to serve as a cake, or as a pudding with apple purée, cream or ice cream.

To serve
Unwrap and thaw at room temperature for 3 hours.
High Quality Storage Life   1 month

Griddle Cakes

Griddle cakes should be cooked as usual and cooled before packing. They are best separated with clingfilm or greaseproof paper, then wrapped in batches in foil or polythene or in a rigid container.

To serve
Thaw in wrappings at room temperature for 1 hour, before buttering.
High Quality Storage Life   2 months

Scones

Scones freeze extremely well. They may be frozen unbaked or baked, but for ease of packing and service, it is best to freeze them in their finished state rather than unbaked. Baked scones are most easily packaged in required quantities in polythene bags (they may be wasted if packed in too large quantities).

To serve unbaked scones
Partly thaw, then cook, or bake in a hot oven without thawing.
High Quality Storage Life   2 weeks
To serve baked scones
Thaw in wrappings at room temperature for 1 hour or at 180°C/350°F/Gas 4 for 10 minutes covered with foil. Alternatively split frozen scones and put under a hot grill.
High Quality Storage Life   2 months

Sponge Cakes

Unbaked sponges should be prepared in freezer-proof baking tins or foil. Cake batter can be stored in cartons if this is easier for packing; it should be thawed in the container before putting into baking tins, but if the mixture thaws too long, the cake will be heavy. Delicate sponges may be frozen in paper or polythene, then packed in boxes to avoid crushing. Sponges should be thawed in wrappings at room temperature if uniced. The wrappings should be removed from iced cakes before thawing. Sponges should not be filled with cream, jam or fruit before freezing. The two layers may be separated by foil, greaseproof paper, polythene or clingfilm before freezing, so that they can be easily separated for filling after thawing.
High Quality Storage Life   10 months (fatless sponges); 4 months (sponges with fat); 2 months (unbaked sponges)

Waffles

Waffles for freezing should not be over-brown. They may be bought or home-made, but are best frozen immediately after cooking and cooling. Pack in usable quantities in foil or polythene.

To serve
Heat unthawed under grill or in oven.
High Quality Storage Life   2 months

Biscuits

Biscuits may be frozen raw or cooked very successfully. Baked biscuits store equally well in tins, however, and are likely to break in the freezer unless very carefully packed. If they are to be frozen, they should be packed in layers in containers with clingfilm or greaseproof paper between layers, and with crumpled up paper in air spaces to safeguard freshness and stop breakages.

Uncooked frozen biscuits are extremely useful, and the frozen dough will give light crisp biscuits. The best way to prepare biscuits is to freeze batches of any recipe in cylinder shapes in polythene or foil, storing them carefully to avoid dents from other packages in the freezer. The unfrozen dough should be left in its wrappings in the refrigerator for 45 minutes until it begins to soften, then cut in slices and baked. If the dough is too soft it will be difficult to cut.
High Quality Storage Life   2 months

BREADS AND OTHER YEASTED MIXTURES

Bread

Both bought and home-baked bread freezes extremely well if fresh at the time of freezing. The length of storage time varies with the type of bread. It is practical to keep one or two loaves for emergency use; baps, rolls and flavoured breads for special meals, unusual bread such as granary loaves or French sticks which may not always be obtainable from local bakers. Bread can be wrapped in heavy foil or polythene for storage, or can be frozen unwrapped for short-term storage.

To serve
Thaw bread in its wrappings at room temperature; a 675g/1½ lb loaf will take about 3 hours. Alternatively, thaw in foil in the oven at 200°C/400°F/Gas 6 for 45 minutes. This second method will, however, make the bread go stale quickly.

Crusty bread is best 'refreshed' in the oven at 200°C/400°F/Gas 6 for 10 minutes after thawing at room temperature.

Sliced bread can be toasted while still frozen if the slices are separated carefully with a knife before toasting.
High Quality Storage Life   4 weeks (white and brown bread); 6 weeks (enriched bread); 1 week (crisp crusted loaves and rolls); 3 days (Vienna loaves and rolls)

Baps

These soft flat rolls are usefully frozen to be used with a variety of fillings for lunch-boxes, or with hamburgers. They may be bought or home-made, and are most easily packed in small quantities in a polythene bag.

To serve
Thaw at room temperature for 45 minutes.
High Quality Storage Life   6 weeks

Brioches

Large or small brioches, either bought or home-made, can be successfully stored in the freezer. After thawing, they can be used on their own, or with a sweet or savoury filling. Brioches can be packed in polythene bags for freezer storage.

To serve
Thaw in wrappings at room temperature for 45 minutes. They can also be heated with the tops cut off and the centres filled with creamed mushrooms, chicken or shrimps.
High Quality Storage Life   6 weeks

Croissants

Fresh croissants can be bought or made at home. They freeze very successfully, but are best packed in boxes since they tend to flake.

To serve
Remove wrappings and heat on baking tray at 180°C/350°F/Gas 4 for 15 minutes.
High Quality Storage Life   1 month

Crumpets

Crumpets are available seasonally, so can usefully be stored for later use. They are best packed in the wrappings in which they are bought, then overwrapped in polythene or foil.

To serve
Thaw at room temperature for 20 minutes before toasting.
High Quality Storage Life   6 weeks

Doughnuts

Doughnuts freeze well, but if filled with jam, will be a little soggy in thawing. Ring doughnuts are, therefore, preferable for freezing. Home-made doughnuts must be well drained when removed from fat, and are best frozen without being rolled in sugar. Doughnuts should be packed in usable quantities in polythene bags.

To serve
Remove from bags and heat immediately at 200°C/400°F/Gas 6 for 8 minutes, then roll in sugar.
High Quality Storage Life   1 month

Danish Pastries

These may be frozen with a light water icing, or without icing. They are best packed in foil trays with a foil covering, or in boxes to avoid crushing. If packed in polythene bags, the pastries bruise and flake.

To serve
Thaw at room temperature for 1 hour, removing wrappings if iced. The pastries may also be lightly heated in a moderate oven.
High Quality Storage Life   2 months

Uncooked Yeast Mixtures

Unbaked bread and buns may be frozen, but proving after freezing takes a long time, and the texture may be heavier. Unbaked dough to be frozen should be allowed to prove once, then shaped for baking, or kept in bulk if this is easier for storage. The surface should be brushed with a little olive oil or unsalted butter to prevent toughening of the crust, and a little extra sugar added to sweet mixtures.

Single loaves or a quantity of dough can be packed in foil or polythene; rolls can be packed in layers separated by clingfilm before wrapping in foil or polythene.

To serve
Thaw in a moist warm place; greater speed in thawing will give a lighter texture loaf. After shaping, prove the mixture again before baking. If the bread has been shaped before freezing, it should be proved once in a warm place before baking:
High Quality Storage Life   2 weeks
Note *Fresh yeast* can be stored in the freezer for 6 months. The yeast is best bought in 225g/8 oz or 450g/1 lb packets, divided into 25g/1 oz cubes, and each cube wrapped in foil or polythene, and then a quantity of these stored in a preserving jar in the freezer. A cube of yeast will be ready for use after 30 minutes at room temperature.

SANDWICHES

Sandwiches freeze extremely well, but their storage life is limited by the type of filling. There is little point in keeping sandwiches longer than 4 weeks. Plain white bread, whole wheat, rye, pumpernickel and fruit breads can be used for frozen sandwiches, together with baps and rolls. Brown bread is good for fish fillings, and fruit bread for cheese or sweet fillings.

Preparation

Soften butter or margarine for spreading the bread for freezer sandwiches but do not allow it to melt. Make sure that fillings are well chilled before use, and that all wrapping materials and prepared breads are ready for use before starting to assemble sandwiches.

Spread fat right to the edges of the bread to prevent fillings soaking in, and spread fillings evenly to ensure even thawing. Stack sandwiches neatly and cut them with a sharp knife, leaving in large portions (such as half-slices) with crusts on; this will prevent the sandwiches drying out and becoming mis-shapen during freezing.

Packing and Freezing

Sandwiches are best packed in groups of six or eight rather than individually. Wrap them tightly in clingfilm, then in foil or polythene. This enables the outer wrapping to be removed for further use and the inner packet to be put straight into a lunch-box. If sandwiches are frozen against the freezer wall, this will result in uneven thawing, and it is best to put packages a few cm/inches from the wall of the freezer. They should be thawed in their wrappings in the refrigerator for 12 hours, or at room temperature for 4 hours.

Types of Sandwiches

Specially prepared types of sandwiches can be frozen ahead for parties or weddings. Sandwiches which are rolled, or formed into pinwheels or ribbons are best frozen in aluminium foil trays to keep their shape, covered with foil and carefully sealed before freezing.

To serve

Thaw for 12 hours in the refrigerator or 4 hours at room temperature. Thawing will be speeded up if the foil is replaced by greaseproof or wax paper when the tray is removed from the freezer.

Pinwheel Sandwiches

Using a sandwich loaf, cut the slices lengthways. Spread with soft butter and filling, and roll bread like a Swiss roll. Pack in foil trays and freeze.

To serve, cut the thawed Swiss roll into slices of the required thickness.

Ribbon Sandwiches

Use three slices of bread for each sandwich, alternating white and brown. Spread with butter and filling and make a triple sandwich. Press lightly under a weight before packing and freezing.

To serve, cut the thawed sandwiches into fingerthick slices.

Rolled Sandwiches

Use finely grained bread and well-creamed butter, and cut bread very thinly. It will be easier to roll the sandwiches if the bread is lightly rolled with a rolling-pin before spreading. Spread with butter and filling, roll sandwiches and pack closely in foil tray to freeze. A creamed filling may be used for these sandwiches, or the bread rolled round canned asparagus tips, or lightly cooked fresh ones.

COOKED FOODS AND GARNISHES

All kinds of cooked food can be frozen for future use. These can be complete dishes, or separate items such as sauces and pasta which can be combined after freezing to make complete meals.

Standard recipes can be followed with a few adjustments. Vegetable and tomato purées or cornflour are better for thickening than flour which can curdle thickened liquids on reheating. Rice, pasta and potatoes become slushy if frozen in liquids.

Note Hard-boiled egg whites, mayonnaise and salad dressings should not be used in recipes for freezing.

Flavourings Spices and seasonings tend to intensify their flavour in the freezer, and recipes should be adjusted accordingly. Fresh herbs are better used than dry herbs, which can taste musty. Onions and garlic tend to develop off-flavours, and also to give their smell to other food in the freezer, so they are best omitted, or used only for dishes which are to be eaten within 2 months.

It is best not to keep cooked dishes longer than 2 months in the freezer, while a life of only 1 month is even better. Cooked dishes will deteriorate in colour, flavour and texture during long storage.

PACKING

Complete dishes can be frozen in the utensils in which they are cooked. They can then be reheated and served in the same container. It is possible to freeze such items as stews in foil-lined ovenglass casseroles, then to remove them and store them without the container. They can quickly be returned to the original dish for reheating and serving. Full details are given on page 31.

It is important to pack cooked dishes in usable portions so that only enough should be reheated which can be eaten at one meal. Cooked dishes should *not* be refrozen.

REHEATING

Frozen cooked dishes are best reheated without thawing. Partial thawing is, of course, sometimes necessary to get food out of a package before reheating.

Pies should be transferred directly from freezer to oven, with an air vent cut for the escape of steam when the pie begins to heat through. Pies should be put into a preheated oven.

Casseroles are best put into a cold oven which is then set to the temperature required; this avoids scorching at the edges.

Soups and Sauces should be gently reheated in a double boiler or saucepan, stirring occasionally to help reconstitute the mixture.

It is important to allow plenty of time for reheating so that the inside of a dish is still not frozen solid when the outside is hot (usually 45–60 minutes in a moderate oven will be required).

Fish

Fish is a perishable food and must be dealt with promptly. Neither cooked nor raw fish must be left standing at room temperature, nor kept for more than a few hours in a domestic refrigerator before freezing.

Dishes made with *raw* fish need to be chosen with care because of the problems of reheating. Grilled or baked dishes with tasty toppings are among the more successful of those so far tested.

Dishes made with *cooked* fish pose no problem in freezing or reheating. Typical examples are fish cakes, fish pies, fish au gratin and kedgeree.

After cooking, the dishes must be cooled as quickly as possible, then chilled in the refrigerator, packaged and frozen promptly. Shallow single layer dishes will freeze and reheat more quickly than deeper dishes. A high quality storage life of 1 month is best for fish dishes.

Poultry

Old birds such as boiling fowls are best frozen after being cooked. The meat should be stripped from the bones and frozen; or it can be made at once into pies or casseroles while the carcass is simmering in the cooking liquid, to make strong stock for freezing. Slices of cooked poultry can be frozen on their own or in sauce (the latter method is preferable to prevent drying out). If the meat is frozen without sauce, the slices should be divided by two sheets of clingfilm and then closely packed together excluding air. Roast and fried poultry which is frozen to eat cold is not particularly successful; on thawing it tends to exude moisture and become flabby.

Game

Any favourite game recipe can be frozen with little adaptation, but, like poultry, is not recommended to be eaten cold.

Hot water crust game pies can be frozen for a short time completely baked, but the flavour deteriorates after about 2 weeks, and it is really best to freeze only small pieces of leftover pie if absolutely necessary. If you very much want to freeze such a pie, it is best baked and cooled before freezing, but without the finishing jelly. This jellied stock can be prepared at the same time as the pie and frozen – it can then be heated and poured through the pie lid during the thawing process; this will accelerate deterioration however and the pie will not keep.

Meat

These dishes are all easy to prepare and freeze well. When a bulk order of meat is purchased, it is a good idea to convert some immediately into cooked dishes as this will save freezer space and provide a number of quickly served meals.

There is little advantage in freezing pre-cooked joints, steaks or chops as the outer surface sometimes develops an off-flavour, and reheating will dry out the meat. Fried meats tend to toughness, dryness and rancidity when frozen. Any combination dishes of meat and vegetables should include undercooked vegetables to avoid softness on reheating. It is very important that all cooked meats should be cooked quickly for freezing.

Joints of meat may be sliced and frozen to serve cold. Slices should be at least ½cm/¼ inch thick, separated by clingfilm or greaseproof paper, and packed tightly together to avoid drying out of surfaces, then put into rigid containers or bags. Meat slices should be thawed for 3 hours in a refrigerator in the container, then separated and spread on absorbent paper to remove moisture. Ham and pork lose colour when stored in this way.

Sliced cold meat may also be packaged with a good gravy. Both meat and gravy must be cooked quickly before packing. The slices in gravy are easiest to handle if packed in foil dishes, then in bags, as the frozen dish may be put straight into the oven in the foil for reheating. If the foil dish is covered with foil before packaging, this foil lid will help to keep the meat moist in reheating. Heat the frozen dish in a warm to moderate oven for 45 minutes–1 hour.

Meat pies can be frozen completely cooked so that they need

only be reheated. Preparation time is, however, saved if the meat filling is cooked and cooled, then topped with pastry to be frozen in its raw state. The time taken to cook the pastry is enough to heat the meat filling, and is little longer than the time needed to reheat the whole pie.

Pies are most easily frozen in foil containers which can be used in the oven for final cooking. If a bottom crust is used, sogginess will be prevented if the bottom pastry is brushed with melted lard or butter just before filling.

Vegetable purée
Cook and sieve the vegetables. Pack in boxes. Small quantities can be frozen in ice cube trays and the cubes transferred to bags for easy storage. To serve, reheat in a double boiler, and add to soups. Vegetable purée has a storage life of 3 months.

Cakes, biscuits and breads
See pages 92–97.

Vegetables in Sauce
Slightly undercook the vegetables. Cook and fold into the sauce. Pack into containers and freeze. To serve, reheat gently in a double boiler.

Curry
Curry freezes extremely well, but being highly spiced, has a limited storage life of 1 month. Curry sauce is also extremely useful to store in the freezer to use for meat, poultry, vegetables or hard-boiled eggs.

Dips
Cocktail party dips for use with crisps, biscuits or raw vegetables, can be frozen if based on cottage or cream cheese. Salad dressing, mayonnaise, hard-boiled egg whites or crisp vegetables should be omitted from the dips before freezing, but can be added during thawing. It is important to label packages carefully with the instructions for finishing a dip before serving. Flavourings such as garlic, onion and bacon can be included before freezing, but careful packing is essential to avoid leakage of flavours to other foods in the freezer. To serve, thaw at room temperature for 5 hours.

Garnishes
It is useful to have a supply in the freezer, which can be prepared at leisure and are quickly available to give colour and flavour to either fresh or frozen foods.

Croûtons Lightly toasted or fried cubes of bread about 1cm/1 inch thick can be frozen for 1 month in polythene bags. They should be thawed in wrappings at room temperature, or can be put directly into hot soup. As an alternative, untreated cubes of bread can be frozen for 2 months, and can be fried while still frozen.

Fruit Strawberries with hulls, and cherries on stalks can be open frozen on trays, then packed into polythene bags. They can be put straight on to puddings or into drinks while still frozen.

Herbs Frozen herbs become limp on thawing, but sprigs of mint can be added to fruit cup straight from the freezer, and sprigs of parsley put on to sandwich plates in their frozen state. Chopped frozen herbs and herb butter can also be used to add to soups or sauces.

Julienne Vegetables Root vegetables such as carrots and turnips can be cut in matchstick slices and frozen in small bags. It is best to blanch then for long-term storage, but this is not necessary if they are to be frozen for less than 1 month. They can be added to soup just before serving.

Gravy
Only unthickened gravy, or that thickened with cornflour, is suitable for freezing. Small quantities can be frozen in ice cubes, wrapping individual cubes in foil for storage. These cubes can be added to soups or casseroles, or heated in a double boiler to serve with meat.

Surplus gravy can also be added to pies or stews for freezing, or poured over cold meat or poultry slices. Both meat and gravy should be completely cold when combined; they are best packed in a foil dish with a lid, and the lid should be retained for reheating at 180°C/350°F/Gas 4 for 35 minutes, before serving.

Parmesan Cheese
Small bags of grated Parmesan cheese may be kept in the freezer for 1 month, but should be well-wrapped. The cheese thaws quickly at room temperature, but a fuller flavour will develop with a longer thawing time.

Pasta
Pasta such as spaghetti and macaroni may be successfully frozen to be used with a variety of sauces. Composite meals, such as macaroni cheese, may also be frozen when cooked. Pasta shapes may be frozen to use with soup, but they should not be frozen in liquid as they become slushy, and so are most conveniently added to soup during the reheating period.

103

Pasta should be slightly undercooked in boiling salted water. After thorough draining, it should be cooled under cold running water in a sieve, then shaken as dry as possible, packed into polythene bags, and frozen. To serve, the pasta is put into a pan of boiling water and brought back to the boil, then simmered until just tender; the time depends on the state in which it has been frozen. Composite dishes can be reheated in a double boiler or in the oven under a foil lid.

Pastry
See pages 89–91.

Pâté
Pâté made from liver, game or poultry, freezes extremely well. It can be packed in individual pots ready for serving, or cooked in loaf tins or terrines, then turned out and wrapped in foil for easy storage. Pâté containing strong seasoning, herbs or garlic should be carefully overwrapped. Any pâté which has exuded fat or excess juices during cooking must be carefully cooled and the excess fat or jelly scraped off before freezing. To serve, thaw small individual containers at room temperature for about 1 hour. Thaw large pâté in wrappings in the refrigerator for about 6 hours, or at room temperature for 3 hours, and use immediately after thawing. Pâté made with smoked fish, such as kipper or cod's roe, can also be frozen successfully, and is best prepared in small containers, well overwrapped. Fish pâté should be thawed in a refrigerator for about 3 hours, stirring occasionally to blend ingredients.

Pizza
Bought or home-made pizza may be frozen, and is useful for entertaining and for snack meals. The pizza is best frozen on a flat foil plate on which it can be baked, wrapped in foil for storage. Anchovies should be omitted from the topping as their saltiness may cause rancidity in the fatty cheese during storage; they can be added at the reheating stage. Fresh rather than dried herbs should be used. To serve, unwrap and thaw at room temperature for 1 hour, then bake at 190°C/375°F/Gas 5 for 25 minutes, and serve very hot.

Puddings
See page 84–87.

Rice
Rice is a useful item for the freezer, to be combined with sauces, or to serve with other freezer dishes. Rice should be slightly undercooked in boiling salted water. After thorough draining it

should be cooled under cold running water in a sieve, then shaken as dry as possible, packed into polythene bags and frozen. To serve, the rice is put into a pan of boiling water until just tender, the time depending on the state in which it has been frozen. Rice can also be reheated in a frying pan with a little melted butter. It can also be made into composite dishes such as Spanish Rice, which can be reheated in a double boiler, or in the oven under a foil lid. It should not, however, be frozen in liquid such as soup, as it then becomes slushy; it is better to freeze the rice separately and add it to the soup when reheating.

Risotto

This is a useful dish for the freezer, either prepared in its most simple form, or with the addition of cooked peas, mushrooms, flaked fish or shellfish, chopped ham or chicken, or chicken livers, any of which should be added during the last 10 minutes' cooking. For a complete meal, a small packet of grated cheese can be attached to the packet of risotto for serving.

Roux

Small quantities of roux made from butter and plain flour can be frozen to assist thickening of hot liquids. 450g/1 lb butter to 225g/8 oz plain flour should be used in making the roux. Put tablespoons of the mixture on baking sheets, and freeze uncovered, then pack in waxed or rigid containers for storage. To use, add frozen spoonfuls of roux to hot liquid, stirring well, and cook gently to the required thickness.

Sauces

Sweet and savoury sauces can be frozen very successfully. Complete sauces can be prepared to use with spaghetti, rice or sweet puddings, or they can be basic white or brown sauces to which other ingredients can be added before use. Sauces for freezing are best thickened by reduction, or with cornflour, as flour-thickened sauces may curdle when reheated. Egg or cream thickening should also be added after freezing and during reheating. Mayonnaise and custard sauces do not freeze well as the ingredients freeze at different temperatures and give unsatisfactory results.

Large quantities of sauce can be frozen in rigid containers, or in brick form using loaf tins. Small quantities can be frozen either in containers or in ice cube trays, then wrapped individually in foil and packed in quantities in polythene bags for easy storage.

Soup

Most soups freeze well, though it is often necessary to adjust recipes to suit freezer conditions. Soup which is thickened with ordinary flour tends to curdle on reheating; cornflour is therefore best used as a thickening agent, since it gives a creamy result. Rice flour can be used but it makes the soup glutinous. Porridge oats can be used for thicker meat soups. Starchy foods such as rice, pasta, barley and potatoes become slushy when frozen in liquid, and should be added during the final reheating after freezing. It is also better to omit milk or cream from frozen soups; they can be added when reheating.

Soup to be frozen should be cooled and surplus fat removed as this will separate in storage and cause off-flavours. Soup should be frozen in leakproof containers, allowing 1cm/½ inch headspace for wide-topped containers and 1.5cm/¾ inch headspace for narrow-topped containers. Rigid plastic containers are useful for storage, but large quantities of soup may be frozen in loaf tins or freezer boxes lined with foil; the solid block can then be wrapped in foil and stored like a brick.

Soup should not be stored for longer than 2 months. It will thicken during freezing, and allowance should be made for this in the recipe so that additional liquid can be added on reheating without spoiling the soup. Seasonings may cause off-flavours, and it is best to season after thawing. Clear soups can be heated in a saucepan over low heat, but cream soups should be heated in a double boiler and well-beaten to keep them smooth.

Stews and Casseroles

There must be plenty of liquid in stews to be frozen to cover the meat completely, or it may dry out. Vegetables are best undercooked to avoid softness. Potatoes, rice or other starch additions should be made during thawing and heating for service, as they become soft when frozen in liquid and tend to develop off-flavours. Sauces and gravies tend to thicken during storage; ordinary flour in a recipe may result in curdling during reheating, and cornflour should be substituted. While almost any recipe can be adapted for freezer use, the fat content should be as low as possible to avoid rancidity. Surplus fat should be removed from the surface of dishes cooled before freezing.

Stews can be packed in freezer-to-oven casseroles, in rigid containers, or in foil-lined casseroles from which the foil package can be removed for storage. Stews should not be packed in very large quantities, as reheating will take a long time; 1.2 litres/2 pints size is the largest practical size. To serve, reheat in a double boiler, or over direct heat if curdling is not likely to occur; or in the original container in a warm to moderate oven for 45 minutes–1 hour.

106

Stock

Stock prepared from meat, poultry, bones and/or vegetables can be stored in the freezer. The stock shold be strained and cooled, and the fat removed. To save freezer space, it is a good idea to concentrate the stock by boiling until the liquid is reduced by half. It can be packed in brick or ice cube form, or in containers, leaving 2.5cm/1 inch headspace. To serve, thaw gently over direct heat and use as required.

5 Recipes

SOUPS

Beetroot Soup

350g/12 oz cooked
   beetroot
1 medium onion
400ml/¾ pint chicken
   stock
3 celery leaves
2.5ml/½ teaspoon salt
pepper
5ml/1 teaspoon sugar
30ml/3 dessertspoons
   lemon juice

Dice the beetroot and put into a liquidizer with the chopped onion, stock, celery, salt, pepper and sugar. Blend until the beetroot is finely chopped. Put into a pan and simmer for 10 minutes. Add the lemon juice and leave until cold. Pack into containers, leaving headspace, and freeze.

To serve
Reheat gently, or thaw and serve cold.
High Quality Storage Life   2 months

Carrot Soup

450g/1 lb carrots
600ml/1 pint water
25g/1 oz butter
3 large tomatoes
salt and pepper

FOR SERVING
600ml/1 pint milk
chopped parsley

Cook the carrots for 30 minutes in the water. Drain, reserving the liquid, and then grate the carrots. Melt the butter and lightly cook the skinned and pipped tomatoes. Add the grated carrot and cook until all the butter is absorbed. Add the carrot cooking liquid and simmer for 30 minutes. Season lightly with salt and pepper, and cool. Pack in a rigid container, leaving headspace, and freeze.

To serve
Reheat gently and when completely thawed, add 600ml/1 pint milk. Simmer until hot and adjust seasoning to taste, then garnish with chopped parsley.
High Quality Storage Life   2 months

Celery Soup

450g/1 lb celery
1 small onion
1.2 litres/2 pints chicken
   stock
15ml/1 tablespoon
   chopped parsley

FOR SERVING
2 egg yolks
150ml/¼ pint single cream
salt and pepper
chopped parsley

Cut the celery into short lengths and chop the onion. Bring the stock to the boil, and add the celery, onion and parsley. Cover and simmer for 30 minutes. Sieve or liquidize until smooth, and cool. Pack into a rigid container, leaving headspace, and freeze.

To serve
Reheat gently until hot. Whip the egg yolks with the cream. Add a little of the soup to the cream mixture and stir well. Gradually add the cream mixture to the soup and heat gently, but do not boil. Season to taste and serve hot with a garnish of chopped parsley.
High Quality Storage Life   2 months

Cock-a-Leekie Soup

1 boiling chicken
450g/1 lb shin of beef
6 leeks
10ml/2 teaspoons salt
5ml/1 teaspoon black
   pepper
125g/4 oz stoned prunes

Wipe the chicken inside and out and put into a large saucepan. Cut meat into small pieces. Slice leeks thinly, using some of the green parts. Add salt and pepper and cover with cold water. Bring to simmering point and cook gently for 4 hours. Add the prunes and simmer for 45 minutes. Take out the chicken and cut flesh into neat small pieces, return to saucepan and reheat. Cool. Pack into containers, leaving headspace, and freeze.

To serve
Reheat gently, adjusting seasoning.
High Quality Storage Life   2 months

Basic Chicken Stock

1 chicken carcass
1 carrot
1 onion
1 stick celery
a sprig of parsley
1.2 litres/2 pints water
a pinch of salt

Break up the carcass and slice the vegetables. Put in a pan with water and salt. Simmer for 2 hours, strain and cool, removing fat from the surface. Pack into containers, leaving headspace, and freeze.

To serve
Thaw in a saucepan over low heat and add to dishes as required.
High Quality Storage Life   2 months

Green Pea Soup

900g/2 lb green peas
  (frozen or fresh)
25g/1 oz butter
1 small onion
1 small lettuce
a pinch of mixed herbs
1.8 litres/3 pints chicken
  stock
salt and pepper

FOR SERVING
45ml/3 tablespoons single
  cream

Put the peas, butter, finely chopped onion, shredded lettuce
and herbs in a pan with a tight-fitting lid and simmer for 10
minutes. Add the stock, salt and pepper and simmer for 1
hour. Put through a sieve or liquidize until smooth, and cool.
Pack in a rigid container, leaving headspace, then freeze.

To serve
Reheat gently and adjust seasoning to taste. Stir in 45ml/3
tablespoons single cream just before serving.
  If liked, fried or toasted bread cubes, or small pieces of crisp
bacon can be used to garnish the soup.
High Quality Storage Life   2 months

Italian Tomato Soup

2 medium onions
1 garlic clove
30ml/2 tablespoons olive
  oil
900g/2 lb ripe tomatoes
salt and pepper
5ml/1 teaspoon sugar
a pinch of mint
a pinch of basil
a pinch of marjoram
1.2 litres/2 pints beef stock

FOR SERVING
50g/2 oz cooked long
  grain rice
25g/1 oz grated Parmesan
  cheese

Chop the onions finely and crush the garlic. Cook them in the
oil until soft and golden. Add the peeled tomatoes cut into
pieces, with the salt, pepper, sugar and herbs. Cover with the
stock and simmer for 30 minutes. Put through a sieve, cool and
pack in a rigid container, leaving headspace, then freeze.

To serve
Reheat gently and add the cooked rice. Just before serving,
sprinkle with cheese.
High Quality Storage Life   2 months

Kidney Soup

225g/8 oz ox kidney
1 small onion
25g/1 oz butter
1.2 litres/2 pints beef stock
1 carrot
a sprig of parsley

Slice the kidney. Cook with the sliced onion in the butter until
the onion is soft and golden. Add the stock, chopped carrot,
herbs and seasoning and simmer for 1½ hours. Put through a
sieve, or blend in a liquidizer and return to the pan. Mix the
cornflour with a little water and stir into the soup. Simmer for

a sprig of thyme
1 bay leaf
salt and pepper
25g/1 oz cornflour

FOR SERVING
30ml/2 tablespoons sherry

5 minutes. Cool and pack into a rigid container, leaving headspace, then freeze.

To serve
Reheat gently until hot, and stir in sherry just before serving.
High Quality Storage Life   2 months

ROB   *727220*
WILL   *730696*

Leek Soup

4 large leeks
25g/1 oz butter
1.8 litres/3 pints water or
   chicken stock
450g/1 lb potatoes
salt and pepper
a pinch of nutmeg

FOR SERVING
150ml/¼ pint single cream
chopped parsley or chives
   (optional)

Cut the leeks in thin rings and cook in the butter over low heat until they begin to soften. Add the water or stock, sliced potatoes and seasonings. Cover and simmer until the vegetables are soft. Blend until smooth. Cool, pack in a rigid container, leaving headspace, and freeze.

To serve

511767.

Reheat gently and just before serving stir in the cream.
Garnish with chopped parsley or chives if liked, and serve with cubes of toasted or fried bread, or with French bread.
High Quality Storage Life   2 months

07836647752.

Minestrone

225g/8 oz lean beef
4 tomatoes
2 stalks celery (with
   leaves)
1 carrot
1 onion
1 small turnip
50g/2 oz shelled peas
50g/2 oz haricot beans
1.2 litres/2 pints water
salt and pepper

FOR SERVING
50g/2 oz pasta
grated Parmesan cheese

Mince the meat, using a coarse screen. Put the finely chopped tomatoes, celery tops, carrot, onion and turnip into a pan with the meat, peas, celery stalks cut into 1cm/½ inch pieces and the haricot beans which have been soaked overnight. Add the water, bring to the boil and simmer for 1 hour. Season lightly with salt and pepper, cool and pack in containers, leaving headspace, then freeze.

To serve
Reheat and add 50g/2 oz pasta which has been cooked in a separate pan for 5 minutes. Simmer for 10 minutes and serve with plenty of grated Parmesan cheese.
High Quality Storage Life   2 months

Onion Soup

675g/1½ lb onions
50g/2 oz butter
1.8 litres/3 pints beef stock
salt and pepper
30ml/2 tablespoons
   cornflour

Slice the onions finely and cook gently in the butter until soft and golden. Add the stock and seasoning, bring to the boil, then simmer for 20 minutes. Thicken with cornflour mixed with a little water. Simmer for a further 5 minutes. Cook and skim off any surplus fat. Pack into rigid containers, leaving headspace, and freeze.

To serve
Reheat gently, stirring well.
High Quality Storage Life 2 months

Oxtail Soup

1 oxtail
seasoned flour
butter
1.5 litres/2½ pints water
2 carrots
2 onions
1 turnip
1 stick celery
25g/1 oz pearl barley
salt

FOR SERVING
2.5ml/½ teaspoon
   Worcestershire sauce
2.5ml/½ teaspoon lemon
   juice

Wipe the oxtail and cut into pieces. Toss in a little seasoned flour and fry in a little butter for 10 minutes. Put in a pan with the water and simmer for 2 hours. Remove meat from bones and return to the stock with the vegetables cut in neat pieces, and pearl barley; season to taste. Simmer for 45 minutes and put through a sieve, or liquidize. Cool and remove fat from the top. Pack in containers, leaving headspace, and freeze.

To serve
Reheat gently in saucepan, adding Worcestershire sauce and lemon juice.
High Quality Storage Life 2 months

Scotch Broth

450g/1 lb lean neck of
   mutton
2.4 litres/4 pints water
1 leek
2 sticks celery
1 onion
1 carrot
1 turnip
a sprig of parsley
salt and pepper

FOR SERVING
30ml/2 tablespoons pearl
   barley

Cut the meat into small squares and simmer in water for 1 hour. Add the diced vegetables, parsley and seasoning, and continue cooking gently for 1½ hours. Cool and remove the fat on the top. Take out the parsley. Pack into containers, leaving headspace, and freeze.

To serve
Reheat gently in saucepan and add the barley, simmering until it is tender.
High Quality Storage Life 2 months

Shrimp Soup

2 sticks celery
125g/4 oz mushrooms
1 small onion
1 carrot
50g/2 oz butter
1.2 litres/2 pints chicken
    stock
salt and pepper
bay leaf
a pinch of nutmeg
30ml/2 tablespoons lemon
    juice
30ml/2 tablespoons white
    wine
175g/6 oz shrimps

FOR SERVING
300ml/½ pint double
    cream

Cut the celery, mushrooms, onion and carrot in small pieces and cook gently in butter for 10 minutes. Add the stock, seasoning, bay leaf, nutmeg and lemon juice, and simmer for 20 minutes. Put through a sieve or liquidize. Add the wine and shrimps and simmer for 5 minutes. Cool and remove fat. Pack into containers, leaving headspace, and freeze.

To serve
Reheat in double boiler, stirring gently. When thawed, stir in 300ml/½ pint double cream and continue reheating without boiling.
High Quality Storage Life   1 month

Spring Chicken Soup

1.35kg/3 lb chicken
2 sticks celery
1 leek
1 carrot
125g/4 oz peas (fresh or
    frozen)
salt and pepper

Remove the giblets from the chicken. Put the chicken into a saucepan, cover with water and bring to the boil. Reduce the heat and simmer for 1 hour. Remove from the cooking liquid and cut the flesh into neat pieces (some of the chicken breast could be used for another meal). Cut the celery and leek into neat pieces and slice the carrot into thin rings. Add to the cooking liquid with the chicken flesh and simmer for 15 minutes. Add the peas and simmer again for 5 minutes. Season lightly and then cool. Pour into a rigid container and freeze, leaving headspace.

To serve
Reheat gently, adjust seasoning and serve hot.
For a richer soup, mix 2 egg yolks with a little milk and pour a little of the hot soup into this mixture. Stir the egg yolk mixture into the soup and heat gently but do not boil.
High Quality Storage Life   2 months

PÂTÉS

Liver Pâté

350g/12 oz pig's liver
225g/8 oz pork fat
5 anchovy fillets
1 small onion
50g/2 oz dry breadcrumbs
300ml/½ pint milk
25g/1 oz butter
25g/1 oz plain flour
1 egg
5ml/1 teaspoon salt
5ml/1 teaspoon pepper
5ml/1 teaspoon ground
  mixed spice
5ml/1 teaspoon ground
  cloves
2.5ml/½ teaspoon sugar
350g/12 oz strips of pork
  fat

This Danish liver pâté is smooth, creamy and firm, and very easy to slice. The strips of pork fat should be cut very thinly for lining the container.

Mince the liver, pork fat, anchovy fillets and onion with the fine blade three times. Soak the breadcrumbs in a little of the milk. Melt the butter, work in the flour and add the rest of the milk. Cook together, stirring well, to make a thick white sauce. Cool and stir in the egg and seasonings. Mix the sauce thoroughly into the liver mixture until smoothly blended, together with the soaked breadcrumbs.

Line a freezer-proof tin or foil container with strips of pork fat so that they overlap slightly and cover the bottom and sides of the container. Put the liver mixture into the container and cover with strips of pork fat. Cover with a double thickness of cooking foil, and put the container into a roasting tin half-full of water. Bake at 180°C/350°F/Gas 4 for 1½ hours. Remove the foil and chill the pâté under weights. Wrap in foil or polythene to freeze.

To serve
Thaw in the refrigerator for 6 hours. Serve with salad or toast, or on open sandwiches, accompanied by pickled cucumbers.
High Quality Storage Life   2 months

Pork and Sausage Pâté

225g/8 oz pig's liver
125g/4 oz lean bacon
225g/8 oz pork
  sausage-meat
25g/1 oz white
  breadcrumbs
125g/4 oz finely chopped
  mushrooms
1.25ml/¼ teaspoon sage
10ml/1 dessertspoon
  tomato chutney

FOR SERVING
chopped gherkins

Put the liver and bacon through the mincer and mix them with all the other ingredients. Mix thoroughly and press into a loaf tin. Cover with foil and bake at 160°C/325°F/Gas 3 for 1½ hours. Leave in the tin under weights until cold. Turn out and wrap in foil or polythene to freeze.

To serve
Thaw in refrigerator overnight. Garnish with chopped gherkins.
High Quality Storage Life   1 month

Farmhouse Pâté

12 rashers streaky bacon
225g/8 oz pig's liver
225g/8 oz stewing veal
1 medium onion
25g/1 oz fresh white
    breadcrumbs
1.25ml/¼ teaspoon sage
15ml/1 tablespoon brandy
    or sherry
salt and pepper
beaten egg

Remove the rind and stretch bacon rashers by drawing the blade of a knife along them. Cut each rasher in half and use to line foil pudding basins. Mince the liver, veal and onion, and mix with the remaining ingredients until well blended, then spoon into prepared basins and press down well. Cover each basin tightly with a piece of foil, then place basins in a roasting tin filled with 2.5cm/1 inch water. Cook at 160°C/325°F/Gas 3 for 1-1½ hours. Loosen lids, and allow pâté to cool. Pour off excess liquid and cover basins with foil, then freeze quickly.

To serve
Thaw in refrigerator for 8 hours, or overnight. Serve with Melba Toast.
High Quality Storage Life 1 month

Chunky Pâté

350g/12 oz belly pork
350g/12 oz bacon pieces
40g/1½ oz crustless white
    bread
freshly ground black
    pepper
2.5ml/½ teaspoon sage
2.5ml/½ teaspoon mustard
    powder
1 egg
45ml/3 tablespoons milk
125g/4 oz liver sausage

Mince the pork, bacon and bread. Mix with the pepper, sage, mustard, egg and milk and beat well. Grease a 450g/1 lb loaf tin and spread in half the meat mixture. Chop the liver sausage in small pieces and cover the meat mixture. Top with the remaining meat mixture. Cover with foil and bake at 180°C/350°F/Gas 4 for 45 minutes. Strain off excess fat. Continue cooking for 15 minutes. Cool in tin and turn out. Wrap in foil or polythene to freeze.

To serve
Thaw in refrigerator for 6 hours, then cut in slices.
High Quality Storage Life 2 months

Chicken Liver Pâté

225g/8 oz chicken livers
75g/3 oz fat bacon
1 small onion
25g/1 oz butter
salt and pepper
2 garlic cloves
1 egg

Cut the livers into small pieces and chop the bacon and onion. Cook the bacon and onion in butter until just soft. Add the livers and cook gently for 10 minutes. Mince very finely and season. Add crushed garlic and beaten egg and put the mixture into individual foil containers. Stand the containers in a roasting tin half-full of water, cover and cook at 180°C/350°F/Gas 4 for 1 hour. Cool completely. Cover containers with foil to freeze.

To serve
Thaw containers in refrigerator for 3 hours and serve with toast.
High Quality Storage Life 1 month

Terrine of Duck

2.3kg/5 lb duck
60ml/4 tablespoons brandy
grated rind and juice of 1
  orange
5ml/1 teaspoon minced
  onion
thyme, parsley, 2 bay
  leaves
1 duck's liver
225g/8 oz veal
175g/6 oz liver pâté
125g/4 oz lean pork
125g/4 oz fresh pork fat
1 egg
salt and black pepper

Skin the duck, taking care to keep the skin intact, and lay aside. Remove the 2 breast fillets, but do not slice them. Remove the rest of the meat from the carcass, scraping all bones clean. Marinate the breast fillets overnight in a mixture of brandy, orange juice, onion, chopped parsley, thyme and crumbled bay leaves and the grated orange rind. Mince the remaining duck meat together with the duck liver, veal, liver pâté, the pork and pork fat. Stir in the liquid and ingredients of the marinade (take out onion). Add the well beaten egg. Season to taste with salt and pepper. Mix well together and fill the skin of the duck in alternate layers of mixture and breast fillets. Wrap the duck skin around and press into a greased tin, the open side of the skin at the bottom. Cover, place in a pan of hot water and bake at 180°C/350°F/Gas 4 for 1¼ hours. Remove cover and weight gently as the pâté cools. Remove surplus fat, unmould and wrap in foil or polythene to freeze.

To serve
Thaw in refrigerator for 8 hours and serve in slices.
High Quality Storage Life 2 months

Potted Crab

125g/4 oz butter
5ml/1 teaspoon black
  pepper
5ml/1 teaspoon ground
  mace
a pinch of Cayenne pepper
225g/8 oz fresh crabmeat
juice of ½ lemon

Heat 15g/½ oz butter in a pan, and add pepper, mace and Cayenne pepper. When the butter is hot, add crab and lemon juice, and stir well until crab is hot but not brown. Pack into small waxed or plastic cartons. Heat the rest of the butter until it is foamy, skim, and pour over the crab, covering it completely. Leave until butter is hard. Cover with lid, seal and freeze.

To serve
Thaw overnight in refrigerator, turn out, and serve with hot toast and lemon slices.
High Quality Storage Life 1 month

Seafood Mousse

300ml/½ pint packet aspic
  powder
225g/8 oz cooked lobster,
  crab or scampi
15ml/1 tablespoon dry
  white wine
150ml/¼ pint double
  cream
salt and Cayenne pepper

FOR SERVING
prawns and sliced
  cucumber

Make up the aspic as directed on the packet, but with only 150ml/¼ pint water. Leave until cold. Pound together the shellfish and wine, and put the mixture through a sieve. Gradually add the aspic, a little at a time. Whip the cream to soft peaks and gradually fold into the crab mixture. It is best if this is done with the crab mixture in a bowl on crushed ice. Add salt and Cayenne pepper to taste. Put into individual soufflé dishes, cover and freeze.

To serve
Thaw in refrigerator for 3 hours and garnish with prawns and sliced cucumber.
High Quality Storage Life 1 month

Potted Shrimps

shrimps
butter
salt and pepper
ground mace and cloves

Cook freshly caught shrimps, cool in cooking liquid, then shell. Pack tightly into waxed cartons. Melt the butter, season with salt, pepper and a little mace and cloves. Cool the butter and pour over the shrimps. Chill until cold. Cover with lids, seal and freeze.

To serve
Thaw in containers at room temperature for 2 hours, or heat in double boiler until butter has melted and shrimps are warm. Serve on toast.
High Quality Storage Life   1 month

Cod's Roe Pâté

350g/12 oz smoked cod's
   roe
150ml/¼ pint double
   cream
1 garlic clove
juice of ½ lemon
10ml/2 teaspoons olive oil
black pepper

Scrape the roe into a bowl and mix with the cream, crushed garlic, lemon juice and oil. Season to taste with pepper and mix well until the pâté is like thick cream. Pack into small containers and overwrap to freeze.

To serve
Thaw in refrigerator for 4 hours, stirring occasionally to blend ingredients. Serve with wedges of lemon and hot toast.
High Quality Storage Life   1 month

Sardine Pâté

225g/8 oz canned sardines
   in oil
juice of ½ lemon
salt and pepper
50g/2 oz melted butter

Bone the sardines and then mash them in a bowl with their skins and oil. For a really smooth pâté, put into a blender. Work in the lemon juice and season well. Press into·a freezer-proof pot and cover with butter. Chill, then cover with foil and freeze.

To serve
Thaw in refrigerator for 6 hours to serve with toast.
High Quality Storage Life   1 month

Smoked Fish Pâté

2 smoked mackerel or
225g/8 oz kipper fillets
225g/8 oz butter
75ml/3 fl oz cream
juice of 1 lemon
salt and pepper

Smoked fish pâtés may be varied according to taste. Those who like a sharp-tasting pâté may like to increase the amount of lemon juice, but others may prefer a milder flavour and use more cream.

Skin and bone the fish and put into a liquidizer. Melt the butter gently and add just enough to let the mixture turn easily in the machine. When it is smooth, put the purée into a bowl and mix with cream, lemon juice, seasoning, and any chosen added flavouring. Put into one large container or individual containers, overwrap and freeze.

To serve
Thaw at room temperature for 3 hours.
High Quality Storage Life   1 month

Kipper Mousse

275g/10 oz kipper fillets
300ml/½ pint single cream
25g/1 oz butter
25g/1 oz plain flour
300ml/½ pint milk
salt and pepper
2 eggs
15g/½ oz gelatine
juice of ½ lemon
30ml/2 tablespoons water

Cook fresh or frozen kippers by grilling or boiling. Skin the fish and flake the flesh. Mix the kippers with a little of the cream and pound to a paste, adding remaining cream (or blend in a liquidizer). Melt the butter and stir in the flour. Cook for 1 minute and then gradually add the milk. Stir over low heat until smooth. Remove from heat, season and beat in egg yolks. Dissolve the gelatine in the lemon juice and water, and heat until syrupy. Stir into the white sauce and leave to cool slightly before folding into the creamed kipper mixture. Whisk egg whites to soft peaks and fold into the kipper mixture. Turn into a freezer-proof dish and leave until cold and set. Cover and freeze.

To serve
Thaw in the refrigerator for 4 hours and serve with thinly sliced cucumber and brown bread and butter.
High Quality Storage Life   1 month

PASTA, PIZZAS, QUICHES AND FLANS

Macaroni Cheese

225g/8 oz macaroni
50g/2 oz butter
50g/2 oz plain flour
750ml/1¼ pints milk
225g/8 oz grated Cheddar
   cheese
salt and pepper

FOR SERVING
rashers of bacon
hard-boiled egg slices

Cook the macaroni as directed on the packet and drain well. Melt the butter and work in the flour. Cook for 1 minute and work in the milk. Stir over gentle heat until the sauce is smooth and creamy. Over very low heat, stir in the grated cheese and seasoning. Mix the macaroni and cheese sauce, then cool. Pack into a foil container and cover with a lid to freeze. If liked, some chopped cooked ham or bacon, chopped cooked onions or mushrooms can be added to the macaroni cheese before freezing.

To serve
Remove lid, cover the container with foil and heat at 200°C/400°F/Gas 6 for 1 hour, removing the foil for the last 15 minutes to brown the top. Garnish with bacon rashers and hard-boiled eggs.
High Quality Storage Life　1 month

Chicken Pompadour

225g/8 oz spaghetti
50g/2 oz butter
350g/12 oz cooked
   chicken
salt and pepper
150ml/¼ pint single cream
1 egg yolk
5ml/1 teaspoon chopped
   parsley

FOR SERVING
tomato or mushroom
   sauce

Cook the spaghetti in plenty of boiling salted water for 10 minutes. Drain thoroughly. Grease a foil pudding basin with half the butter and line it with the spaghetti, twisting it round to fit the basin. Chop the chicken and mix with salt, pepper, cream, egg yolk and parsley. Put into the spaghetti-lined basin and top with the remaining spaghetti. Cover with greased paper and foil, and steam for 1 hour. Cool, and pack in polythene to freeze.

To serve
Put the basin with a covering of foil into a pan of boiling water and steam for 1 hour. Turn out and serve with hot tomato or mushroom sauce.
High Quality Storage Life　2 months

Spring Chicken Soup (page 113)

Leek Soup (page 111)

LEFT *Spinach Flan* (page 126)

RIGHT *Liver Pâté* (page 114)

OPPOSITE *Quiche Lorraine* (page 125)

Macaroni Cheese (page 120)

Spaghetti Bolognese

30ml/2 tablespoons oil
50g/2 oz onions
450g/1 lb raw minced beef
400g/14 oz canned
    tomatoes
50g/2 oz concentrated
    tomato pureé
300ml/½ pint beef stock
a pinch of marjoram
1 bay leaf
salt and pepper
450g/1 lb spaghetti

Heat the oil and fry the chopped onions and beef until golden. Add the tomatoes with the juice, pureé, stock and herbs, with salt and pepper to taste. Simmer for at least 45 minutes, stirring occasionally. If liked, use a little red wine in place of some of the stock. A chopped chicken liver and a crushed garlic clove give added richness and flavour to the sauce. Remove the bay leaf before freezing the dish.

While the sauce is cooking, cook the spaghetti in a large pan of boiling salted water for about 12 minutes until tender but still firm. Drain very well and put in the middle of a large foil container. Put the sauce round the spaghetti, cover with a lid, and freeze. The pasta in composite dishes should be placed in the middle of the container as it heats more quickly than the sauce and can dry out when reheated. The sauce can be packed separately in a rigid container for freezing, to be paired with freshly cooked pasta.

To serve
Remove lid and cover the container with foil. Heat at 190°C/375°F/Gas 5 for 45 minutes. If the sauce is frozen separately, reheat it gently in a double saucepan.
High Quality Storage Life 2 months

Cannelloni

12 cannelloni
5ml/1 teaspoon oil
125g/4 oz streaky bacon
450g/1 lb raw minced beef
1 large onion
50g/2 oz concentrated
    tomato purée
2.5ml/½ teaspoon mixed
    herbs
450ml/¾ pint cheese
    sauce (25g/1 oz butter,
    25g/1 oz flour, 50g/2 oz
    grated hard cheese,
    450ml/¾ pint milk)

Cook the cannelloni as directed on the packet, then drain thoroughly. Heat the oil and fry the finely chopped bacon for 3 minutes. Stir in the beef and onion, and cook for 10 minutes. Drain off the surplus fat. Stir the tomato purée and herbs into the meat mixture. Fill the cannelloni with the meat mixture and arrange in a greased freezer container. Season the cheese sauce well and pour over the cannelloni. Cool, cover with foil or a lid, and freeze.

To serve
Remove lid and bake at 190°C/375°F/Gas 5 for 1 hour.
High Quality Storage Life 2 months

Spinach Noodles with Cheese

450g/1 lb noodles
1 large onion
1 garlic clove
15g/½ oz butter
225g/8 oz lean bacon
450g/1 lb spinach
300ml/½ pint soured
  cream
salt and pepper
a pinch of nutmeg
200g/7 oz Gruyère cheese

Cook the noodles in boiling water from 6–8 minutes until tender, then drain thoroughly. Chop the onion finely and crush the garlic clove and cook in the butter until soft and golden. Chop the bacon and cook with the onion until soft. Stir the onion and bacon into the noodles and arrange in a freezer-to-table container. Wash the spinach very well and put into a saucepan without any water. Cook over gentle heat until the spinach is soft. Drain very thoroughly and press out any liquid. Mash the spinach with a potato masher and then work in the soured cream, salt, pepper and nutmeg. Arrange in the centre of the noodles. Cool completely and cover with thin slices of cheese. Cover with foil or a lid to freeze.

To serve
Remove lid and cover dish with foil. Heat at 180°C/350°F/Gas 4 for 40 minutes. Remove foil and continue cooking for 15 minutes until the cheese has melted.
High Quality Storage Life 1 month

Gnocchi

1 medium onion
1 bay leaf
600ml/1 pint milk
75g/3 oz semolina
salt and pepper
40g/1½ oz grated Cheddar
  cheese
15g/½ oz butter
5ml/1 teaspoon made
  mustard
50g/2 oz melted butter
50g/2 oz grated Cheddar
  cheese

Put the onion into a pan with the bay leaf and milk. Cover, and bring slowly to the boil. Remove from the heat and leave to stand for 5 minutes, then take out the onion and bay leaf. Stir in the semolina and mix well. Add salt and pepper and simmer for 15 minutes until creamy. Put to one side, stir in the cheese, butter and mustard, and spread out the mixture on a tin or plate about 1.75cm/¾ inch thick. Leave until cold and set, then cut into 5cm/2 inch squares. Pack in layers in a foil tray, brushing each layer with melted butter and sprinkling with grated cheese. Cover and freeze.

To serve
Thaw at room temperature for 1 hour, then uncover and bake at 180°C/350°F/Gas 4 for 45 minutes until golden and crisp.
High Quality Storage Life 2 months

Fish Lasagne

175g/6 oz green lasagne
450g/1 lb smoked cod or
  haddock
450ml/¾ pint water
1 bay leaf
salt and pepper
1 small onion
1 celery stick
75g/3 oz butter
75g/3 oz plain flour
600ml/1 pint milk
75g/3 oz grated Cheddar
  cheese

Cook the lasagne in a large pan of boiling salted water for 10 minutes. Drain thoroughly. Put the fish, water, bay leaf and seasoning into a pan and bring to the boil, then simmer gently for 10 minutes. Strain the liquid and reserve. Flake the fish. Chop the onion and celery and fry in the butter until soft and golden. Add the flour and cook for 1 minute. Gradually add the milk and the reserved fish stock. Cook for 5 minutes over low heat, then season to taste and add the grated cheese.

Line a greased freezer dish with the lasagne. Cover with half the fish and one-third of the sauce. Cover with lasagne, the remaining fish and half the remaining sauce. Finish with a layer of lasagne and the remaining sauce. Cool completely, cover with a lid, and freeze.

To serve
Remove lid and cover the container with foil. Heat at 190°C/375°F/Gas 5 for 45 minutes. Remove foil and continue heating for 20 minutes.
High Quality Storage Life   2 months

Quick Mushroom Pizza

350g/12 oz self-raising
  flour
5ml/1 teaspoon salt
150ml/¼ pint cooking oil
90ml/6 tablespoons water
175g/6 oz lean bacon
175g/6 oz onions
450g/1 lb mushrooms
pepper
a pinch of rosemary
125g/4 oz grated Gruyère
  cheese
25g/1 oz grated Parmesan
  cheese

Mix the flour and salt and mix with the oil and water to make a soft dough. Divide into 2 pieces and roll to make a soft dough, then roll out into large thin rounds. Bake at 220°C/450°F/Gas 8 for 15 minutes and cool. Put the chopped bacon into a pan and heat gently until the fat runs. Stir in the chopped onions and continue cooking until the onions are soft and golden. Add the chopped mushrooms and cook until they are just soft. Season with pepper and rosemary and spread the mixture on the 2 baked circles. Top with a thick crust of grated cheese. Cool, then wrap in foil or polythene to freeze.

To serve
Unwrap and cover loosely with foil. Bake from frozen at 180°C/350°F/Gas 4 for 45 minutes. Remove foil and continue heating for 10 minutes.
High Quality Storage Life   1 month

123

Pizza with Anchovies and Olives

8g/¼ oz fresh yeast or
   5ml/1 teaspoon dried
   yeast
150ml/¼ pint warm water
8g/¼ oz lard
225g/8 oz strong plain
   flour (white or white
   and brown mixed)
5ml/1 teaspoon salt
olive oil

FILLING
olive oil
350g/12 oz cheese
450g/1 lb sliced or canned
   tomatoes
pepper
5ml/1 teaspoon fresh
   thyme, oregano,
   marjoram or basil

FOR SERVING
anchovy fillets
black olives

Blend the fresh yeast into the warm water, or reconstitute the dried yeast as directed on the packet. Leave for 10 minutes. Rub the fat into the flour and salt. Mix the yeast liquid into the dry ingredients and work to a firm dough, adding extra flour if needed, until the dough leaves the bowl clean. Turn it on to a lightly floured surface and knead until it feels smooth and elastic. Leave the dough to rise in a lightly greased polythene bag until doubled in size.

Turn the risen dough on to a board. Flatten with the knuckles or a rolling-pin to a long strip. Brush with oil and roll up like a Swiss roll. Repeat this 3 times in all. Divide the dough into 4 pieces if making individual pieces, and roll each piece into a flat circle to fit 17.5cm/7 inch foil plates, or roll out the dough to fit 1 large foil plate.

To make the filling, brush the dough with olive oil and cover with alternate layers of cheese, tomato and seasoning, finishing with a layer of cheese. Bake on the top shelf of an oven at 230°C/450°F/Gas 8 for 25–30 minutes. Cool, then wrap in foil and freeze.

To serve
Unwrap and thaw at room temperature for 1 hour. Garnish with anchovy fillets and olives, and heat at 190°C/375°F/Gas 5 for 25 minutes.
High Quality Storage Life   2 months

Prawn Pizza

BASE DOUGH
225g/8 oz self-raising flour
2.5ml/½ teaspoon salt
40g/1½ oz butter
about 150ml/¼ pint milk

TOPPING
125g/4 oz grated Cheddar
   cheese
5ml/1 teaspoon mustard
   powder
2.5ml/½ teaspoon mixed
   herbs
225g/8 oz tomatoes
225g/8 oz peeled prawns
18 black stoned olives
paprika

For base dough, sift together the flour and salt and rub in the butter until the mixture is like fine breadcrumbs. Bind with milk to form soft dough. Roll out lightly to a 30cm/12 inch circle on a baking sheet.

For the topping, mix grated cheese, mustard and herbs in a basin. Sprinkle over the dough. Arrange thinly sliced tomatoes on top and then the prawns. Place olives in circle. Sprinkle with paprika. Bake at 200°C/400°F/Gas 6 for 30 minutes. Cool and pack in foil or polythene to freeze.

To serve
Unwrap and reheat at 200°C/400°F/Gas 6 for 25 minutes.
High Quality Storage Life   1 month

Quiche Lorraine

225g/8 oz shortcrust pastry
15g/½ oz butter
1 small onion
25g/1 oz streaky bacon
1 egg
1 egg yolk
50g/2 oz grated Cheddar
   cheese
150ml/¼ pint creamy milk
salt and pepper

Roll out the pastry and line a flan ring. Bake the pastry blind at 200°C/400°F/Gas 6 for 15 minutes. Melt the butter and cook the chopped onion and bacon until golden. Put into the pastry case. Lightly beat together the egg, egg yolk, cheese and milk. Season with pepper and a little salt, if the bacon is not very salty. Pour into the pastry case. Bake at 190°C/375°F/Gas 5 for 30 minutes. Cool. Open freeze, then wrap in foil or polythene, or put into a box, and store.

To serve
Thaw at room temperature to serve cold. If preferred hot, unwrap and heat at 180°C/350°F/Gas 4 for 20 minutes.
High Quality Storage Life   2 months

Prawn Quiche

125g/4 oz shortcrust pastry
1 small onion
25g/1 oz butter
175g/6 oz peeled prawns
salt and black pepper
15ml/1 tablespoon
   chopped parsley
1 egg
1 egg yolk
150ml/¼ pint single cream
25g/1 oz Gruyère cheese

Roll out the pastry and line a flan ring. Bake the pastry blind at 200°C/400°F/Gas 6 for 15 minutes. Grate the onion and fry it gently in butter until yellow. Add the prawns, salt and pepper, and put the mixture into a pastry case. Sprinkle on the parsley. Lightly beat together the eggs, cream and grated cheese, and pour over the prawns. Bake at 180°C/350°F/Gas 4 for 40 minutes until just firm. Open freeze, then wrap in foil or polythene, or put into a box, and store.

To serve
Thaw at room temperature for 3 hours, or unwrap and reheat at 180°C/350°F/Gas 4 for 20 minutes.
High Quality Storage Life   1 month

Mushroom Flan

225g/8 oz shortcrust pastry
1 medium onion
15g/½ oz butter
225g/8 oz button
   mushrooms
15ml/1 tablespoon lemon
   juice
2 eggs
150ml/¼ pint single cream
salt and pepper
5ml/1 teaspoon chopped
   fresh parsley

Roll out the pastry to line a flan ring and bake blind at 200°C/400°F/Gas 6 for 15 minutes. Chop the onion finely and cook in the butter until soft and golden. Stir in the chopped mushrooms and lemon juice, and cook for 2 minutes. Cool. Beat the eggs and cream together and then stir in the mushrooms and onion. Season well and add the parsley. Pour into the pastry case. Bake at 200°C/400°F/Gas 6 for 40 minutes. Cool. Open freeze, then wrap in foil or polythene, or put into a box, and store.

To serve
Unwrap and reheat from frozen at 180°C/350°F/Gas 4 for 45 minutes.
High Quality Storage Life   2 months

Spinach Flan

450g/1 lb shortcrust pastry
675g/1½ lb spinach
50g/2 oz butter
2 eggs
225g/8 oz full fat soft
   cream cheese
50g/2 oz grated Parmesan
   cheese
salt and pepper
a pinch of ground nutmeg

Roll out the pastry to line a flan ring and bake blind at 200°C/400°F/Gas 6 for 15 minutes. Wash the spinach very well and then put into a pan with the butter. Cover and cook for about 8 minutes until soft. Drain well and press out excess moisture. Put into a bowl and add the eggs and cream cheese beaten together. Stir in the grated Parmesan cheese, salt, pepper and nutmeg. Put into the pastry case. Cool. Open freeze, then wrap in foil or polythene, or put in a box, and store.

To serve
Unwrap and return flan to flan ring. Bake from frozen at 230°C/450°F/Gas 8 for 15 minutes, and then at 190°C/375°F/Gas 5 for 25 minutes. Leave to stand for 5 minutes before removing flan ring. Serve hot or cold.
High Quality Storage Life   1 month

Chicken Flan

225g/8 oz shortcrust pastry
1 eating apple
1 small onion
15g/½ oz butter
15g/½ oz curry powder
2 eggs
150ml/¼ pint milk
salt and pepper
175g/6 oz cooked chicken

Roll out the pastry to line a flan ring and bake blind at 200°C/400°F/Gas 6 for 15 minutes. Chop the apple and onion finely and cook in the butter for 3 minutes over low heat. Add the curry powder and stir over heat for 1 minute. Cool, then mix with the beaten eggs, milk, salt and pepper. Dice the chicken and arrange in the pastry case. Pour on the curry mixture and bake at 200°C/400°F/Gas 6 for 35 minutes. Cool. Open freeze, then wrap in foil or polythene, or put into a box, and store.

To serve
Thaw in wrappings at room temperature to serve cold. To serve hot, unwrap and reheat from frozen at 180°C/350°F/Gas 4 for 40 minutes.
High Quality Storage Life   2 months

FISH AND SHELLFISH

Fish Florentine

675g/1½ lb white fish
    fillet, skinned
salt and pepper
450g/1 lb frozen leaf
    spinach or 675g/1½ lb
    fresh spinach
300ml/½ pint white sauce
    (25g/1 oz butter, 25g/1
    oz flour, 300ml/½ pint
    milk)
30ml/2 tablespoons grated
    Parmesan or dry
    Cheddar cheese
a shake of Cayenne
    pepper
salt and pepper
50g/2 oz grated Cheddar
    cheese

This dish freezes very successfully provided it is made with freshly cooked white fish. The spinach too should be freshly cooked and well drained and dried.

Divide the fish into 4 portions, season lightly and bake or steam until just cooked. Drain and allow to cool. Cook the frozen spinach according to the directions on the packet. If fresh spinach is used, wash thoroughly, then cook without additional water in a covered pan. Drain very thoroughly, pressing out as much water as possible. Season lightly, and leave to cool.

Add the 30ml/2 tablespoons cheese and seasoning to the white sauce, and cook gently for 2–3 minutes. Arrange the spinach to cover the bottom of a lightly buttered foil baking dish. Place the fish portions on top, and coat evenly with the cheese sauce. Sprinkle the surface with grated Cheddar cheese. When quite cold, cover the dish with foil, and freeze.

To serve
Heat with the foil cover at 180°C/350°F/Gas 4 for 20 minutes.
High Quality Storage Life   1 month

Fish Pie (1)

225g/8 oz cooked halibut
3 tomatoes
125g/4 oz button
  mushrooms
juice of ½ lemon
15ml/1 tablespoon
  chopped parsley
25g/1 oz butter
25g/1 oz plain flour
300ml/½ pint milk
salt and pepper
a pinch of ground nutmeg
350g/12 oz puff pastry
beaten egg

Cut the fish into pieces and arrange in layers with sliced tomatoes and mushrooms in a freezer-proof pie dish or foil container, sprinkling the layers with lemon juice and parsley. Melt the butter and stir in the flour. Cook for 1 minute and blend in the milk. Stir over gentle heat until the sauce thickens. Season with salt, pepper and nutmeg and pour over the fish. Cool and cover with pastry. Brush with beaten egg. Bake at 220°C/425°F/Gas 7 for 30 minutes. Cool and pack in polythene to freeze.

To serve
Reheat from frozen at 180°C/350°F/Gas 4 for 50 minutes.
High Quality Storage Life   1 month

Fish Pie (2)

450g/1 lb freshly boiled
  potatoes
salt and pepper
25g/1 oz butter
15-30ml/1–2 tablespoons
  milk
450g/1 lb cooked white
  fish fillet (575g/1¼ lb
  raw fish)
300ml/½ pint white sauce
  (25g/1 oz butter, 25g/1
  oz flour, 300ml/½ pint
  milk)
15ml/1 tablespoon lemon
  juice
15ml/1 tablespoon
  chopped fresh parsley
25g/1 oz grated dry cheese

Mash the potatoes, season lightly, add the butter and enough milk to make a stiff but spreadable mixture. Remove any skin and bones from the fish, and flake coarsely. Stir in the white sauce, lemon juice, parsley and seasoning. Turn into a foil baking dish. Spread the potato mixture over the fish, and mark the surface with a fork. Sprinkle with cheese and leave to cool. When quite cold, cover with foil and freeze.

To serve
Uncover, and cook at 200°C/400°F/Gas 6 for 1 hour, until hot through and browned.
High Quality Storage Life   1 month

Fish Cakes

225g/8 oz cooked white
  fish
225g/8 oz mashed
  potatoes
10ml/2 teaspoons chopped
  parsley
25g/1 oz melted butter
salt and pepper
beaten egg
breadcrumbs

Flake the fish and mix with the potatoes, parsley, melted butter, salt and pepper; bind with a little egg. Divide the mixture into 8 portions and form into flat cakes. Coat with egg and breadcrumbs and fry until golden. Cool quickly, open freeze and pack in bags for storage.

To serve
Thaw by reheating in the oven or frying pan.
High Quality Storage Life 1 month

Kedgeree

125g/4 oz long grain rice
225g/8 oz cooked smoked
  haddock fillet
50g/2 oz butter
10ml/2 teaspoons lemon
  juice
salt and pepper
15ml/1 tablespoon
  chopped fresh parsley

FOR SERVING
1 sliced hard-boiled egg

Cook the rice in plenty of fast boiling salted water until just tender. Drain and spread out to dry and cool. Free the haddock of all skin and bone, and flake the fish coarsely. When both are quite cold, mix the rice and haddock together thoroughly, and add other ingredients. Fill into a suitable container, seal, and freeze.
Note Use a firm rice which retains its texture, and take care not to overcook it. Italian long grain rice gives very good results. Cook the rice in plain salted water, not in the liquid in which the fish was cooked.

To serve
Heat gently, breaking up the frozen block with a fork. Cover, and cook over a low heat. Pile on to a hot serving dish and garnish with a sliced hard-boiled egg.
High Quality Storage Life 1 month

Fish Pudding

450g/1 lb haddock
75g/3 oz shredded suet
75g/3 oz breadcrumbs
10ml/2 teaspoons chopped
  parsley
5ml/1 teaspoon chopped
  onion
2 eggs
300ml/½ pint milk
salt and pepper

The fish should not be cooked for this dish, but may be fresh or thawed frozen fish.

Remove any skin and bone and chop the flesh finely. Mix with the suet, breadcrumbs, parsley, onion, beaten eggs and milk. Season well with salt and pepper. Put into a well-greased foil pudding basin, cover with greased paper and foil, and steam the pudding for 1 hour. Cool and pack in polythene to freeze.

To serve
Put the basin with a covering of foil into a pan of boiling water and steam for 45 minutes. Turn out and serve with parsley, tomato or mushroom sauce.
High Quality Storage Life 1 month

Fish Puffs

125g/4 oz plain flour
2.5ml/½ teaspoon salt
15ml/1 tablespoon cooking
  oil
150ml/¼ pint lukewarm
  water
225g/8 oz flaked cooked
  fish
15ml/1 tablespoon lemon
  juice
30ml/2 tablespoons
  chopped capers
2 stiffly beaten egg whites
fat or oil for deep frying

Sift together the flour and salt and then mix to a thick batter with the oil and water. Add the fish, lemon juice and capers. Fold in the egg whites. Deep fry dessertspoonsful of the mixture in hot fat or oil and cook until the puffs are golden-brown and crisp. Cool, pack in polythene bags and freeze.

To serve
Thaw for 30 minutes at room temperature, then fry in hot oil or fat until crisp.
High Quality Storage Life 1 month

Fish Rarebit

350g/12 oz white fish
  fillet, skinned
salt and pepper
125g/4 oz coarsely grated
  Cheddar cheese

Arrange fish in a lightly oiled shallow ovenproof dish. Season. Sprinkle thickly with grated cheese to cover the fish completely. Grill gently until the fish is lightly cooked and the topping golden. This will take from 5–8 minutes depending on the thickness of the fish. Leave in a cold place to cool quickly. When quite cold, cover with foil and freeze immediately.

To serve
Uncover, and put into an oven preheated to 200°C/400°F/Gas 6 for 30 minutes.
High Quality Storage Life 1 month

Sea Pie

125g/4 oz shortcrust pastry
225g/8 oz cooked cod or
  haddock
125g/4 oz prawns or
  shrimps
25g/1 oz butter
25g/1 oz plain flour
300ml/½ pint milk
75g/3 oz grated cheese
50g/2 oz mushrooms
salt and pepper

FOR SERVING
hard-boiled egg slices

Line a freezer-proof or foil pie plate with pastry and bake blind for 15 minutes. Flake the fish and prepare prawns or shrimps if fresh. Melt butter, add flour and cook gently for 1 minute. Stir in milk, and bring to the boil, stirring all the time. Add fish, prawns or shrimps, cheese, mushrooms and seasoning. Cool slightly and pour into the pastry case. Bake at 200°C/400°F/Gas 6 for 20 minutes. Cool completely. Pack in polythene or foil to freeze.

To serve
Thaw at room temperature for 3 hours to eat cold, or reheat at 180°C/350°F/Gas 4 for 30 minutes to eat hot. Serve garnished with slices of hard-boiled eggs.
High Quality Storage Life 1 month

Smoked Haddock Cobbler

450g/1 lb smoked haddock
  fillet
400ml/¾ pint milk
25g/1 oz butter
25g/1 oz plain flour
15ml/1 tablespoon lemon
  juice
30ml/2 tablespoons
  chopped parsley
salt and pepper

TOPPING

50g/2 oz butter
225g/8 oz self-raising flour
1.25ml/¼ teaspoon salt
5ml/1 teaspoon mustard
  powder
75g/3 oz grated Cheddar
  cheese
150ml/¼ pint milk

Poach the fish in the milk for 15 minutes and reserve the milk. Flake the fish. Melt the butter, stir in the flour and then the reserved milk. Return to the heat and stir until the sauce thickens. Add the flaked fish, lemon juice, parsley, salt and pepper. Spoon into a greased ovenware or freezer dish.

To make the topping, rub the butter into the sifted flour and salt until the mixture is like fine breadcrumbs. Stir in the mustard and 50g/2 oz cheese. Add enough milk to mix to a soft light dough. Knead lightly and roll out to a rectangle about 22.5 × 10cm/9 × 4 inches. Divide into 6 rectangles and cut each in half diagonally to make triangles. Arrange, slightly overlapping, on top of the fish mixture. Brush with a little milk and sprinkle with the remaining cheese. Bake at 220°C/425°F/Gas 7 for 25 minutes. Cool and wrap in foil or polythene for freezing.

To serve
Reheat from frozen at 180°C/350°F/Gas 4 for 1 hour.
High Quality Storage Life   1 month

Halibut in Tomato Sauce

1 large onion
50g/2 oz olives
50g/2 oz mushrooms
15ml/1 tablespoon cooking
  oil
425g/15 oz canned
  tomatoes
2.5ml/½ teaspoon mixed
  herbs
salt and pepper
4 halibut steaks

Fry sliced onion, olives and mushrooms in oil for 10 minutes. Add tomatoes, herbs and seasoning and bring to boil. Simmer for 10 minutes. Meanwhile, grill or fry halibut steaks and place in rigid container. Pour the sauce over the fish, cool, cover and freeze.

To serve
Reheat at 150°C/300°F/Gas 2 for 40 minutes.
High Quality Storage Life   1 month

Cod with Curry Sauce

25g/1 oz butter
1 small onion
1 tomato
1 small apple
salt
10ml/2 teaspoons curry
    paste
10ml/2 teaspoons lemon
    juice
25g/1 oz flour
a pinch of sugar
300ml/½ pint water
450g/1 lb cod steaks

Fresh or frozen cod steaks may be used for this dish. There is no need to thaw the frozen steaks first.

Melt the butter. Chop the onion finely and skin and slice the tomato and apple. Fry the onion, tomato and apple gently until browned lightly. Stir in salt, curry paste, lemon juice, flour and sugar and cook gently for 3 minutes. Stir in the water and bring to the boil, stirring well. Add the fish, cover and simmer for 15 minutes. Cool and pack in foil tray, covering the fish with sauce. Cover and freeze.

To serve
Cover tray with a piece of foil and heat at 180°C/350°F/Gas 4 for 40 minutes.
High Quality Storage Life   1 month

Scallops with Mushrooms

8 scallops
300ml/½ pint dry white
    wine
1 small onion
parsley, thyme and bay
    leaf
125g/4 oz butter
juice of 1 lemon
125g/4 oz small
    mushrooms
15ml/1 tablespoon plain
    flour
salt and pepper
50g/2 oz grated cheese

FOR SERVING
buttered breadcrumbs

Clean scallops and put in a pan with wine, chopped onion and herbs. Simmer for 5 minutes but no longer as they become tough. Drain scallops, reserving the liquid. Melt half the butter, add lemon juice and cook sliced mushrooms until just soft. Drain mushrooms. Add remaining butter to the pan, work in flour, and pour in the liquid from scallops. Simmer for 2 minutes. Season with salt and pepper and add grated cheese. Cut scallops in pieces, mix with mushrooms and a little sauce, and divide between 8 scallop shells or individual dishes. Coat with remaining sauce. Put shells on to trays, cool, open freeze, then wrap in foil for storage.

To serve
Heat frozen scallops at 200°C/400°/Gas 6 for 20 minutes, after sprinkling surface with a few buttered breadcrumbs which may also be frozen.
High Quality Storage Life   1 month

POULTRY AND GAME

Chicken Croquettes

350g/12 oz cooked
  chicken
25g/1 oz butter
25g/1 oz plain flour
150ml/¼ pint chicken
  stock or milk
50g/2 oz mushrooms
5ml/1 teaspoon chopped
  parsley
salt and pepper
beaten egg
breadcrumbs

Mince the chicken finely. Melt the butter, work in the flour and add the stock or milk gradually, stirring well. Chop the mushrooms and add them with the parsley to the sauce. Cook for 3 minutes. Add the minced chicken, mix well and season. Turn the mixture on to a plate and cool. Cut into equal-sized pieces and roll into thick finger shapes, or form into flat cakes. Coat with beaten egg, dust with breadcrumbs and fry on both sides until golden. Cool and pack in rigid container to freeze.

To serve
Without thawing, cook on both sides in hot fat until golden and hot right through. Croquettes may also be reheated at 180°C/350°F/Gas 4 for 25 minutes.
High Quality Storage Life   2 months

Chicken in Tomato Sauce

900g/2 lb cooked chicken
400g/14 oz canned
  tomatoes
1 garlic clove
1 medium onion
1 green pepper
60ml/4 tablespoons olive
  oil
5ml/1 teaspoon basil
2.5ml/½ teaspoon
  marjoram
15ml/1 tablespoon
  concentrated tomato
  purée
salt and pepper
15ml/1 tablespoon white
  wine
6 drops Tabasco sauce

FOR SERVING
chopped parsley

Cut the chicken into neat pieces. Put the tomatoes and juice through a sieve. Crush the garlic and chop the onion and pepper finely. Cook the garlic, onion and pepper in hot oil until just soft. Stir in the tomatoes, herbs, tomato purée, salt, pepper, wine and Tabasco sauce. Simmer for 15 minutes. Stir in the chicken and cook for 5 minutes. Pack into a foil container when cool, and cover with a lid for freezer storage.

To serve
Replace lid with foil and heat at 180°C/350°F/Gas 4 for 1 hour. Sprinkle with chopped parsley before serving.
High Quality Storage Life   2 months

Chicken in Curry Sauce

1.35kg/3 lb chicken pieces
2 medium onions
15ml/1 tablespoon curry
  powder
600ml/1 pint chicken stock
  (from cooking chicken
  pieces)
15ml/1 tablespoon
  cornflour
15ml/1 tablespoon vinegar
15ml/1 tablespoon brown
  sugar
15ml/1 tablespoon chutney
15ml/1 tablespoon sultanas

Simmer the chicken pieces in water until tender, drain off the stock, and keep the chicken warm. Fry the sliced onions in a little butter until soft, add curry powder and cook for 1 minute. Slowly add the chicken stock and the cornflour blended with a little water. Add remaining ingredients and simmer for 5 minutes. Add the chicken pieces and simmer for 15 minutes. Cool. Pack in rigid containers to freeze.

To serve
Heat gently in double boiler.
High Quality Storage Life   1 month

Chinese Drumsticks

6–8 chicken drumsticks
15ml/1 tablespoon soy
  sauce
75ml/5 tablespoons clear
  honey
50g/2 oz soft butter

Brush each drumstick with soy sauce. Beat the honey and butter together and completely cover each drumstick with this mixture. Place the drumsticks in a large pan that has been lined with foil and bake at 230°C/450°F/Gas 8 for 30 minutes. Turn the pieces frequently, being careful not to pierce the skin, and baste with the honey and butter mixture. The honey will turn a rich dark brown and completely seal the skin. Lower the heat to 180°C/350°F/Gas 4, cover and bake for another 45 minutes. Cool and pack in a polythene bag to freeze.

To serve
Put drumsticks on a baking sheet, and heat at 180°C/350°F/Gas 4 for 1 hour.
High Quality Storage Life   2 months

Country Chicken

25g/1 oz butter
30ml/2 tablespoons
  cooking oil
1.35–1.6kg/3–3½ lb
  chicken
175g/6 oz unsmoked
  streaky bacon
125g/4 oz mushrooms
45ml/3 tablespoons
  chicken stock
a pinch of garlic salt
4 skinned tomatoes
1 bay leaf

Heat the butter and oil in a large pan. Add the chicken and brown all over. Place in a warm casserole and add the chopped bacon and mushrooms; cook for 3–4 minutes. Add the stock and seasoning, then pour over the chicken. Cover the casserole and cook at 180°C/350°F/Gas 4 for 1 hour. Add the sliced tomatoes and bay leaf and continue cooking for 30 minutes. Cool, pack in a rigid container and freeze.

To serve
Reheat at 180°C/350°F/Gas 4 for 1 hour.
High Quality Storage Life   2 months

Country Chicken Pie

1.8kg/4 lb chicken
3 rashers streaky bacon
15ml/1 tablespoon
  chopped parsley
a pinch of mixed herbs
salt and pepper
cornflour
350g/12 oz shortcrust
  pastry

Remove the giblets from the bird. Put the chicken into a pan with all the giblets except the liver (save that for an omelet or pâté) and just cover with water. Bring to the boil, then reduce heat and simmer for 1½ hours. Cool and remove the chicken meat from the bones. Arrange the chicken meat in layers in a pie dish which will go in the freezer, along with the chopped bacon, parsley and herbs. Season each layer lightly with salt and pepper. Thicken the chicken stock with a little cornflour and cover the chicken. Cool completely and cover with the pastry. Bake at 230°C/450°F/Gas 8 for 45 minutes. Cool and pack into a polythene bag to freeze.

To serve
Reheat at 180°C/350°F/Gas 4 for 1 hour, covering the pastry if it becomes too brown. The pie may be frozen with uncooked pastry, and should then be baked straight from the freezer at 230°C/450°F/Gas 8 for 45 minutes, then at 190°C/375°F/Gas 5 for 20 minutes.
High Quality Storage Life   2 months

Kedgeree (page 129)

ABOVE *Halibut in Tomato Sauce* (page 132) *and* BELOW *Sea Pie* (page 131)

ABOVE *Country Chicken Pie* (page 136) *and* BELOW *Coq au Vin* (page 137)

Duck with Orange (page 139)

Coq Au Vin

2 × 1.35kg/2 × 3 lb
  chicken or chicken
  joints
225g/8 oz bacon
50g/2 oz butter
50ml/2 fl oz oil
20 small onions
30ml/2 tablespoons brandy
salt and pepper
15ml/1 tablespoon
  concentrated tomato
  purée
600ml/1 pint red wine
a sprig of parsley
a sprig of thyme
1 bay leaf
a pinch of ground nutmeg
1 garlic clove
350g/12 oz button
  mushrooms
25g/1 oz butter
15g/½ oz cornflour

FOR SERVING
chopped parsley
triangles of fried bread

Joint the chicken if using a whole one. Cut the bacon in strips and simmer in a little water for 10 minutes. Drain well. Heat the butter and oil together and fry the bacon lightly until brown. Remove from the pan and brown the onions in the fat. Remove the onions and cook the chicken joints for about 10 minutes until golden on all sides. Add the bacon and onions, cover and cook over low heat for 10 minutes. Pour on the brandy and ignite it, rotating the pan until the flame dies out. Season with salt and pepper, and add the tomato purée, wine, herbs, nutmeg and crushed garlic. Cover and simmer for 1 hour. Remove the chicken pieces and put into a freezer container.

Cook the mushrooms in butter until just tender and add to the chicken pieces. Stir the cornflour into a little water and add to the cooking liquid. Simmer until smooth and creamy. Cool and pour over the chicken and mushrooms. Cover and freeze.

To serve
Transfer the dish to an ovenware container, cover and heat at 200°C/400°F/Gas 6 for 45 minutes. Garnish with parsley and triangles of fried bread.
High Quality Storage Life   2 months

Chicken Crumble

175g/6 oz shortcrust pastry
300ml/½ pint white sauce
  (25g/1 oz butter, 25g/1
  oz flour, 300ml/½ pint
  milk)
350g/12 oz cooked
  chicken
15ml/1 tablespoon
  chopped parsley
12 capers
salt and pepper
25g/1 oz fresh
  breadcrumbs

Roll out the pastry and line a foil pie dish. Bake blind at 200°C/400°F/Gas 6 for 15 minutes. Heat the white sauce and add the chopped chicken, parsley and capers, and season to taste. Cool completely and put into the pastry case. Sprinkle with breadcrumbs. Cover with foil and freeze.

To serve
Reheat at 180°C/350°C/Gas 4 for 45 minutes.
High Quality Storage Life   2 months

Farmhouse Chicken

4 chicken portions
seasoned flour
25g/1 oz butter
30ml/2 tablespoons oil
2 onions
2 carrots
1 green pepper
400ml/¾ pint chicken
    stock
a pinch of tarragon

FOR SERVING
150ml/¼ pint single cream

Coat the chicken portions with the flour. Melt the butter and oil together and fry the chicken quickly until golden on all sides. Transfer to a casserole. Chop the onions, and slice the carrots and green pepper. Cook these in the fat until soft and golden, and add to the chicken. Pour in the stock and add the tarragon. Cover and cook at 180°C/350°F/Gas 4 for 1¼ hours. Cool, pack in a foil container, cover and freeze.

To serve
Reheat at 160°C/325°F/Gas 3 for 1 hour and stir in the single cream just before serving.
High Quality Storage Life   2 months

Casserole of Chicken Livers

225g/8 oz mushrooms
2 green peppers
45ml/3 tablespoons butter
675g/1½ lb chicken livers
1 bay leaf
salt and pepper
125ml/4 fl oz red wine

FOR SERVING
chopped parsley

Toss whole mushrooms and chopped peppers in 15ml/1 tablespoon of the butter. Put the rest in a casserole and slightly brown the livers. Add the mushrooms, peppers, bay leaf, salt and pepper and the red wine. Simmer for 10 minutes. Cool, pack in a rigid container and freeze.

To serve
Reheat in double saucepan and garnish with some chopped parsley.
High Quality Storage Life   2 months

Turkey Roll

350g/12 oz cold turkey
225g/8 oz cooked ham
1 small onion
a pinch of mace
salt and pepper
2.5ml/½ teaspoon mixed
    fresh herbs
1 egg
breadcrumbs

Mince the turkey, ham and onion finely and mix with mace, salt and pepper and herbs. Bind with beaten egg. Put into a greased dish or tin (loaf tin, cocoa tin lined with paper, or a stone marmalade jar), cover and steam for 1 hour. While warm, roll in breadcrumbs, then cool completely. Pack in foil or in a polythene bag to freeze.

To serve
Thaw at room temperature for 1 hour, and slice to serve with salads or sandwiches.
High Quality Storage Life   1 month

Duck with Orange

125g/4 oz streaky bacon
1 medium onion
1 carrot
45ml/3 tablespoons plain
   flour
15ml/3 teaspoons
   concentrated tomato
   purée
125g/4 oz mushrooms
400ml/¾ pint stock
60ml/4 tablespoons sherry
1 duck
75g/3 oz butter
juice of 2 oranges
salt and pepper
2 oranges

Cut the bacon in small pieces and put over gentle heat to extract the fat. Remove the bacon pieces, and add the sliced onion and carrot to the fat. Cook over low heat till lightly browned. Stir in the flour and cook till brown, then add tomato purée and sliced mushrooms. Pour on the stock slowly, and stir in the sherry. Cook very gently till mushrooms are tender, then strain in this sauce. Joint the duck and fry in butter until golden-brown. Put the duck into a casserole. Pour on the sauce, and the juice of 2 oranges. Season well, cover, and cook at 180°C/350°F/Gas 4 for 1 hour. Remove the orange skins, and cut into fine slices. Add to the casserole 15 minutes before the end of cooking. Cool, pack into a rigid container and freeze.

To serve
Reheat at 160°C/325°F/Gas 3 for 1 hour.
High Quality Storage Life   2 months

Duck with Cherries

1.8–2.3kg/4–5 lb duck
50g/2 oz butter
225g/8 oz black cherries
150ml/¼ pint stock
1 wineglass Madeira or
   sherry
salt and pepper
10ml/1 dessertspoon
   cherry brandy

Roast the duck with the butter inside. Remove the duck from tin and pour off the fat. Cut the duck into large pieces. Put the stoned cherries, stock, Madeira or sherry, salt and pepper in the roasting tin, bring to the boil and simmer until cherries are tender. Remove from heat, stir in the cherry brandy and pour over the duck. Cool. Pack into rigid plastic containers (cherry juice may leak through waxed containers), then freeze.

To serve
Thaw at room temperature for 1 hour, and reheat gently in double boiler.
High Quality Storage Life   2 months

Hunter's Casserole

3 rashers streaky bacon
4–6 rabbit portions
15ml/1 tablespoon flour
salt and pepper
1 onion
2 medium carrots
125g/4 oz mushrooms
15ml/1 tablespoon
   concentrated tomato
   purée
25g/1 oz butter or bacon
   fat
900ml/1½ pints water or
   stock

Cut the bacon into small pieces and fry them until lightly browned. Dip the rabbit portions in the flour seasoned with salt and pepper, and also fry until lightly browned. Chop the onion and cook until soft and yellow. Put the bacon, rabbit and onion into a casserole. Add the sliced carrots, mushrooms and tomato purée. Stir the flour into the fat in the frying pan and cook until browned. Add to the casserole together with the water or stock. Cover and cook at 180°C/350°F/Gas 4 for 1½ hours. Cool, pack into a rigid container and freeze.

To serve
Reheat at 180°C/350°F/Gas 4 for 1 hour.
High Quality Storage Life 2 months

Rabbit Pie

1 rabbit
seasoned flour
350g/12 oz fat bacon
1 onion
5ml/1 teaspoon chopped
   parsley
150ml/¼ pint water or
   stock
350g/12 oz puff pastry

Joint the rabbit and soak the pieces in cold water for 1 hour. Dry them and toss in seasoned flour. Put a layer into a pie dish and sprinkle with pieces of bacon, onion and parsley. Continue in alternate layers, seasoning well until the dish is full. Add the water or stock and cover with pastry. Bake at 200°C/400°F/Gas 6 for 1½ hours. Cool, pack in foil or polythene and freeze.
Note The pie can also be made with boned rabbit meat; the bones should then be used for the stock. Ham or bacon, and forcemeat balls can be added for extra richness.
To serve
Thaw at room temperature for 3 hours to serve cold, or reheat at 180°C/350°F/Gas 4 for 1 hour.
High Quality Storage Life 2 months

Normandy Rabbit

1 young rabbit
75g/3 oz butter
4 garlic cloves
15ml/1 tablespoon
    concentrated tomato
    purée
300ml/½ pint cider
salt and pepper

FOR SERVING
chopped parsley

Soak the rabbit joints in cold water for 30 minutes, then drain. Cover with fresh cold water and simmer for 30 minutes. Drain well and remove meat from bones in large neat pieces. Fry the rabbit in the butter with the crushed garlic cloves until just golden. Stir in the tomato purée and add the cider and seasoning. Simmer for 10 minutes and cool. Pack into a rigid container, making sure the rabbit pieces are covered with sauce, then freeze.

To serve
Reheat gently on low heat, or in a low oven, and serve garnished with plenty of chopped parsley.
High Quality Storage Life   2 months

MEAT

Beef in Cider

675g/1½ lb stewing steak
40g/1½ oz cornflour
salt and pepper
30ml/2 tablespoons oil
2 onions
1 garlic clove
2 carrots
2 oranges
150ml/¼ pint cider
600ml/1 pint beef stock

Trim the meat, cut into cubes and coat in the seasoned cornflour. Heat the oil and fry the meat, sliced onion and chopped garlic. Remove to a casserole. Add the carrots cut into matchsticks. Thinly peel the oranges, remove the white pith, blanch the peel for a few minutes, then cut in thin strips. Add to the meat and vegetables. Squeeze the juice from the oranges and add to the cider. Add the beef stock. Pour over the meat and vegetables. Cover and cook for 1¼ hours at 180°C/350°F/Gas 4. Cool, pack in a rigid container and freeze.

To serve
Reheat at 160°C/325°F/Gas 3 for 1 hour.
High Quality Storage Life   2 months

Beef Mexicano

8 small onions
900g/2 lb stewing beef
seasoned flour
25g/1 oz dripping
400g/14 oz canned
    tomatoes
15ml/1 tablespoon made
    mustard
15ml/1 tablespoon chutney
15ml/1 tablespoon honey
15ml/1 tablespoon cherry
    or blackcurrant jam
2 garlic cloves

Peel onions and leave whole. Trim excess fat off the meat and cut into 5cm/2 inch cubes. Toss the meat in seasoned flour. Heat dripping in a large pan and brown the meat. Add tomatoes with their juice, and the mustard, and blend well together. Add all the other ingredients, stir well and adjust seasoning. Transfer to an oven casserole with a fitting lid and simmer for 2 hours at 160°C/325°F/Gas 3. Cool, pack into a rigid container and freeze.

To serve
Reheat at 160°C/325°F/Gas 3 for 1 hour.
High Quality Storage Life 2 months

Beef Olives

450g/1 lb chuck steak
25g/1 oz fat
2 onions
2 carrots
bay leaf
salt and pepper
300–400ml/½–¾ pint hot
    beef stock
15g/½ oz flour

FORCEMEAT
75g/3 oz breadcrumbs
50g/2 oz shredded suet
juice of ½ lemon
15ml/1 tablespoon
    chopped parsley
15ml/1 tablespoon thyme
1 onion
beaten egg

Cut the meat into thin slices, about 10 × 7.5cm/4 × 3 inches. Spread on a board and flatten each piece.

Mix the ingredients together for the forcemeat and spread some on each piece of meat. Roll up and secure with fine string or cotton. Heat the fat and fry the meat and chopped onion in it, add the chopped carrot, bay leaf, seasoning and stock. Cover and simmer until tender. Remove the string and thicken the gravy by blending in 15g/½ oz flour and bringing to the boil. Cool, pack in a rigid container and freeze, covering the meat with gravy.

To serve
Reheat in a covered dish in the oven at 190°C/375°F/Gas 5 for 1 hour.
High Quality Storage Life 2 months

142

Beef with Walnuts

675g/1½ lb topside of beef
15ml/1 tablespoon bacon fat
12 small onions
a pinch of sugar
25g/1 oz flour
1 wineglass red wine
bay leaf
a sprig of thyme
a sprig of parsley
1 garlic clove
5ml/1 teaspoon salt
stock
50g/2 oz shelled walnuts
25g/1 oz butter
1 celery heart

Cut the meat into large cubes and fry in the bacon fat. Remove to casserole and fry the onions in the same fat with a pinch of sugar until they start to colour. Work in the flour, cook for 3 minutes, then add the wine. Add to the meat the bay leaf, thyme, parsley and garlic clove crushed with salt. Pour on hot stock to cover, put on a lid and cook at 160°C/325°F/Gas 3 for 1½ hours. After 1 hour, toss the walnuts in hot butter, and add the celery heart cut into small strips. Cook for 3 minutes, then add to the meat in the casserole. Cool, pack in a rigid container and freeze.

To serve
Reheat at 160°C/325°F/Gas 3 for 1 hour.
High Quality storage Life 2 months

Carbonnade of Beef

675g/1½ lb topside of beef
seasoned flour
50g/2 oz butter
2 onions
300ml/½ pint beer
300ml/½ pint stock
1 garlic clove
1 bay leaf
a sprig of parsley
a sprig of thyme
10ml/2 teaspoons sugar
10ml/2 teaspoons vinegar

Cut beef in slices and dust with seasoned flour. Melt butter and colour beef lightly on both sides. Put into a casserole. In the butter, soften the sliced onions without colouring, then put into the casserole. Add beer, stock, crushed garlic, herbs, sugar and vinegar. Cook at 160°C/325°F/Gas 3 for 1½ hours. Cool, pack into rigid container and freeze.

To serve
Reheat at 160°C/325°F/Gas 3 for 1 hour.
High Quality Storage Life 2 months

Southern Beef

675g/1½ lb chuck steak
15ml/1 tablespoon olive oil
3 tomatoes
50g/2 oz mushrooms
150ml/¼ pint stock
12 pitted black olives
1 clove garlic
2.5ml/½ teaspoon salt
1.25ml/¼ teaspoon pepper
a pinch of basil
1 bay leaf

Cut steak into 1cm/½ inch slices, and brown well in hot oil. Pour off fat. Add the quartered tomatoes, sliced mushrooms, stock, olives, crushed garlic, salt and pepper, and herbs to the meat. Put into casserole, cover and cook at 160°C/325°F/Gas 3 for 2 hours. Cool, pack in rigid container and freeze.

To serve
Reheat at 160°C/325°F/Gas 3 for 45 minutes.
High Quality Storage Life 2 months

Ginger Beef Casserole

450g/1 lb chuck steak
50g/2 oz fat
30ml/2 tablespoons soy
  sauce
7.5ml/1½ teaspoons
  ground ginger
5ml/1 teaspoon sugar
water
1 onion
1 turnip

Cut the meat in cubes and brown in hot fat. Put into a casserole with the soy sauce, ginger, sugar and water, just to cover the meat. Cover and cook at 180°C/350°F/Gas 4 for 1 hour. Add the quartered vegetables, cover and cook for 30 minutes. Cool, pack in a rigid container and freeze.

To serve
Reheat at 160°C/325°F/Gas 3 for 1 hour.
High Quality Storage Life   2 months

Spiced Beef Casserole

900g/2 lb chuck or brisket
  beef
50g/2 oz butter
2 large onions
1 garlic clove
300ml/½ pint stock or
  water
150ml/¼ pint red wine
350g/12 oz carrots
10ml/2 teaspoons
  concentrated tomato
  purée
1 bay leaf
a sprig of parsley
a sprig of thyme
1.25ml/¼ teaspoon
  ground mace
2.5ml/¼ teaspoon caraway
  seeds
salt and pepper
225g/8 oz large
  mushrooms
15ml/1 tablespoon
  cornflour

Cut the meat into cubes and remove excess fat. Melt the butter and brown the meat all over. Add the sliced onions and crushed garlic and continue cooking for 5 minutes. Add the stock, wine, sliced carrots, tomato purée, herbs, spices and seasoning. Cover and simmer for 1 hour. Add the thickly sliced mushrooms and continue cooking for 30 minutes. Take out the herbs. Mix the cornflour with a little water and stir into the pan. Bring to the boil, and stir for a few minutes until the gravy is smooth and creamy. Cool and pack into a foil container, covering with a lid to freeze.

To serve
Replace lid with foil and reheat at 180°C/350°F/Gas 4 for 1 hour.
High Quality Storage Life   2 months

Goulash

900g/2 lb chuck steak or
  pork
30ml/2 tablespoons bacon
  fat
6 medium onions
30ml/2 tablespoons
  paprika
2.5ml/½ teaspoon salt
2 green peppers

FOR SERVING
soured cream or yoghurt
  (optional)

Cut the meat into cubes. Put half into a pan and cook in its own fat until lightly browned. Transfer to a saucepan. Rinse out the frying pan with 300ml/½ pint water and add this water to the meat. Repeat the process with the remaining meat. Melt the fat and cook the coarsely chopped onions until soft and golden. Stir in the paprika and salt, and add to the meat with the chopped green peppers. Cover and simmer for about 2 hours until the meat is tender. Cool, pack in a rigid container, and freeze.

To serve
Reheat gently and serve with noodles or plain boiled potatoes. Some soured cream or yoghurt may be stirred into the goulash just before serving.
High Quality Storage Life   2 months

Stuffed Cabbage Rolls

450g/1 lb minced cold
  meat
25g/1 oz butter
1 small onion
30ml/2 tablespoons
  cooked rice
5ml/1 teaspoon chopped
  parsley
salt and pepper
stock
12 medium-sized cabbage
  leaves

Cook the meat in the butter with the finely chopped onion until the meat begins to colour. Mix with rice, parsley, salt, pepper and enough stock to moisten, and cook for 5 minutes. Blanch cabbage leaves in boiling water for 2 minutes and drain well. Put a spoonful of filling on each leaf, and form into a parcel. Put parcels close together in a covered oven dish and cover with stock. Cook at 180°C/350°F/Gas 4 for 45 minutes and then cool. Put into a foil container, cover and freeze.

To serve
Remove lid and reheat at 180°C/350°F/Gas 4 for 1 hour with a covering of foil so that the cabbage leaves remain soft.

If liked, thicken the cooking liquid with a small ball of butter and flour worked together and stirred in about 5 minutes before serving time.
High Quality Storage Life   2 months

Beef Galantine

1 medium onion
350g/12 oz fresh beef
50g/2 oz fresh white
  breadcrumbs
75g/3 oz shredded suet
salt and pepper
5ml/1 teaspoon mixed
  herbs
1 egg

FOR SERVING
crisp breadcrumbs

Grate the onion, and mince the meat. Mix with all ingredients, binding with the egg. Form into a neat roll or oblong. Dip a cloth in boiling water, flour well, and put the galantine in this. Steam for 2¾ hours. Unwrap the cloth and cool the galantine completely. Pack in foil or polythene to freeze.

To serve
Thaw in refrigerator for 6 hours, or at room temperature for 3 hours. Roll galantine in crisp breadcrumbs just before serving.
High Quality Storage Life   2 months

Beef and Potato Pie

25g/1 oz dripping
2 medium onions
15ml/1 tablespoon flour
15ml/1 tablespoon curry
  powder
300ml/½ pint stock
450g/1 lb minced beef
salt and pepper
10ml/1 tablespoon tomato
  chutney
675g/1½ lb potatoes
15g/½ oz butter
25g/1 oz Cheddar cheese

Melt the dripping in a saucepan, and gently fry the thinly sliced onions until soft. Stir in the flour and curry powder, cook for a minute or two, then slowly add the stock. Bring to the boil, lower the heat, and simmer until the sauce has thickened. Stir in the meat, breaking up any lumps. Cover and cook over low heat for 20 minutes. Add the salt, pepper and chutney, mix with a spoon and cook for another 15 minutes or until the meat is tender.

Meanwhile, peel and boil the potatoes. When they are cooked, drain well, season, stir in the butter and grated cheese, and mash well.

When the meat is ready, transfer to a foil dish, cover with the potato mixture and cook at 220°C/425°F/Gas 7 for about 15 minutes until the potato topping is lightly browned. Cool, cover with a foil lid and freeze.

To serve
Remove the lid and heat at 180°C/350°F/Gas 4 for 45 minutes.
High Quality Storage Life   2 months

Meat and Potato Loaf

1 onion
25g/1 oz fat
5ml/1 teaspoon mustard
  powder
900g/2 lb fresh minced
  meat (any mixture of
  beef, pork or veal)
15ml/1 tablespoon
  chopped parsley
2 grated carrots
salt and pepper
2 potatoes
1 egg

Chop and fry the onion in the fat until soft. Stir in the mustard powder. Put the meat into a mixing bowl. Add the onion, parsley and grated carrots, and mix thoroughly. Season to taste. Peel the potatoes, cut into cubes and add to the meat. Bind with the lightly beaten egg. Shape into a loaf or turn into a greased loaf tin. Bake at 190°C/375°F/Gas 5 for 1 hour. Cool, wrap in foil or polythene and freeze.

To serve
Reheat at 180°C/350°F/Gas 4 for 45 minutes.
High Quality Storage Life   2 months

Saunder's Old English Pie

25g/1 oz lard
1 onion
675g/1½ lb raw minced
  beef
15g/½ oz cornflour
30ml/2 tablespoons
  Worcestershire sauce
30ml/2 tablespoons water
15ml/1 tablespoon
  concentrated tomato
  purée
salt and pepper
2 eggs
25g/1 oz flour
450g/1 lb mashed potatoes

Heat the lard in a pan and fry the onion for 2 minutes. Add the minced beef and fry gently for 5 minutes. Cover the pan and cook slowly for 30 minutes. Blend the cornflour with the sauce and the water and stir into the mince with tomato purée. Return to the boil, cook for 1 minute and season. Cool.

Beat the eggs and flour into the potatoes. Grease a loose bottomed cake tin and spread one-third of the potato mixture on the base. Use one-third of the mixture to line sides of tin to a height of approximately 3.5cm/2½ inches. Spoon in the mince and cover with remaining one-third of potato mixture. Make sure the meat is completely covered with the potato. Bake at 190°C/375°F/Gas 5 for 45 minutes until the top of the potato is well browned. Leave for 5 minutes before removing from tin and removing base of tin. Cool completely, wrap in foil and freeze.

To serve
Return to cake tin and heat at 180°C/350°F/Gas 4 for 45 minutes. Leave for 5 minutes and turn out.
High Quality Storage Life   2 months

Little Meat Balls

350g/12 oz minced fresh beef
125g/4 oz minced fresh pork
50g/2 oz dry white breadcrumbs
300ml/½ pint creamy milk
1 small onion
salt and pepper
25g/1 oz butter

Mix together the beef and pork. Soak the breadcrumbs in the milk. Chop the onion finely and cook in the butter until soft and golden. Mix the breadcrumbs and onion with the meat and season well. The mixture will be soft. Shape into small balls and fry a few at a time in butter until evenly browned, shaking the pan to keep the meat balls round. Drain each batch and cool. Pack in bags or rigid containers to freeze.

To serve
Thaw in wrappings in refrigerator for 3 hours to eat cold with salad. To serve hot, fry quickly in hot fat, or heat in gravy or tomato sauce.
High Quality Storage Life 2 months

Cornish Pasties

225g/8 oz plain flour
salt and pepper
175g/6 oz lard
45–60ml/3–4 tablespoons water
50g/2 oz carrot
75g/3 oz onion
175g/6 oz potato
225g/8 oz lean beef
2.5ml/½ teaspoon mustard powder
beaten egg

Put the flour and a pinch of salt into a bowl and rub in the lard. Add enough water to make a firm dough. Rest the pastry for about 1 hour. Mix the chopped vegetables, beef, mustard, salt and pepper. Roll out the pastry on a floured surface to a thickness of ½cm/¼ inch. Cut out rounds 15cm/6 inches in diameter. Place 45ml/3 tablespoons of the mixture on each round. Moisten the edges of the pastry, fold over and flute to seal. Put the pasties on a baking tray and cut 2 small slits in the top of each. Brush with beaten egg. Bake at 200°C/400°F/Gas 6 in the centre of the oven for 15 minutes. Reduce heat to 180°C/350°F/Gas 4 and cook for 30 minutes until golden. Cool, pack in foil or polythene, and freeze.

To serve
Thaw for 3 hours at room temperature to serve cold. Reheat at 180°C/350°F/Gas 4 for 30 minutes to serve hot.
High Quality Storage Life 2 months

Steak and Kidney Pie

450g/1 lb chuck steak
125g/4 oz kidney
25g/1 oz dripping
400ml/¾ pint beef stock
salt and pepper
15g/½ oz cornflour
225g/8 oz puff pastry

Cut the steak and kidney into neat pieces and fry until brown in the dripping. Add stock and seasoning and simmer for 2 hours. Mix the cornflour with a little water. Stir into the hot mixture, and simmer for a few minutes until the gravy is smooth and creamy. Pour into a foil dish, or into a pie dish which will withstand freezer temperatures. Cool the meat, cover with pastry, pack into a polythene bag and freeze.

To serve
Bake from frozen at 200°C/400°F/Gas 6 for 50 minutes until pastry is crisp and golden.
High Quality Storage Life   2 months

Breast of Veal with Sausage Stuffing

1.35kg/3 lb boned breast
   of veal
225g/8 oz pork
   sausage-meat
salt and pepper
150ml/¼ pint water
60ml/4 tablespoons bottled
   sauce
1 onion

Spread the veal with the sausage-meat, roll it up, and tie it securely. Sprinkle the meat with salt and pepper and brown it all over in a little hot fat. Add the water, sauce and sliced onion, cover and simmer for 2 hours. Cool and remove surplus fat. Pack in a rigid container to freeze.

To serve
Reheat at 180°C/350°F/Gas 4 for 1 hour.
High Quality Storage Life   1 month

Veal with Olives

450g/1 lb stewing veal
45ml/3 tablespoons olive
   oil
2 onions
30ml/2 tablespoons flour
½ glass white wine
300ml/½ pint stock
125g/4 oz mushrooms
30ml/2 tablespoons
   concentrated tomato
   purée
1 garlic clove
12 pitted green olives
pepper

Cut veal in pieces and fry in oil till golden. Slice onions and fry till golden. Sprinkle in flour, and cook till brown. Stir in wine and stock, bring to boil, and add sliced mushrooms, tomato purée and crushed garlic. Cover and cook at 160°C/325°F/Gas 3 for 1 hour. Add olives and a good shake of pepper 5 minutes before cooking finishes. Cool, pack in rigid container and freeze.

To serve
Reheat at 160°C/325°F/Gas 3 for 1 hour.
High Quality Storage Life   2 months

Spring Veal

450g/1 lb stewing veal
50g/2 oz butter
12 button onions
25g/1 oz plain flour
600ml/1 pint beef stock
salt and pepper
a bunch of mixed herbs
225g/8 oz French beans
1 firm lettuce heart
225g/8 oz shelled peas
225g/8 oz new carrots

FOR SERVING
450g/1 lb new potatoes

Cut the meat into cubes. Melt the butter and fry the meat until golden. Lift out the meat and place in a casserole. Add the whole onions to the fat and fry over low heat until golden. Stir in the flour and cook for 1 minute. Add the stock, salt, pepper and herbs, and simmer for 5 minutes. Pour over the veal, stir well and cover. Cook at 160°C/325°F/Gas 3 for 1 hour. Cut the beans in chunks and the lettuce heart into quarters. Add the beans, lettuce heart, peas and carrots to the casserole, cover and continue cooking for 30 minutes. Cool, pack in a rigid container and freeze.

To serve
Return to casserole, cover and heat at 160°C/325°F/Gas 3 for 30 minutes, then add the potatoes and cook for another 30 minutes.
High Quality Storage Life   1 month

Brown Veal Casserole

675g/1½ lb stewing veal
3 rashers bacon
2 carrots
2 onions
1 stick celery
50g/2 oz butter
50g/2 oz flour
600ml/1 pint water
10ml/1 dessertspoon
    concentrated tomato
    purée
10ml/1 dessertspoon
    Worcestershire sauce
5ml/1 teaspoon meat
    extract
2 sprigs parsley
salt and pepper
2 strips lemon rind
15ml/1 tablespoon dry
    sherry

Cut veal in cubes, bacon and carrots in narrow strips, and slice the onions finely. Cut the celery in small chunks. Melt butter, lightly colour the vegetables, and remove to a casserole. Sprinkle the flour into the remaining butter, cook till brown, then gradually add the water and stir till the sauce thickens. Add tomato purée, Worcestershire sauce, meat extract, parsley, salt and pepper, and the lemon rind from which the white pith has been removed. Bring to the boil, then add the sherry. Put the meat in the casserole with the vegetables, pour over the sauce, mix well, and cover tightly. Cook at 150°C/300°F/Gas 2 for 2 hours. Cool, pack in a rigid container and freeze.

To serve
Reheat at 160°C/325°F/Gas 3 for 45 minutes.
High Quality Storage Life   2 months

Spanish Veal Rolls

4 veal escalopes
125g/4 oz butter
1 medium onion
125g/4 oz mushrooms
50g/2 oz stuffed green
  olives
50g/2 oz fresh white
  breadcrumbs
1 egg
salt and pepper
25g/1 oz plain flour
150ml/¼ pint chicken
  stock
juice of 1 orange
15ml/1 tablespoon sherry

FOR SERVING
150ml/¼ pint single cream
25g/1 oz stuffed green
  olives

Make sure that the veal is very thin.

Melt half the butter and fry the chopped onion until soft and golden. Add the chopped mushrooms and cook for 2 minutes. Chop the olives and stir into the pan with the breadcrumbs. Remove from the heat and work in the beaten egg, salt and pepper. Spread this mixture on the veal slices, roll up and secure with string. Melt the remaining butter and fry the veal rolls until golden and cooked through. Put into a shallow freezer container. Stir the flour into the pan juices and add the stock slowly, stirring to mix well. Add the orange juice and sherry, and simmer for 1 minute. Pour over the veal, cool completely and cover for freezing.

To serve
Reheat at 160°C/325°F/Gas 3 for 1 hour. Lift the veal rolls on to a serving dish and keep warm. Stir the cream into the sauce and heat gently without boiling. Pour over the veal and garnish with sliced olives.
High Quality Storage Life   1 month

Tarragon Veal

675g/1½ lb stewing veal
50g/2 oz butter
15g/½ oz plain flour
300ml/½ pint dry white
  wine
15ml/1 tablespoon
  chopped fresh tarragon

FOR SERVING
2 hard-boiled eggs

Cut the veal into cubes and brown on all sides in the butter. Sprinkle in the flour and cook for 2 minutes. Add the wine and simmer for 2 minutes. Turn into a casserole, cover and cook at 160°C/325°F/Gas 3 for 1 hour. Stir in the tarragon and continue cooking for 10 minutes. Cool completely and pack in a rigid container to freeze.

To serve
Reheat at 160°C/325°F/Gas 3 for 1 hour and serve sprinkled with finely chopped hard-boiled eggs.
High Quality Storage Life   2 months

Veal in Tomato Sauce

900g/2 lb veal shoulder
30ml/2 tablespoons olive
  oil
1 garlic clove
225g/8 oz button
  mushrooms
10 button onions
salt and pepper
4 large tomatoes
150ml/¼ pint dry white
  wine
300ml/½ pint chicken
  stock
a sprig of parsley
a sprig of thyme

Cut the veal into cubes and brown in the hot oil. Lift it out and put to one side. Cook the crushed garlic, sliced mushrooms and whole onions in the oil over low heat until just soft. Put into a casserole and mix with the meat. Season well with salt and pepper. Chop the skinned tomatoes. Stir into the oil and add the wine, stock and herbs. Simmer gently, stirring well, to make a smooth sauce. Remove the herbs and pour the sauce over the meat and vegetables. Cover and cook at 160°C/325°F/Gas 3 for 1¼ hours. Cool, pack in a rigid container and freeze.

To serve
Return to the casserole and reheat at 160°C/325°F/Gas 3 for 1 hour.
High Quality Storage Life   2 months

Ossi Buchi

2 veal shins
1 carrot
2 onions
30ml/2 tablespoons olive
  oil
225g/8 oz canned
  tomatoes
a sprig of parsley
a sprig of thyme
1 bay leaf
600ml/1 pint beef stock
salt and pepper

FOR SERVING
grated rind of ½ lemon
finely chopped parsley

Cut the veal into 7.5cm/3 inch lengths. Slice the carrot and onions. Heat the oil and fry the meat, carrot and onions until golden-brown. Add the tomatoes and their liquid, the herbs, stock and seasoning. Cover and simmer for 1½ hours. Remove the herbs, cool and pack in a rigid container to freeze.

To serve
Reheat at 160°C/325°F/Gas 3 for 1 hour. Serve sprinkled with lemon rind and parsley, with an accompaniment of boiled rice.
High Quality Storage Life   2 months

Goulash (page 145)

Steak and Kidney Pie (page 149)

RIGHT *Stuffed Cabbage Rolls* (page 133)

Breast of Veal with Sausage Stuffing (page 149)

Kidneys in Red Wine (page 163)

Burgundy Lamb

125g/4 oz bacon
1 medium onion
1 garlic clove
675g/1½ lb leg or
    shoulder of lamb
15ml/1 tablespoon flour
1 medium carrot
15ml/1 tablespoon
    concentrated tomato
    purée
125g/4 oz button
    mushrooms
400ml/¾ pint red wine
salt and pepper
5ml/1 teaspoon sugar

Fry the chopped bacon in a large deep frying pan until crisp. Remove from the pan. Fry the sliced onion and crushed garlic in the bacon fat until golden-brown. Cut the lamb into 2.5cm/1 inch cubes, dust with flour, and add to the onion with the sliced carrot. Fry for 10–15 minutes until the meat is brown on all sides. Return the bacon to the pan with the tomato purée, mushrooms, red wine, salt, pepper and sugar, and bring to the boil. Place in a large casserole and cook at 180°C/350°F/Gas 4 for 1½ hours. Cool, pack into a rigid container and freeze.

To serve
Reheat at 180°C/350°F/Gas 4 for 1 hour.
High Quality Storage Life   2 months

Lamb and Lentil Bake

675g/1½ lb middle and
    scrag end of lamb
2 onions
125g/4 oz lentils (soaked
    overnight)
425g/15 oz canned
    tomatoes
300ml/½ pint stock
salt and pepper

FOR SERVING
chopped parsley

Cut the lamb in pieces and brown in its own fat. Lift out the lamb pieces into a casserole. Slice the onions and cook in the remaining fat until soft and golden. Add to the lamb with the drained lentils, tomatoes in their juice, stock, salt and pepper. Cover and cook at 180°C/350°F/Gas 4 for 1¼ hours. Cool and pack in rigid or foil container to freeze.

To serve
Reheat at 180°C/350°F/Gas 4 for 1 hour and sprinkle with chopped parsley before serving.
High Quality Storage Life   2 months

Sweet and Sour Lamb

675g/1½ lb boned breast of
  lamb
1 medium onion
1 medium carrot
300ml/½ pint stock
15ml/1 tablespoon vinegar
10ml/2 teaspoons
  cornflour
10ml/2 teaspoons soy
  sauce
10ml/2 teaspoons brown
  sugar

Cut the meat into thin strips and fry in its own fat until crisp. Drain off fat. Add the sliced onion and carrot to the lamb with the stock. Add the vinegar, cornflour blended with a little water, soy sauce and sugar. Cover and simmer for 1 hour. Cool and pack in a rigid or foil container to freeze.

To serve
Reheat gently in a double saucepan and serve with rice or noodles.
High Quality Storage Life   2 months

Spiced Lamb Hotpot

900g/2 lb stewing lamb
1 onion
2 sticks celery
225g/8 oz carrots
5ml/1 teaspoon tarragon
5ml/1 teaspoon paprika
salt and pepper
a pinch of grated nutmeg
900ml/1½ pints water
25g/1 oz cornflour
15ml/1 tablespoon vinegar
15ml/1 tablespoon
  mustard powder
5ml/1 teaspoon chopped
  parsley

Cut the meat into small joints. Arrange the sliced onion, celery and carrots in layers in a flameproof casserole with the meat. Season with tarragon, paprika, salt, pepper and a pinch of nutmeg. Cover with water, and cook at 160°C/325°F/Gas 3 for 1½ hours. Blend cornflour, vinegar, mustard and parsley with 15ml/1 tablespoon of cold water. Add 30ml/2 tablespoons of hot stock and stir; blend with meat in casserole, allow to thicken over heat. Cool, pack in rigid container and freeze.

To serve
Reheat at 160°C/325°F/Gas 3 for 1 hour.
High Quality Storage Life   2 months

Cumberland Cutlets

8 best end neck lamb
  cutlets
oil
1 small onion
1 garlic clove
125g/4 oz mushrooms
1 red pepper
15ml/1 tablespoon
  concentrated tomato
  purée
150ml/¼ pint stock
15ml/1 tablespoon lemon
  juice
10ml/2 teaspoons sugar
salt and pepper

Fry the cutlets in hot oil until brown on both sides. Remove from the pan and place in a casserole. Fry the chopped onion and garlic until soft and the sliced mushrooms until lightly browned. Drain and place in the casserole with the cutlets. Add the sliced red pepper. Mix together with tomato purée, stock and lemon juice and pour into the casserole. Season with sugar, salt and pepper. Cover and bake at 180°C/350°F/Gas 4 for 45 minutes. Allow to cool. Put chops and sauce in foil container, seal, and freeze.

To serve
Reheat at 190°C/375°F/Gas 5 for 45 minutes.
High Quality Storage Life   2 months

Pot-Roasted Stuffed Shoulder of Lamb

900g/2 lb shoulder lamb
dripping
2 onions
½ parsnip
2 sticks celery
2 carrots
salt and pepper
thyme, parsley and bay
  leaf

STUFFING
175g/6 oz pork
  sausage-meat
225g/8 oz apricots
50g/2 oz breadcrumbs
salt and pepper

Have the lamb boned. Mix all the stuffing ingredients together in a bowl and stuff the lamb. Tie into a round shape. Heat the dripping in frying pan and brown meat on all sides. Place in a saucepan and surround meat with the chopped vegetables. Add seasoning and herbs and cover with tight-fitting lid. Cook slowly over heat until meat is tender. The meat may also be cooked in a casserole at 160°C/325°F/Gas 3 for 2½ hours. Pack in a rigid or foil container and freeze.

To serve
Reheat in a covered dish at 160°C/325°F/Gas 3 for 1¼ hours.
High Quality Storage Life   2 months

Savoury Lamb Pie

450g/1 lb fillet of neck of
   lamb
2 large onions
3 lamb's kidneys
5ml/1 teaspoon sage
300ml/½ pint stock
salt and pepper
125g/4 oz button
   mushrooms
flour

PASTRY
125g/4 oz plain flour
50g/2 oz margarine
25g/1 oz grated Cheddar
   cheese
beaten egg

Ask the butcher to cut the fillet from the neck of lamb, and
then cut the meat into 2.5cm/1 inch cubes. Fry the lamb in its
own fat. Add the chopped onions, chopped kidneys, sage, stock
and seasoning. Bring to the boil, cover and simmer for 1 hour.
Add the mushrooms and then thicken the liquid with a little
flour if a thick sauce is liked. Put into a freezer-proof pie dish
or foil container.

Make the pastry with the flour, fat and grated cheese and
mix with a little cold water to a stiff dough. Roll out the pastry
and cover the pie. Brush with beaten egg and bake at
200°C/400°F/Gas 6 for 30 minutes. Cool, pack in a polythene
bag and freeze.

To serve
Reheat at 180°C/350°F/Gas 4 for 50 minutes.
High Quality Storage Life   2 months

Lamb Meat Loaf

225g/8 oz bacon rashers
450g/1 lb lean shoulder
   lamb
10ml/1 dessertspoon
   Tabasco sauce
1.25ml/¼ teaspoon
   marjoram
5ml/1 teaspoon mustard
   powder
5ml/1 teaspoon clear
   honey
120ml/8 tablespoons fresh
   white breadcrumbs
1 egg
salt and black pepper

Line a loaf tin with the bacon rashers. Mince the lamb. Blend
all the ingredients together in a bowl, and season well. Pack
the mixture into the prepared loaf tin. Cook at
180°C/350°F/Gas 4 for 1 hour. Turn out of the tin. Cool, wrap
in foil or polythene and freeze.

To serve
Thaw in the refrigerator for 6 hours to serve cold.
High Quality Storage Life   2 months

Braised Pork and Tomatoes

50g/2 oz lard
900g/2 lb hand of pork
2 chopped onions
6 tomatoes
salt and pepper
150ml/¼ pint dry cider

Heat the lard in a frying pan and brown the meat on all sides. Remove the meat. Fry the chopped onions for a few minutes, then add the sliced tomatoes and seasoning, and toss in the fat to coat. Place the vegetables in a casserole, place the meat on the vegetables and pour over the cider. Place in the oven and cook at 160°C/325°F/Gas 3 for 1½ hours. When cooked, slice the meat and surround with the braised vegetables. Pack in a foil dish, cover and freeze.

To serve
Reheat at 180°C/350°F/Gas 4 for 45 minutes.
High Quality Storage Life   2 months

Cassoulet

225g/8 oz butter beans
15ml/1 tablespoon cooking oil
1 large onion
125g/4 oz streaky bacon
900g/2 lb belly pork
225g/8 oz garlic sausage
750ml/1¼ pints stock
225g/8 oz canned tomatoes
15g/½ oz parsley and thyme and 1 bay leaf
salt and pepper
125g/4 oz fresh breadcrumbs

Soak beans in water overnight. Heat the oil in pan and fry the chopped onion and bacon for 3 minutes. Add the cubed pork and fry gently for 5 minutes, turning the meat. Drain the butter beans and add with the cubed garlic sausage, stock, tomatoes with juice, herbs and seasoning. Bring to the boil, stirring. Transfer to a large foil container, cover and bake at 160°C/325°F/Gas 3 for 1½ hours. Remove the herbs, sprinkle the top with breadcrumbs and bake, uncovered, for 30 minutes. Cool, cover and freeze.

To serve
Uncover and reheat at 180°C/350°F/Gas 4 for 1 hour.
High Quality Storage Life   2 months

Pork Pulao

60ml/4 tablespoons
  vegetable oil
1 onion
30ml/2 tablespoons curry
  powder
1.25ml/¼ teaspoon
  ground ginger
400ml/¾ pint stock
450g/1 lb lean cooked
  pork
1 cooking apple
15ml/1 tablespoon sultanas
1.25ml/¼ teaspoon salt
225g/8 oz long grain rice

Heat the oil and fry the finely chopped onion until brown. Remove the onion from the pan. Fry the curry powder and ginger until dark brown. Return the onion to the pan and add the stock, diced meat and apple, sultanas and salt. Heat through quickly, reduce the heat, cover and simmer for 15 minutes. Add the rice and simmer very gently until all the liquid is absorbed. The rice should be dry and fluffy. Cool and pack in a polythene bag or rigid container to freeze.

To serve
Reheat at 150°C/300°F/Gas 2 for 45 minutes in an uncovered dish, stirring occasionally with a fork.
High Quality Storage Life　1 month

Pork with Orange Sauce

6 large lean pork chops
seasoned flour
oil
2 medium onions
300ml/½ pint orange juice
  (fresh, canned or
  frozen)
30ml/2 tablespoons
  vinegar
15ml/1 tablespoon brown
  sugar

FOR SERVING
fresh orange slices or
  segments

Toss the meat very lightly in a little seasoned flour and cook in a little oil until browned. Remove from the oil and cook the sliced onions until just soft. Return the chops and onions to the pan, pour over the orange juice, vinegar and sugar, and simmer gently for 30 minutes until the chops are cooked through. Cool. Pack in foil trays, cover with sauce, cover with a foil lid and freeze.

To serve
Heat with the lid on at 180°C/350°F/Gas 4 for 45 minutes. Garnish with fresh orange slices or segments.
High Quality Storage Life　2 months

Cranberry Pork Chops

4 pork chops
salt and pepper
225g/8 oz cranberries
50g/2 oz honey
30ml/2 tablespoons water

Heat a little fat in a thick pan and brown the chops on both sides. Put them into a foil freezer tray and season with salt and pepper. Crush the cranberries and mix them with the honey and water. Pour over the chops, cover and bake at 180°C/350°F/Gas 4 for 45 minutes. Cool and cover with a lid for freezing.

To serve
Reheat at 180°C/350°F/Gas 4 for 45 minutes.
High Quality Storage Life   2 months

Pork Fricassée

575g/1¼ lb hand of pork
2 onions
150ml/¼ pint white wine
   or cider
1 bay leaf
1 sprig of thyme
2 parsley stalks
salt and pepper
25g/1 oz butter
25g/1 oz flour
75ml/3 fl oz milk
125g/4 oz mushrooms

Place the pork in a casserole and add the chopped onions, wine or cider, bay leaf, thyme, parsley and seasoning. Cover and cook at 160°C/325°F/Gas 3 for 1½ hours. Remove the herbs and strain off the liquid. Melt the butter in a pan, stir in the flour and cook for 2 minutes. Make up the milk to 300ml/½ pint with meat juices, and add slowly to the roux mixture. Season to taste. Pour over the meat, add the mushrooms and return to the oven for another 20 minutes. Cool, pack in a rigid container and freeze.

To serve
Reheat gently in double boiler and serve with boiled rice.
High Quality Storage Life   2 months

Lincolnshire Haslet

900g/2 lb lean pork
1 small onion
225g/8 oz stale bread
15g/½ oz salt
5ml/1 teaspoon pepper
5ml/1 teaspoon sage

Mince the meat and onion coarsely. Cut the bread into cubes and soak in a little water. Squeeze out the moisture and mix the bread with the meat. Season with the salt, pepper and finely chopped sage. Put into a loaf tin and bake at 180°C/350°F/Gas 4 for 1 hour. Cool in the tin and turn out. Wrap in foil or polythene to freeze.

To serve
Thaw at room temperature for 3 hours and serve in slices with salad.
High Quality Storage Life   2 months

Winter Pork Pudding

175g/6 oz self-raising flour
125g/4 oz shredded suet
salt and pepper
150ml/¼ pint milk
350g/12 oz belly pork
1 onion or leek
1 large potato
5ml/1 teaspoon sage
60ml/4 tablespoons cider

Mix the flour, suet and seasoning together to a soft dough with the milk. Roll out the pastry to a round.

Put the pork, onion or leek and the potato into a foil pudding basin. Add the sage, and season to taste. Moisten with cider. Cover the top with the pastry. Place a piece of buttered foil over the top and steam for 2 hours. Cool. Cover the top with foil and freeze.

To serve
Put the basin into boiling water and boil for 1 hour. Serve with rich gravy.
High Quality Storage Life   2 months

Pork and Apple Pie

25g/1 oz lard
2 large onions
3 sticks celery
675g/1½ lb pork spare rib
   or shoulder chops cut
   into 2.5cm/1 inch cubes
30ml/2 tablespoons
   Worcestershire sauce
300ml/½ pint chicken
   stock
15ml/1 tablespoon
   cornflour
30ml/2 tablespoons water
salt and pepper
1 large cooking apple

PASTRY
175g/6 oz flour
1.25ml/¼ teaspoon salt
40g/1½ oz lard
40g/1½ oz butter
30ml/2 tablespoons water
beaten egg

Heat lard in a pan and fry the chopped onion and celery gently for 5 minutes. Add the pork and fry, turning occasionally, for a further 10 minutes. Add Worcestershire sauce and stock, cover and simmer for 30 minutes. Blend cornflour with water and stir into saucepan. Bring back to the boil, season, add the chopped apple and leave to cool. Place in a freezer-proof pie dish or foil container.

For the pastry, sift together the flour and salt. Rub in fats until the mixture resembles fine breadcrumbs. Add water and mix to a firm dough. Knead lightly until smooth. Roll out and use to cover the pie dish. Decorate the top with leaves made from pastry trimmings. Brush with beaten egg. Bake at 200°C/400°F/Gas 6 for 30–35 minutes until the pastry is golden. Cover and freeze.

To serve
Thaw in wrappings at room temperature to eat cold, or reheat at 180°C/350°F/Gas 4 for 1 hour to eat hot. Alternatively the pie may be frozen with a cooked filling and uncooked pastry if this is preferred.
High Quality Storage Life   2 months

Pork and Sausage Plait

125g/4 oz belly pork
225g/8 oz pork
   sausage-meat
salt and pepper
5ml/1 teaspoon basil
beaten egg
225g/8 oz puff pastry

Chop or mince the pork very finely. Mix thoroughly with sausage-meat, seasoning, herbs and half the beaten egg. Form into a long roll 10cm/4 inches thick. Roll out pastry to an oblong 25cm/10 inches long. Place meat roll down the centre leaving equal borders cut obliquely in 1cm/½ inch wide strips, and brush with beaten egg. Fold alternate strips across filling to form a plait. Glaze with beaten egg and bake at 200°C/400°F/Gas 6 for 30 minutes. Cool. Cover and freeze.

To serve
Reheat in low oven, or thaw and serve cold.
High Quality Storage Life   2 months

Bacon in Madeira

50g/2 oz lard
1 carrot
1 turnip
1 onion
900g/2 lb collar bacon in
   one piece
125g/4 oz mushrooms
1 bay leaf
1 sprig thyme
1 sprig parsley
400ml/¾ pint stock
60ml/4 tablespoons
   Madeira

Melt lard and toss diced carrot, turnip and onion till lightly golden. Drain and put into a casserole. Put bacon piece in the hot fat and fry on both sides for 5 minutes. Put on top of vegetables in casserole, add mushrooms, bay leaf, thyme and parsley, and pour over the stock mixed with the Madeira. Cover and cook at 160°C/325°F/Gas 3 for 1 hour. Remove herbs, cool, pack in rigid container and freeze.

To serve
Reheat at 160°C/325°F/Gas 3 for 1 hour.
High Quality Storage Life   1 month

Bacon Pasties

350g/12 oz shortcrust
   pastry
175g/6 oz streaky bacon
125g/4 oz lamb's kidneys
1 large onion
225g/8 oz raw minced
   beef
salt and pepper
2.5ml/½ teaspoon
   Worcestershire sauce

Roll out pastry and cut six 17.5cm/7 inch rounds. Chop bacon, kidneys and onion finely and mix with minced beef. Season well with salt, pepper and Worcestershire sauce. Put a spoonful of mixture on each round and form into pasty shapes, sealing edges well. Put on a baking sheet and bake at 220°C/425°F/Gas 7 for 45 minutes. Cool and pack in polythene to freeze.

To serve
Thaw for 2 hours at room temperature.
High Quality Storage Life   1 month

Faggots

675g/1½ lb pig's liver
4 rashers back bacon
2 onions
175g/6 oz soft
 breadcrumbs
75g/3 oz shredded suet
10ml/2 teaspoons sage
5ml/1 teaspoon basil
salt and pepper

Mince the liver and bacon together and chop the onions finely. Mix them together with the breadcrumbs, suet, herbs, salt and pepper. Form the mixture into 8 balls and put them closely together into a foil baking tin. Bake at 180°C/350°F/Gas 4 for 30 minutes. Cool, cover with foil and freeze.

To serve
Heat at 180°C/350°F/Gas 4 for 45 minutes, divide the faggots with a knife, and serve with rich brown gravy and pease pudding.
High Quality Storage Life 2 months

Liver and Sausage Bake

225g/8 oz pig's liver
225g/8 oz sausages
25g/1 oz butter
2 medium onions
225g/8 oz tomatoes
salt and pepper
a pinch of sage
300ml/½ pint stock

Cut the liver into thin slices. Skin the sausages and cut in slices. Melt the butter and cook the sliced onions until soft but not brown. Drain off fat. Arrange onions, liver, sausages and sliced tomatoes in layers in a foil container, seasoning each layer with salt, pepper and sage. Pour over the stock, cover and cook at 180°C/350°F/Gas 4 for 30 minutes. Cool, cover with a lid and freeze.

To serve
Replace lid with foil and cook at 160°C/325°F/Gas 3 for 1 hour.
High Quality Storage Life 2 months

Liver in Wine

350g/12 oz calf's liver
3 onions
30ml/2 tablespoons olive
 oil
1 wineglass red wine
1 wineglass water
10ml/2 teaspoons brown
 sugar
a sprig of parsley
salt and pepper

Cut the liver in cubes, and slice the onions. Heat the oil, and toss the liver and onions quickly till brown. Add wine, water, sugar, parsley, salt and pepper to taste. Cover and cook at 160°C/325°F/Gas 3 for 45 minutes. Cool, pack into a rigid container and freeze.

To serve
Reheat at 160°C/325°F/Gas 3 for 45 minutes.
High Quality Storage Life 2 months

Kidneys in Red Wine

10 lamb's kidneys
40g/1½ oz butter
1 small onion
1 garlic clove
125g/4 oz small button
    mushrooms
15g/½ oz plain flour
150ml/¼ pint red wine
60ml/4 tablespoons beef
    stock
salt and pepper
5ml/1 teaspoon made
    mustard

FOR SERVING
chopped parsley

Cut the kidneys in half. Melt the butter and cook the kidneys for 3 minutes. Remove them and put into a small pan. Cook the chopped onion, crushed garlic and sliced mushrooms in the fat for 2 minutes and stir in the flour. Pour in the wine and stock and bring to the boil. Add the kidneys and season with salt, pepper and mustard. Simmer for 10 minutes. Cool and pack in a rigid container to freeze.

To serve
Reheat gently until piping hot and serve garnished with chopped parsley.
High Quality Storage Life   2 months

Oxtail Stew

1 oxtail
butter or dripping
1 small onion
2 cloves
½ blade mace
parsley, thyme and bay
    leaf
1 small carrot
6 peppercorns
juice of 1 lemon
600ml/1 pint water
25g/1 oz flour
15ml/1 tablespoon bottled
    brown sauce

FOR SERVING
225g/8 oz mixed
    vegetables
    (celery/carrots, peas)

Cut the oxtail into neat joints and fry in a little butter or dripping until brown. Put into a saucepan and add the chopped onion, cloves, mace, herbs, carrot, peppercorns, lemon juice and water. Bring to the boil, cover and simmer for 3 hours. Take out the oxtail pieces and strain the cooking liquid. Melt a little butter, stir in the flour and cook for 2 minutes. Gradually add the cooking liquid and stir until boiling. Add the oxtail and the sauce and simmer for 15 minutes. Cool completely and remove any fat. Put into a foil dish or rigid container, cover and freeze.

To serve
Reheat at 180°C/350°F/Gas 4 for 1 hour, adding the mixed vegetables for the last 20 minutes.
High Quality Storage Life   2 months

Pressed Ox Tongue

1 ox tongue
1 carrot
1 onion
2 sticks celery
parsley, thyme and bay
    leaf
10 peppercorns

Soak the tongue overnight if it has been salted. Put in a large pan with cold water and bring slowly to the boil. Drain tongue, cover with fresh water and bring to the boil again. Add chopped carrot, onion, celery, bunch of herbs and peppercorns. Cover and simmer for 3 hours. Cool in the liquid, then remove bones, fat and gristle and skin. Curl tongue into a round cake tin or soufflé dish and cover with weights. Leave in a cold place for 12 hours. Pack tongue in freezer paper and overwrap with polythene.

To serve
Thaw in refrigerator overnight.
High Quality Storage Life   2 months

VEGETABLE DISHES

Mixed Vegetable Casserole

900g/2 lb assorted
    vegetables, eg a mixture
    of carrots, parsnips,
    potatoes, onions, celery,
    peppers and tomatoes
3 rashers bacon
50g/2 oz butter
50g/2 oz flour
15ml/1 tablespoon made
    mustard
300ml/½ pint milk
salt and pepper
75g/3 oz grated cheese

Dice the vegetables and cook in boiling salted water for 10 minutes. Drain and reserve 300ml/½ pint of the vegetable stock. Derind the bacon rashers, cut into strips and dry fry. Melt butter in a pan, remove from the heat and stir in the flour and mustard. Add the milk and vegetable stock and bring to the boil, stirring continuously. Simmer for 10 minutes until thick. Pour half the sauce on the bottom of a foil freezer dish, add the cooked vegetables and bacon pieces. Season well with salt and pepper and cover with the rest of the sauce. Sprinkle the grated cheese on top. Bake for 20 minutes at 180°C/350°F/Gas 4. Cool, cover with a lid and freeze.

To serve
Uncover, and heat at 180°C/350°F/Gas 4 for 35 minutes.
High Quality Storage Life   1 month

Bean Casserole

350g/12 oz butter beans
1.8 litres/3 pints water
1 glass red wine
350g/12 oz bacon
2 garlic cloves
salt and pepper
350g/12 oz potatoes
275g/10 oz runner beans

FOR SERVING
sliced tomatoes
chopped parsley

Soak the butter beans overnight in the water. The next day, add the wine and the bacon, bring to the boil, and simmer for 1 hour. Add the crushed garlic cloves to the pot. Season with salt and pepper. Peel the potatoes and slice, add to the pot and simmer for a further 10 minutes; then add the runner beans. Simmer for a further 15 minutes. Leave to cool, put in a rigid container and freeze.

To serve
Reheat thoroughly. Add the sliced tomatoes and chopped parsley 5 minutes before serving.
High Quality Storage Life   2 months

Beans in Tomato Sauce

30ml/2 tablespoons olive oil
1 large onion
1 small green pepper
225g/8 oz tomatoes
5ml/1 teaspoon salt
1.25ml/¼ teaspoon black pepper
bay leaf
a pinch of marjoram
675g/1½ lb French beans
1 garlic clove

Heat the oil in a pan and toss the chopped onion and pepper in the oil for 10 minutes. Add the peeled and chopped tomatoes to the onions, together with the salt, pepper and herbs. Bring to the boil and then simmer for 20 minutes. Cut the beans into pieces and add them to the tomatoes. Simmer over a low heat for 20 minutes, add the crushed garlic and continue cooking for 10 minutes. Cool and pack into a rigid container to freeze.

To serve
Turn into a pan, cover and cook slowly till thawed.
High Quality Storage Life   2 months

Chicory with Cheese

4 chicory heads
stock or water flavoured with lemon juice
4 slices cooked ham
25g/1 oz butter
4 slices Cheddar cheese
25g/1 oz breadcrumbs

Cook the chicory in a little stock, or in some water with lemon juice for 25 minutes. Drain well and wrap each chicory head in a piece of ham. Butter a foil freezer container and put in the chicory and ham. Cover with cheese and sprinkle with the breadcrumbs and flakes of butter. Bake at 190°C/375°F/Gas 5 for 15 minutes. Cool, cover and freeze.

To serve
Uncover and reheat at 180°C/350°F/Gas 4 for 30 minutes.
High Quality Storage Life   1 month

165

Baked Leeks

16 large or 24 small leeks
water or chicken stock
75ml/5 tablespoons butter
30ml/2 tablespoons double
    cream
salt and black pepper

FOR SERVING
grated cheese
bacon rasher

Put the leeks in a large pan. Add water or chicken stock barely to cover, and simmer with lid on for 5 minutes. Drain leeks and transfer to a foil freezer dish. Add butter and cream and bake at 180°C/350°F/Gas 4, turning occasionally, for 10 minutes. Season with salt and pepper to taste. Cool, cover and freeze.

To serve
Uncover, sprinkle with grated cheese, cover with a rasher of bacon and heat at 180°C/350°F/Gas 4 for 35 minutes.
High Quality Storage Life   1 month

Ratatouille

3 small aubergines
salt and pepper
45ml/3 tablespoons olive
    oil
2 medium onions
2 garlic cloves
4 small courgettes
450g/1 lb ripe tomatoes
2 small green or red
    peppers

FOR SERVING
chopped parsley

Cut the unpeeled aubergines into 1cm/½ inch rings. Place in a colander and sprinkle with salt. Heat the oil and cook the chopped onions and crushed garlic until the onions are just soft and golden. Rinse the aubergines and dry the slices on kitchen paper. Add to the onion with the unpeeled courgette slices, skinned tomatoes and diced peppers. Season with salt and pepper, cover and simmer for 45 minutes, stirring occasionally, until the oil has been absorbed. Cool, pack in a rigid container and freeze.

To serve
Thaw at room temperature for 3 hours and garnish with chopped parsley to serve cold. Ratatouille may also be reheated very gently. It is good with meat, poultry or fish, or may be served on its own as a first course.
High Quality Storage Life   2 months

Potato Croquettes

900g/2 lb potatoes
5ml/1 teaspoon salt
a pinch of white pepper
25g/1 oz butter
2 eggs
2 egg yolks
75ml/3 fl oz milk
15ml/1 tablespoon salad
oil
40g/1½ oz plain flour
50g/2 oz dry breadcrumbs

Peel the potatoes and cut them in small pieces. Cook them in boiling salted water until tender, and drain well. Shake over a low heat until they are dry and then mash them smoothly. Beat in the salt and pepper, butter, 1 egg and egg yolks. Form into sausage shapes (this amount will make about 10 croquettes). Beat the remaining egg with the milk and oil. Dip the croquettes into the flour, then into the egg mixture and the breadcrumbs. Put on to a tray or baking sheet and open freeze. Pack in a rigid container with foil or film between the layers, and store.

To serve
Fry frozen croquettes in deep fat until golden. Drain well before serving.
High Quality Storage Life   2 months

Stuffed Artichokes

4 globe artichokes
125g/4 oz cooked ham
1 small onion
50g/2 oz frozen peas
1 garlic clove
300ml/½ pint stock

FOR SERVING
butter
salt and pepper
4 shelled prawns

Clean artichokes and cook them in boiling water until tender (frozen ones can be used). Mince the ham and chop the onion. Mix together the ham, peas, chopped onion and crushed garlic and stuff the artichokes. Put the stock into a foil freezer container, and pack the artichokes in close together. Cover and cook at 180°C/350°F/Gas 4 for 20 minutes. Cool, cover and freeze.

To serve
Remove cover and heat at 180°C/350°F/Gas 4 for 20 minutes. Add butter, salt and pepper and continue heating for 15 minutes. Lift on to a dish, and garnish each artichoke with a prawn. Serve the liquid separately.
High Quality Storage Life   2 months

Stuffed Courgettes in Tomato Sauce

6 courgettes
1 small onion
225g/8 oz minced cooked
 meat
50g/2 oz fresh
 breadcrumbs
salt and pepper

SAUCE
400g/14 oz canned
 tomatoes
1 small onion
1 garlic clove
15g/½ oz butter
15g/½ oz plain flour
salt and pepper

Split the courgettes in half lengthways and place in an ovenware dish. Mix the chopped onion with the meat, breadcrumbs and seasoning. Fill the courgettes with this mixture.

To make the sauce, simmer the tomatoes in their juice, with the finely chopped onion and crushed garlic for 10 minutes, and then put through a sieve. Melt the butter and work in the flour. Cook for 1 minute and add the sieved tomato mixture. Season well and simmer for 10 minutes. Pour over the courgettes. Cover with foil and bake for 30 minutes at 180°C/350°F/Gas 4. Cool and cover with foil to freeze (the dish may be cooked in a foil container and then covered with a card lid if preferred).

To serve
Cover with foil and heat at 180°C/350°F/Gas 4 for 30 minutes. Remove foil and continue heating for 15 minutes.
High Quality Storage Life 2 months

Stuffed Onions

4 large onions
225g/8 oz cooked minced
 beef or lamb
50g/2 oz fresh
 breadcrumbs
150ml/¼ pint brown
 gravy
5ml/1 teaspoon
 concentrated tomato
 purée
salt and pepper
dripping

Boil the onions until just tender. Remove centres and chop finely. Mix with meat, breadcrumbs and gravy, tomato purée, salt and pepper. Fill onions with this mixture and put into a baking tin with a little dripping. Sprinkle with a few breadcrumbs and bake at 200°C/400°F/Gas 6 for 45 minutes, basting well. Cool. Pack in foil tray, covering with foil, to freeze.

To serve
Heat at 180°C/350°F/Gas 4 for 45 minutes and serve with gravy.
High Quality Storage Life 1 month

Stuffed Aubergines (page 169)

Bean Casserole (page 165)

Ratatouille (page 166)

ABOVE *Baked Leeks* (page 166) *and* BELOW *Stuffed Peppers* (page 169)

Stuffed Peppers

4 large green or red
  peppers
25g/1 oz butter
225g/8 oz raw minced beef
1 small onion
75g/3 oz cooked
  long grain rice
5ml/1 teaspoon marjoram
10ml/2 teaspoons chopped
  parsley
10ml/2 teaspoons
  concentrated tomato
  purée
30ml/2 tablespoons stock
  or water
salt and pepper

Slice the top off each pepper and remove seeds and
membranes. Put the peppers into a pan and cover with boiling
water. Boil for 5 minutes and drain well. Melt the butter and
brown the meat with the finely chopped onion. Remove from
the heat and stir in the rice, the chopped tops of the peppers,
herbs, tomato purée and stock or water. Season well with salt
and pepper. Fill the peppers with the mixture and place them
in a greased foil container. Bake at 180°C/350°F/Gas 4 for 30
minutes. Cool, cover with a lid and freeze.

To serve
Remove lid and heat peppers at 180°C/350°F/Gas 4 for 45
minutes. Serve with additional tomato sauce if liked.
High Quality Storage Life   2 months

Stuffed Aubergines

2 aubergines
salt
40g/1½ oz cooked rice
50g/2 oz chopped ham
5ml/1 teaspoon onion
5ml/1 teaspoon parsley
25g/1 oz butter
25g/1 oz mushrooms
2.5ml/½ teaspoon grated
  lemon rind
1 egg
salt and pepper

FOR SERVING
4 slices Cheddar cheese

Cut the aubergines in half lengthways. Scoop out the seeds and
sprinkle the insides well with salt. Let them lie, cut side
downwards for an hour. Mix together the rice, ham, chopped
onion and parsley, softened butter, chopped mushrooms, lemon
rind, egg, salt and pepper. Drain the aubergines and wipe
them. Fill them with the stuffing, piling it high, and place them
in a greased foil freezer container. Cover with a piece of
greased paper and bake at 180°C/350°F/Gas 4 for 45 minutes.
Cool, cover and freeze.

To serve
Remove cover, place a slice of cheese on each stuffed
aubergine, and heat at 180°C/350°F/Gas 4 for 20 minutes. This
is good served with a hot tomato sauce.
High Quality Storage Life   1 month

Sweet and Sour Red Cabbage

15g/½ oz butter
1 medium onion
15ml/1 tablespoon brown
  sugar
15ml/1 tablespoon cider
  vinegar
900g/2 lb red cabbage
salt and pepper
150ml/¼ pint cider
2 small tart apples

Melt the butter and fry the sliced onion until soft. Add the sugar, vinegar and the cabbage which has been finely shredded. Add salt and pepper and the cider and cover tightly. Simmer for 1 hour. Peel and core the apples and cut them into slices. Stir into the cabbage and continue cooking for 1 hour. Pack into a rigid container and freeze.

To serve
Heat gently in a double saucepan, or in a moderate oven, and serve with pork, bacon or goose.
High Quality Storage Life   2 months

SAUCES AND STUFFINGS

Apple Sauce

apples
water or dry cider
sugar
lemon juice

Slice the apples without peeling them. Put them into a casserole with just enough water or dry cider to cover them. Cover and cook at 160°C/325°F/Gas 3 for 45 minutes until the apples are soft. Put through a sieve and sweeten to taste, adding a good squeeze of lemon juice. Do not oversweeten, as apple sauce is usually needed as an accompaniment for duck or pork. Cool and pack into small rigid containers, and freeze.

To serve
Thaw for 3 hours at room temperature.
High Quality Storage Life   12 months

Cranberry Sauce

350g/12oz sugar
400ml/¾ pint water
450g/1 lb cranberries

Dissolve the sugar in the water over gentle heat, add the cranberries and cook gently for 15 minutes until the cranberries pop. Cool. Pack in small waxed containers to freeze.

To serve
Thaw at room temperature for 3 hours.
High Quality Storage Life   12 months

170

Gooseberry Sauce

450g/1 lb gooseberries
30ml/2 tablespoons water
25g/1 oz butter
50g/2 oz sugar

Wash the gooseberries but do not top and tail them. Put them into a pan with the water and butter, cover and cook for 15 minutes on low heat. When the berries are soft, put through a sieve, extracting as much liquid as possible. Reheat the purée with the sugar, stirring until it has dissolved. Cool and pack in small containers to freeze.

To serve
Reheat gently and use with fish, or with ices or steamed puddings.
High Quality Storage Life   2 months

Hot Tartare Sauce

25g/1 oz butter
25g/1 oz flour
300ml/½ pint milk
5ml/1 teaspoon capers
5ml/1 teaspoon chopped
   gherkins
5ml/1 teaspoon chopped
   parsley
salt and pepper

Melt butter in a pan, stir in flour and cook gently for 2 minutes. Add milk and slowly bring to boil, stirring continuously until sauce thickens. Add the remaining ingredients and season to taste. Cool. Pour into rigid containers, leaving headspace, and freeze.

To serve
Heat gently in double saucepan and stir until sauce melts and just comes to boiling point.
High Quality Storage Life   2 months

Maître d'Hôtel Butter

50g/2 oz butter
10ml/2 teaspoons lemon
   juice
10ml/2 teaspoons chopped
   parsley
salt and pepper

Cream the butter and work in the other ingredients. Form the butter into a cylinder shape and wrap in foil or polythene, then freeze.

To serve
Unwrap the butter and cut the cylinder in slices to form round pats. Serve on grilled meat or fish, or on vegetables.
High Quality Storage Life   2 months

Piquant Parsley Sauce

300g/11 oz soured cream
grated rind and juice of ½
   small lemon
10ml/2 teaspoons
   concentrated tomato
   purée
45ml/3 tablespoons
   chopped parsley
salt and pepper

Combine all the ingredients and season to taste. Spoon into rigid container and freeze.

To serve
Thaw for 3 hours at room temperature or 8 hours in refrigerator, whisk well and adjust seasoning.
High Quality Storage Life   2 months

Tomato Sauce

25g/1 oz butter
1 small onion
1 small carrot
450g/1 lb ripe tomatoes
25g/1 oz ham
600ml/1 pint stock
a sprig of parsley
a sprig of thyme
1 bay leaf
25g/1 oz cornflour

Melt the butter and fry the sliced onion and carrot until soft and golden. Add the sliced tomatoes, chopped ham, stock and herbs and simmer for 30 minutes. Put through a sieve, and return to a clean saucepan. Mix the cornflour with a little water and stir into the sauce. Simmer for 5 minutes, stirring well. Cool and pack in a rigid container to freeze.

To serve
Reheat in a double saucepan, or in a bowl over hot water, stirring gently.
High Quality Storage Life   12 months

Brandy Butter

50g/2 oz butter
50g/2 oz icing sugar
30ml/2 tablespoons brandy

Cream the butter and sugar and work in the brandy. Pack in small rigid containers, pressing down well, and freeze.

To serve
Thaw in refrigerator for 1 hour before serving with puddings or mince pies.
High Quality Storage Life   12 months

Cherry Sauce

450g/1 lb black cherries,
  fresh or canned
juice and grated rind of
  1 lemon
125g/4 oz sugar
15ml/1 tablespoon
  maraschino
15ml/1 tablespoon cherry
  brandy

If using fresh cherries, stone and simmer them in very little water until tender. If they are canned, drain only. Mix the lemon juice and rind, sugar and liqueurs and simmer in the top of a double saucepan until the sugar has dissolved and the liquid is hot. If the sugar does not melt easily, add 30ml/2 tablespoons juice from the cherries. When the sugar has dissolved, put over direct heat, add the cherries and simmer for 7 minutes. Cool and pack in a rigid container to freeze.

To serve
Thaw at room temperature for 3 hours, or reheat in the top of a double saucepan. This can be used over ice cream, hot puddings or mousses.
High Quality Storage Life   2 months

Chocolate Sauce

300ml/½ pint milk
15g/½ oz cornflour
15g/½ oz cocoa
25g/1 oz sugar

Heat the milk to boiling point. Mix the cornflour and cocoa with a little water. Add a little of the hot milk, blend well, and add to the remaining milk. Add the sugar and cook for 3 minutes, stirring well, until the sauce is thick. Cool and pack into a rigid container, leaving headspace, and freeze.

To serve
Reheat gently in a double saucepan to serve over ice cream or puddings.
High Quality Storage Life   2 months

Lemon Sauce

300ml/½ pint water
juice and rind of 1 lemon
25g/1 oz cornflour
30ml/2 tablespoons sugar
25g/1 oz butter

Boil the water with the lemon juice and rind. Mix the cornflour with a little cold water and then add to the hot liquid together with the sugar. Stir over gentle heat until the sauce is smooth. Cool and stir in the butter. Pack in a rigid container, leaving headspace, and freeze.

To serve
Heat gently in a double saucepan to serve with puddings.
High Quality Storage Life   2 months

Spiced Apple Sauce

450g/1 lb cooking apples
125g/4 oz sugar
1.25ml/¼ teaspoon
 cinnamon
1.25ml/¼ teaspoon
 nutmeg
30ml/2 tablespoons water

Peel and core the apples and cut them into quarters. Put into a pan with the sugar, spices and water. Simmer for 25 minutes until the apples are soft. Beat lightly and cool. Pack into a rigid container and freeze.

To serve
Heat very gently, stirring well, and serve with fruit puddings.
High Quality Storage Life   2 months

Strawberry Sauce

450g/1 lb strawberries
175g/6 oz caster sugar
juice of 2 lemons

Sieve the fruit. Stir in sugar and strained lemon juice and continue stirring until the sugar has dissolved. Pack into rigid containers to freeze.

To serve
Thaw in refrigerator and serve cold over ice cream, cakes or puddings.
High Quality Storage Life   12 months

Basic Poultry Stuffing

1 egg
50g/2 oz shredded suet
125g/4 oz fresh
 breadcrumbs
10ml/2 teaspoons chopped
 parsley
5ml/1 teaspoon chopped
 thyme
5ml/1 teaspoon grated
 lemon rind
salt and pepper

Mix all the ingredients, beginning with the beaten egg. Pack into a polythene bag for freezer storage.

To serve
Thaw in refrigerator for 2 hours and then stuff the bird. This stuffing may also be used for whole fish such as haddock, cod or mackerel.
High Quality Storage Life   1 month

Cherry Stuffing

150g/5 oz breadcrumbs
150g/5 oz sausage-meat
75g/3 oz grated apple
65g/2½ oz maraschino
   cherries
1 egg
salt and pepper

Mix the breadcrumbs, sausage-meat and apple. Cut the cherries in half and add to the breadcrumbs, together with the egg, salt and pepper. Pack in cartons or polythene bags to freeze.

To serve
Thaw in refrigerator for 12 hours before stuffing duck.
High Quality Storage Life 2 weeks

Chestnut Stuffing

450g/1 lb chestnuts
milk
50g/2 oz fresh white
   breadcrumbs
25g/1 oz melted butter
10ml/2 teaspoons fresh
   mixed herbs
2 eggs
salt and pepper
a pinch of mustard
   powder

Peel the chestnuts, then simmer in a little milk until tender. Sieve and mix with breadcrumbs, butter, herbs and eggs. Add salt and pepper and a pinch of dry mustard. Pack in cartons or polythene bags to freeze.

To serve
Thaw in refrigerator for 12 hours before stuffing the bird.
High Quality Storage Life 1 month

Green Pepper and Sausage Stuffing

1 green pepper
50g/2 oz calf's or chicken's
   liver
1 small onion
15g/½ oz butter
225g/8 oz sausage-meat
175g/6 oz fresh white
   breadcrumbs
5ml/1 teaspoon fresh
   mixed herbs
15ml/1 tablespoon
   chopped parsley
2.5ml/½ teaspoon salt
a pinch of pepper
1 egg

Blanch the pepper in boiling water for 1 minute, then cut into small squares. Fry the chopped liver and onion gently in butter for 2–3 minutes. Mix all the ingredients well together, then cool and pack in cartons or polythene bags to freeze.

To serve
Thaw in refrigerator for 12 hours before stuffing bird.
High Quality Storage Life 1 month

Orange Stuffing

175g/6 oz breadcrumbs
2 large oranges
50g/2 oz melted butter
5ml/1 teaspoon celery salt
1 egg
5ml/1 teaspoon chopped
   parsley
5ml/1 teaspoon chopped
   sage

Put the breadcrumbs into a mixing bowl. Grate the rind from the oranges and squeeze the juice from one of them. Strip all the pith from the other orange and cut the sections into small pieces. Mix the orange sections, rind and juice, breadcrumbs, butter, celery salt, egg, parsley and sage thoroughly. Pack in cartons or polythene bags to freeze.

To serve
Thaw in refrigerator for 12 hours before stuffing duck.
High Quality Storage Life   1 month

Sage and Onion Stuffing

4 medium onions
125g/4 oz breadcrumbs
25g/1 oz butter
6 sage leaves
salt and pepper

Put the onions into a pan of cold water, bring to the boil and boil for 5 minutes. Strain off this water and cover the onions with fresh boiling water. Cook till tender, then drain them and chop the onions finely. Mix with the breadcrumbs, butter, sage, salt and pepper. Cool. Pack in cartons, sealing carefully to avoid cross-flavouring in the freezer.

To serve
Thaw in refrigerator for 12 hours before stuffing duck or goose.
High Quality Storage Life   1 month

Sausage Stuffing

450g/1 lb sausage-meat
50g/2 oz streaky bacon
liver from turkey or
   chicken
1 onion
1 egg
50g/2 oz fresh white
   breadcrumbs
salt and pepper
10ml/2 teaspoons fresh
   mixed herbs
stock

Put sausage-meat in a bowl. Mince the bacon, liver and onion. Mix with the sausage-meat, egg, breadcrumbs, seasoning and herbs, and moisten with a little stock if necessary. Pack in cartons or polythene bags to freeze.

To serve
Thaw in refrigerator for 12 hours before using to stuff bird.
High Quality Storage Life   2 weeks

PUDDINGS AND ICES

Apple and Rhubarb Fool

450g/1 lb rhubarb
450g/1 lb apples
125g/4 oz granulated sugar
60ml/4 tablespoons water

Cut the rhubarb into 2.5cm/1 inch pieces. Put the sliced apple, rhubarb, sugar and water in a saucepan, cover and cook very gently until soft. Mix well together. Liquidize or sieve into a smooth purée. Pack in a rigid container and freeze.

To serve
Thaw in refrigerator for 3 hours, and serve with cream.
High Quality Storage Life   12 months

Baked Apple Dumplings

225g/8 oz shortcrust pastry
4 small cooking apples
25g/1 oz seedless raisins
25g/1 oz brown sugar
25g/1 oz softened butter
1.25ml/¼ teaspoon
   ground cinnamon
beaten egg or milk

Roll out the pastry and cut into 4 squares. Peel and core the apples and put one in the centre of each piece of pastry. Fill centres of apples with a mixture of raisins, sugar, butter and cinnamon. Enclose the apples completely in pastry, sealing the edges well. Brush over with a little beaten egg or milk and bake at 220°C/425°F/Gas 7 for 25 minutes. Cool and pack in a foil tray. Cover with foil and freeze.

To serve
Thaw at room temperature for 3 hours to serve cold, or reheat if liked. Sprinkle with caster sugar or serve with hot apricot jam or custard.
High Quality Storage Life   2 months

Baked Cheesecake

50g/2 oz crushed digestive
   biscuit crumbs
450g/1 lb cottage cheese
5ml/1 teaspoon lemon
   juice
5ml/1 teaspoon grated
   orange rind
15ml/1 tablespoon
   cornflour
30ml/2 tablespoons double
   cream
2 eggs
125g/4 oz caster sugar

Butter the sides and line the base of a loose-bottomed cake tin with buttered paper. Sprinkle with biscuit crumbs. Sieve cottage cheese and mix with lemon juice, orange rind and cornflour. Whip cream and stir in. Beat the yolks until thick, then stir into the cheese mixture. Beat egg whites until stiff and beat in half the sugar, then stir in remaining sugar. Fold into the cheese mixture and put into the baking tin. Bake at 180°C/350°F/Gas 4 for 1 hour and leave to cool in the oven. Remove from tin. Open freeze and wrap in foil, and then in a box to avoid crushing.

To serve
Thaw in refrigerator for 8 hours.
High Quality Storage Life   1 month

Cheesecake with Strawberries

225g/8 oz crushed
   digestive biscuit crumbs
50g/2 oz melted margarine
350g/12 oz full fat cream
   cheese
75g/3 oz caster sugar
2 eggs
grated rind and juice of 1
   lemon
1 envelope or 15ml/3
   teaspoons gelatine
30ml/2 tablespoons water
300ml/½ pint double
   cream

FOR SERVING
fresh or frozen
   strawberries

Put the crumbs in a basin and stir in the melted margarine. Press into a greased loose-bottomed cake tin. Bake at 180°C/350°F/Gas 4 for 10 minutes, then cool. Cream the cheese with the sugar and egg yolks until light and fluffy. Add the grated lemon rind. Dissolve the gelatine in the water and heat gently until syrupy. Stir in the lemon juice and beat into the cream cheese mixture. Whisk the egg whites until stiff and whip the cream to soft peaks. Fold the cream into the cheese mixture and finally fold in the egg whites. Chill and then open freeze until solid. Remove from the tin, wrap in foil and then in a box for storage.

To serve
Thaw at room temperature for 3 hours. Top with strawberries and continue thawing for 1 hour.
High Quality Storage Life   1 month

Lemon Cheesecake

125g/4 oz finely crushed
  digestive biscuit crumbs
75g/3 oz melted margarine
25g/1 oz soft brown sugar
225g/8 oz full fat soft
  cream cheese
75g/3 oz caster sugar
2 eggs
150g/5 oz lemon yoghurt
juice and rind of ½ lemon
15g/½ oz gelatine
60ml/4 tablespoons water
150ml/¼ pint double
  cream

FOR SERVING
whipped cream or fresh or
  canned fruit or grated
  chocolate

Put the crumbs in a basin and stir in the melted margarine mixed with the sugar. Press into the base of a greased loose-bottomed cake tin, and leave in a cold place for a few minutes until firm.

Cream the cheese and sugar until smooth and gradually work in the egg yolks, yoghurt, lemon rind and juice. Dissolve the gelatine in water and heat gently until syrupy. Cool slightly and add to the cheese mixture. Whip the cream lightly and fold into the mixture. Whisk the egg whites to soft peaks and fold into the mixture. Pour over the base and chill until firm.

Remove from the tin, leaving the cheesecake on the metal base. Open freeze and when firm, turn upside-down on to a piece of foil. Ease away the metal base of the cake tin. Wrap the foil round the cheesecake, put in a box and store.

Note If lemon yoghurt is not available, use natural yoghurt and then add the juice and rind of 1 lemon.

To serve
Thaw in refrigerator without wrappings for 6 hours. Decorate if liked with whipped cream, fresh or canned fruit, or grated chocolate.
High Quality Storage Life   1 month

Spiced Cheesecake

225g/8 oz shortcrust pastry
125g/4 oz cottage cheese
50g/2 oz honey
50g/2 oz caster sugar
2.5ml/½ teaspoon
  cinnamon
2 eggs

FOR SERVING
cinnamon and caster sugar

Line a deep foil pie plate with the pastry. Sieve the cottage cheese and mix with the honey, sugar, cinnamon and beaten eggs. Pour into the pastry case. Bake at 190°C/375°F/Gas 5 for 35 minutes. Cool and pack in foil or polythene and then in a box to freeze.

To serve
Thaw in refrigerator for 6 hours. Sprinkle the top with a mixture of cinnamon and caster sugar before serving.
High Quality Storage Life   1 month

Sultana Cheesecake

175g/6 oz crushed
   digestive biscuit crumbs
75g/3 oz melted butter
225g/8 oz full fat cream
   cheese
25g/1 oz cornflour
150ml/¼ pint milk
2 eggs
50g/2 oz caster sugar
grated rind and juice of 1
   medium lemon
50g/2 oz sultanas

Put the crumbs in a basin and stir in the melted butter. Press into a foil pie plate. Leave in a cold place for 1 hour to set. Beat the cream cheese in a basin. Blend the cornflour with the milk in a pan, bring to the boil and stir until it thickens. Simmer, stirring, for 2 minutes. Add the egg yolks, sugar, lemon rind and juice. Cook gently for 2 minutes, then cool. Whisk the egg whites until stiff. Fold the cream cheese into the cooled sauce with the sultanas and egg whites. Pour into the pie plate and allow to stand in a cool place for 2 hours. Wrap in foil and then in a box to freeze.

To serve
Thaw at room temperature for 3 hours.
High Quality Storage Life   1 month

Berkshire Pigs

225g/8 oz shortcrust pastry
1 large eating apple
50g/2 oz currants
25g/1 oz soft brown sugar
5ml/1 teaspoon ground
   mixed spice
10ml/2 teaspoons chopped
   mixed peel
25g/1 oz butter
currants

Roll out the pastry into a rectangle and cut into 3 oblong pieces. Mix the chopped apple, currants, sugar, spice and peel, and divide the mixture between the 3 pieces of pastry. Put a small piece of butter on each. Fold the pastry so that the join is on the top and pinch together to make an edge on the 'backbone'. Pull out one end of the roll to form a tail, and the other end to form a head. Put 3 currants for eyes and nose. Form small pieces of pastry for ears. Bake at 200°C/400°F/Gas 6 for 25 minutes. Pack in polythene to freeze.

To serve
Thaw at room temperature for 4 hours to eat cold, or reheat from frozen at 180°C/350°F/Gas 4 for 35 minutes.
High Quality Storage Life   2 months

Blackcurrant Pie

225g/8 oz shortcrust pastry
450g/1 lb blackcurrants
125g/4 oz soft brown
  sugar
10ml/2 teaspoons plain
  flour
cold milk
caster sugar

Roll out the pastry and use half to line a foil pie plate. Mix the currants with the sugar and flour and put on the pastry base. Cover with the remaining pastry and seal the edges firmly. Brush with a little milk and sprinkle with sugar. Bake at 220°C/425°F/Gas 7 for 15 minutes, then reduce to 180°C/350°F/Gas 4 for 20 minutes. Cool completely, wrap in foil or polythene and freeze.

To serve
Thaw at room temperature for 3 hours to serve cold, or reheat from frozen at 180°C/350°F/Gas 4 for 40 minutes.
High Quality Storage Life 2 months

Bread Pudding

225g/8 oz stale white
  bread
40g/1½ oz shredded suet
25g/1 oz chopped mixed
  peel
50g/2 oz sultanas
50g/2 oz currants
2.5ml/½ teaspoon ground
  allspice
a pinch of ground nutmeg
40g/1½ oz sugar
1 egg
25ml/1 fl oz milk

Break the bread into small pieces and soak in cold water until soft. Drain and squeeze out surplus liquid. Mix the suet, peel, dried fruit, spices and sugar with the bread and beat in the egg and milk. Put into a greased roasting tin or foil dish and bake at 160°C/325°F/Gas 3 for 2 hours. If made in a foil dish, put on a lid for freezing; if made in a roasting tin, turn out and wrap in polythene to freeze.

To serve
Thaw at room temperature for 3 hours to serve in the traditional manner as a cake, cut in squares. For a pudding, reheat in a low oven when thawed and serve with custard.
High Quality Storage Life 2 months

Charlotte Marsala

225g/8 oz sponge fingers
Marsala
150g/5 oz butter
150g/5 oz icing sugar
5 egg yolks
150g/5 oz walnuts

FOR SERVING
whipped cream

Dip the sponge fingers quickly into the Marsala and arrange them close together round the sides and on the bottom of a greased loose-bottomed cake tin. Cream the butter and work in the sugar and egg yolks until the mixture is light and fluffy. Add the chopped walnuts and press the mixture lightly into the centre of the tin. Cover and freeze until firm. Remove from the tin and wrap in foil or polythene for storage.

To serve
Thaw at room temperature for 3 hours, and decorate with whipped cream.
High Quality Storage Life   2 months

Cherry Crumble

675g/1½ lb stoned
  cherries
75ml/5 tablespoons water
25g/1 oz caster sugar
50g/2 oz butter
125g/4 oz self-raising flour
50g/2 oz soft brown sugar
a pinch of ground mixed
  spice

Put the cherries, water and sugar into a freezer-proof pie dish. Mix the butter into the flour and rub until the mixture is like fine breadcrumbs. Stir in the sugar and spice and mix thoroughly. Sprinkle on top of the cherries. Bake at 190°C/375°F/Gas 5 for 45 minutes until the top is golden. Cool and cover with foil or polythene to freeze. The crumble may be frozen uncooked, but as it is good to eat cold, it is more useful to store it ready-cooked.
Note Gooseberries or blackberries are also good for this crumble, but may need a little more sugar to sweeten them.

To serve
Thaw at room temperature for 4 hours to eat cold with cream, or reheat at 180°C/350°F/Gas 4 for 45 minutes to serve hot with custard.
High Quality Storage Life   2 months.

Chocolate Drop Sponge Pudding

125g/4 oz plain chocolate
125g/4 oz butter
125g/4 oz caster sugar
2 eggs
225g/8 oz plain flour
10ml/2 teaspoons baking
    powder
milk

Cut the chocolate into small pieces with a sharp knife. Cream the butter and sugar and work in the eggs gradually. Sift together the flour and baking powder, and fold it into the butter mixture, adding enough milk to give a soft dropping consistency. Stir in the chocolate pieces. Put into a freezer-proof pudding basin, cover with foil and steam for 1 hour. The pudding can also be baked at 220°C/425°F/Gas 7 for 15 minutes, then at 190°C/375°F/Gas 5 for 30 minutes. Cool, cover and freeze.

To serve
Steam for 1 hour, or thaw first and reheat at 180°C/350°F/Gas 4 for 45 minutes. Serve with hot jam or chocolate sauce.
High Quality Storage Life   2 months

Chocolate Orange Mousse

175g/6 oz plain chocolate
300ml/½ pint water
15g/½ oz butter
3 eggs
juice of 1 small orange
FOR SERVING
whipped cream
grated chocolate

Shred the chocolate into a small pan, and heat gently with the water to a thick cream. Cool slightly and beat in the butter. Add egg yolks one at a time, and then the orange juice. Whisk the egg whites until stiff and fold into the chocolate mixture. Put into a serving dish which will go into the freezer. Pack into polythene or foil to freeze.

To serve
Thaw in refrigerator for 2 hours and decorate with cream and grated chocolate.
High Quality Storage Life   1 month

Chocolate Whisky Gâteau

16 sponge fingers
125g/4 oz butter
125g/4 oz caster sugar
3 eggs
125g/4 oz plain chocolate
30ml/2 tablespoons whisky

Grease a loose-bottomed cake tin very lightly with butter and put the sponge fingers round the edge so that they fit close together. Cream the butter and sugar, and gradually work in the egg yolks. Melt the chocolate over hot water and gradually whip it into the butter mixture, together with the whisky. Whisk the egg whites until they are stiff and dry, and fold them into the chocolate mixture. Pour into the tin and chill. Open freeze, then remove from the tin and wrap in foil or polythene to store.

To serve
Thaw in refrigerator for 2 hours.
High Quality Storage Life 1 month

Citrus Soufflé

1 envelope or 15ml/3
   teaspoons gelatine
75ml/3 fl oz hot water
175g/6 oz caster sugar
3 eggs
30ml/2 tablespoons orange
   juice
grated rind and juice of 1
   lemon
300ml/½ pint double
   cream
50g/2 oz chopped nuts

Prepare the soufflé dish by cutting a collar of greaseproof paper long enough to go around the outside of the dish with about 7.5cm/3 inches overlap. Fold in half lengthways and secure into position so that the collar stands above the top of the dish by about 5cm/2 inches. Dissolve the gelatine in the hot water. Cool. Whisk the sugar and egg yolks until thick and light in colour. Add the juices and rind and continue whisking for another minute. Stir in the gelatine mixture, and set aside to thicken slightly. Whip the cream and fold in gently. Whisk the egg whites until stiff and fold gently into the mixture. Turn into the soufflé dish. Stand in a cool place until set. Remove the paper collar. Decorate the sides with chopped nuts. Wrap the sides with clingfilm and open freeze. Wrap in foil or polythene and store.

To serve
Remove the outer wrapping and place a piece of clingfilm on the top. When thawed, carefully remove the top film and, just before serving, remove the piece around the sides.
High Quality Storage Life 1 month

Chocolate Orange Mousse (page 183)

LEFT *Nut Ice Cream* (page 194)

BELOW *Ice Cream Layer Cake* (page 197)

Chocolate Ice Cream (page 193)

Tangerine Ice (page 195)

Lemon Cheesecake (page 179)

Rum Babas (page 190)

Crunchy Apricot Crumble

225g/8 oz cooked apricots
50g/2 oz caster sugar
50g/2 oz plain flour
2.5ml/½ teaspoon baking
    powder
50g/2 oz rolled oats
75g/3 oz Demerara sugar
50g/2 oz butter

Arrange the apricots in a foil container. Sprinkle over the caster sugar. Mix together the flour, baking powder, oats and Demerara sugar and rub in the butter. Sprinkle over the fruit. Cover with a lid and freeze.

To serve
Remove the lid and bake at 200°C/400°F/Gas 6 for 45 minutes, and serve with cream.
High Quality Storage Life   2 months

Fresh Fruit Mousse

150ml/¼ pint fruit purée
25g/1 oz caster sugar
150ml/¼ pint double
    cream
2 egg whites
juice of ½ lemon
colouring

Mix the fruit purée and sugar. Whip cream lightly, and whisk egg whites stiffly. Add lemon juice to the fruit, then fold in the cream and egg whites. A little colouring may be added if fruit is pale. Pack in serving dish, then in foil or polythene to freeze.

To serve
Thaw in refrigerator for 2 hours.
High Quality Storage Life   1 month

Fruit Flan

175g/6 oz plain flour
a pinch of salt
15ml/1 tablespoon icing
    sugar
75g/3 oz butter
2 egg yolks
15ml/1 tablespoon iced
    water

FOR SERVING
fruit
apricot jam or redcurrant
    jelly

Sift the flour, salt and sugar on to a board. Make a well in the centre and put in the butter cut into small pieces. Add the egg yolks and work together with a palette knife until the mixture is like breadcrumbs. Sprinkle in the water and knead the dough on a lightly floured board until smooth. Chill in the refrigerator for 30 minutes and then roll out carefully to fit a flan tin. Bake blind at 220°C/425°F/Gas 7 for 15 minutes, then continue baking for about 10 minutes until the pastry is crisp and golden. Cool and wrap in foil to freeze.

To serve
Unwrap and thaw on a serving plate at room temperature for 1 hour. Arrange fruit in the flan case and brush thickly with hot sieved apricot jam or redcurrant jelly.
High Quality Storage Life   2 months

Gooseberry Crumb Tart

225g/8 oz shortcrust pastry
450g/1 lb gooseberries
125g/4 oz soft
  breadcrumbs
45ml/3 tablespoons melted
  butter
3 eggs
50g/2 oz sugar

FOR SERVING
caster sugar

Line a foil pie plate with the pastry. Cook the gooseberries in just enough water to cover until they are soft, and sweeten to taste. Rub through a sieve and mix with the breadcrumbs, butter, eggs and sugar. Pour into the pastry case and bake at 180°C/350°F/Gas 4 for 40 minutes. Cool, cover and freeze.

To serve
Thaw at room temperature for 3 hours to serve cold, and sprinkle with caster sugar. To serve hot, heat at 180°C/350°F/Gas 4 for 30 minutes, and sprinkle with caster sugar.
High Quality Storage Life   2 months

Lemon Flummery

300ml/½ pint water
20g/¾ oz butter
1 lemon
25g/1 oz plain flour
125g/4 oz caster sugar
2 eggs

FOR SERVING
chopped nuts or crushed
  digestive biscuits

Boil together the water, butter and grated rind of the lemon. Mix the flour and sugar in a bowl and pour on the hot liquid, whisking well. Return to the pan and whisk in 2 egg yolks. Bring slowly to the boil, and cook gently for 10 minutes. Add the juice of the lemon to the pan, and fold in the stiffly whisked egg whites. Pour into a serving dish which will go in the freezer. Chill until set, then wrap in foil or polythene, and freeze.

To serve
Thaw in the refrigerator for 3 hours. Sprinkle the top with chopped nuts or crushed biscuits.
High Quality Storage Life   1 month

Mincemeat Carousel

225g/8 oz plain flour
salt
50g/2 oz margarine
50g/2 oz white fat
10ml/1 dessertspoon caster
  sugar
10ml/1 dessertspoon
  ground almonds
1 egg yolk
60ml/4 tablespoons
  mincemeat
425g/15 oz canned peach
  slices

Make up the pastry by sifting the flour with a pinch of salt and rubbing in the fats. Stir in sugar and ground almonds, mix with the egg yolk and about 45ml/3 tablespoons of water to make a fairly soft dough. Knead lightly until smooth, wrap in greaseproof paper and allow to chill before using.

Line a fluted flan ring or foil dish with three-quarters of the pastry. Spread mincemeat over the base with drained peach slices arranged in a circle on top. Cover the top with the remaining pastry, rolled out to fit. Cut a 5cm/2 inch circle from the centre, using a pastry cutter if available. Seal edges firmly. Brush with water, sprinkle on a little caster sugar and bake at 190°C/375°F/Gas 5 for about 40 minutes until golden-brown. Cool. Place the pie in a rigid container so that it will not be knocked, then freeze.

To serve
Allow to thaw at room temperature, and heat through at 190°C/375°F/Gas 5 for about 30 minutes before serving. Custard, whipped cream or ice cream go well with this pie.
High Quality Storage Life 1 month

Nesselrode Mousse

5 eggs
1.25ml/¼ teaspoon cream
  of tartar
125g/4 oz caster sugar
a pinch of salt
30ml/2 tablespoons light
  rum
10ml/2 teaspoons lemon
  juice
400ml/¾ pint double
  cream
125g/4 oz chopped mixed
  glacé fruit

FOR SERVING
glacé cherries
angelica

Beat the egg whites with the cream of tartar until soft peaks are formed. Gradually add 75g/3 oz of the sugar, beating well after each addition until peaks are stiff. Beat the egg yolks and salt until thick and lemon coloured and gradually beat in the remaining sugar. Continue beating while adding the rum and lemon juice. Beat the cream until stiff. Carefully fold the rum mixture, cream and glacé fruit into the egg white mixture and turn into the serving bowl in which the mousse is to be frozen. Pack by wrapping serving dish in foil or polythene, then freeze.

To serve
Thaw at room temperature for 1 hour and decorate with cherries and angelica.
High Quality Storage Life 1 month

Pancakes

125g/4 oz plain flour
1.25ml/¼ teaspoon salt
1 egg
1 egg yolk
300ml/½ pint milk
15ml/1 tablespoon oil or
   melted butter

Sift the flour and salt and mix in the egg and egg yolk with a little milk. Work together until creamy, and gradually add the remaining milk, beating to a smooth batter. Fold in the oil or melted butter. Fry large thin pancakes. When cool, pack in layers separated by clingfilm, then wrap in foil or a polythene bag to freeze.

To serve
Separate the pancakes, put on a baking sheet and cover with foil. Heat at 150°C/300°F/Gas 2 and fill with jam, or serve with sugar and lemon juice. The pancakes may also be thawed at room temperature and filled with a savoury filling, then covered with a cheese, mushroom or tomato sauce for reheating.
High Quality Storage Life   2 months

Peach Pie

225g/8 oz puff pastry
450g/1 lb fresh or canned
   peach halves
3 eggs
125g/4 oz icing sugar
125g/4 oz ground almonds

Line a deep foil pie plate with the pastry. Arrange the peach halves on this, cut side down. Beat the eggs well and work in the icing sugar and almonds. Pour over the peaches. Bake at 190°C/375°F/Gas 5 for 35 minutes. Cool, wrap in foil or polythene and freeze.

To serve
Heat at 180°C/350°F/Gas 4 for 30 minutes.
High Quality Storage Life   2 months

Raspberry Pudding

450g/1 lb raspberries
125g/4 oz caster sugar
25g/1 oz butter
125g/4 oz fresh white
  breadcrumbs
3 eggs

FOR SERVING
icing sugar

Heat raspberries gently with sugar until the juice runs. Put through a sieve, reheat gently and add butter. Pour over the breadcrumbs and leave for 30 minutes. Add the beaten eggs, mix well and put into an ovenproof dish. Bake at 180°C/350°F/Gas 4 for 1 hour. Cool, wrap in foil or turn out when cool and wrap in foil, then freeze.

To serve
Thaw at room temperature for 3 hours, dust with icing sugar and serve with cream.
High Quality Storage Life   2 months

Raspberry Tart

175g/6 oz plain flour
a pinch of ground
  cinnamon
a pinch of salt
125g/4 oz butter
125g/4 oz caster sugar
1 egg
1 egg yolk
125g/4 oz almonds or
  walnuts
grated rind of 1 lemon
225g/8 oz raspberry jam
  (or sweetened raspberry
  pulp)
beaten egg

FOR SERVING
icing sugar

Sieve the flour and cinnamon on to a board with a pinch of salt. Make a well in the centre and put in the butter cut in small pieces, with the sugar, egg and egg yolk. Chop the nuts very finely. Add to the flour mixture with the lemon rind and work together using a palette knife to form a soft dough. Chill in the refrigerator for 1 hour. Roll out very carefully 1cm/½ inch thick and line a flan ring, trimming the edges. Fill the pastry case with jam or raspberry pulp. Roll out the pastry trimmings and cut strips. Arrange them to form a lattice. Brush with beaten egg and bake at 190°C/375°F/Gas 5 for 30 minutes. Cool and wrap in foil or polythene to freeze.

To serve
Thaw at room temperature for 3 hours and dust with icing sugar just before serving.
High Quality Storage Life   2 months

Rum Babas

125g/4 oz plain flour
a pinch of salt
8g/¼ oz fresh yeast or
   5ml/1 teaspoon dried
   yeast
120ml/8 tablespoons warm
   milk
1 egg
40g/1½ oz melted butter
25g/1 oz raisins

SYRUP
50g/2 oz sugar
150ml/¼ pint water
a squeeze of lemon juice
30ml/2 tablespoons rum

FOR SERVING
rum
whipped cream

Sift the flour and salt into a warm bowl. Blend the fresh yeast in the warm milk or reconstitute the dried yeast as directed on the packet. Mix with the flour and leave in a warm place for 20 minutes until the surface is covered with bubbles. Gradually add the egg, melted butter and raisins, and then knead well for 10 minutes. Put the dough into individual greased and dusted pudding moulds and leave in a warm place until it reaches the top of the moulds. Bake at 230°C/450°F/Gas 8 for 15 minutes. Reduce to 190°C/375°F/Gas 5 and cook for 15 minutes.

To make the syrup, dissolve the sugar in the water and lemon juice and boil for 2 minutes. Cool and add the rum. Turn out the babas on a rack and soak with the rum syrup while still hot. Baste with the syrup until it is all absorbed. Pack into individual rigid containers and freeze.

To serve
Thaw at room temperature for 3 hours without wrappings. Sprinkle with a little rum, and fill with whipped cream.
High Quality Storage Life   2 months

Spiced Apple Pudding

450g/1 lb cooking apples
50g/2 oz butter or
   margarine
225g/8 oz self-raising flour
175g/6 oz caster sugar
grated rind and juice of ½
   lemon
2 beaten eggs
60ml/4 tablespoons milk
75g/3 oz soft brown sugar
5ml/1 teaspoon mixed
   spice
25g/1 oz walnut halves

Line and grease a square cake tin or foil freezer tray. Cover the thinly sliced apples with water. Rub butter or margarine into flour and add caster sugar. Add grated lemon rind, juice, eggs and milk, and mix to a soft dropping consistency. Drain apples well.

Spoon half the cake mixture into the prepared tin and spread evenly. Arrange half the apples over the cake mixture. Mix together brown sugar and mixed spice and sprinkle half of it over the apples. Spoon in the remaining cake mixture and spread as evenly as possible. Arrange remaining apple slices on top and sprinkle with remaining sugar mixture. Decorate with walnuts. Bake at 180°C/350°F/Gas 4 for 1½ hours. Cool, leave in tin, and wrap with foil, or put into a polythene bag to freeze.

To serve
Thaw at room temperature for 3 hours. Serve cold as a cake, or reheat at 180°C/350°F/Gas 4 to use as a pudding with custard, cream or ice cream.
High Quality Storage Life   2 months

Strawberry Betty

450g/1 lb strawberries
juice of ½ lemon
50ml/2 fl oz white wine
125g/4 oz brown sugar
8 thick slices bread
50g/2 oz sugar
5ml/1 teaspoon grated
   lemon rind
25g/1 oz butter

Mix the strawberries with the lemon juice, wine and brown sugar. Put into a foil freezer container. Trim the crusts from the bread slices, and cut the bread into 1cm/½ inch cubes. Mix the bread, sugar and grated lemon rind and put on top of the strawberries. Dot with flakes of butter. Bake at 180°C/350°F/Gas 4 for 30 minutes. Cool, cover and freeze.

To serve
Heat at 180°C/350°F/Gas 4 for 30 minutes and serve warm with cream.
High Quality Storage Life   2 months

Summer Fruit Bowl

450g/1 lb gooseberries
125g/4 oz redcurrants
150ml/¼ pint water
175g/6 oz caster sugar
125g/4 oz raspberries
125g/4 oz blackberries

Put the gooseberries and redcurrants in the water with the sugar and bring slowly to the boil. Simmer very gently for 5 minutes without breaking the fruit. Cool and stir in the raspberries and blackberries. Pack in waxed or rigid containers and freeze.

To serve
Thaw in refrigerator for 3 hours and serve with cream.
High Quality Storage Life   12 months

Spiced Orange Pudding

75g/3 oz butter
50g/2 oz soft brown sugar
grated rind of 1 orange
75g/3 oz black treacle
1 egg
175g/6 oz self-raising flour
5ml/1 teaspoon ground
   cinnamon
40g/1½ oz chopped glacé
   cherries
50g/2 oz seedless raisins

FOR SERVING
juice of 2 oranges
150ml/¼ pint water
15ml/1 tablespoon
   cornflour
sugar

Cream the butter, sugar and orange rind until light and fluffy, and beat in the treacle. Whisk the egg and add gradually, and stir in the sifted flour and cinnamon. Add the cherries and raisins, and put into a greased pudding basin. Cover with foil and steam for 1½ hours. Cool, cover and freeze.

To serve
Steam for 1 hour and serve with orange sauce made by cooking the juice of 2 oranges, 150ml/¼ pint water and 15ml/1 tablespoon cornflour, and sweetening to taste.
High Quality Storage Life   1 month

191

Basic Custard Ice

300ml/½ pint milk
1 vanilla pod
2 egg yolks
50g/2 oz sugar
a pinch of salt
150ml/¼ pint double
cream

Scald the milk with vanilla pod, remove the pod and pour milk on to egg yolks which have been lightly beaten with sugar and salt. Cook in a double boiler until mixture coats the back of a spoon. Cool and strain. Stir in the cream. Pour into freezing trays and beat twice during a total freezing time of 3 hours. Pack into containers, cover and freeze.
High Quality Storage Life 3 months

Basic Cream Ice

600ml/1 pint thin cream
1 vanilla pod
75g/3 oz sugar
a pinch of salt

Heat the cream with vanilla pod, remove from heat, stir in sugar and salt, and cool. Remove vanilla pod and freeze mixture to a mush. Beat well in a chilled bowl, and continue freezing for a total of 2 hours. Pack into containers, cover and freeze.
High Quality Storage Life 3 months

Basic Gelatine Ice

400ml/¾ pint creamy milk
1 vanilla pod
10ml/1 dessertspoon
gelatine
75g/3 oz sugar
a pinch of salt

Heat 150ml/¼ pint milk with the vanilla pod to boiling point. Soak the gelatine in 30ml/2 tablespoons water, and heat the bowl standing in hot water until the gelatine is syrupy. Pour the warm milk on to the gelatine, stir in the sugar and salt, and add the remaining milk. Remove the vanilla pod. Put into a freezing tray and beat twice during 3 hours freezing time. Pack into containers, cover and freeze. This mixture is particularly good with added flavourings.
High Quality Storage Life 3 months

Rich Ice Cream

2 eggs
75g/3 oz caster sugar
400ml/¾ pint milk
10ml/2 teaspoons gelatine
30ml/2 tablespoons hot
  water
300ml/½ pint double
  cream
5ml/1 teaspoon vanilla
  essence

Whisk the eggs with the sugar and milk in a basin over a pan of hot water until the mixture thickens. Cool. Dissolve the gelatine in the hot water. Cool. Add to the custard. Whip the cream and carefully fold into the mixture. Add the vanilla essence. Pour into a freezing tray and freeze until firm around the edges. Turn into a bowl. Beat until smooth. Return to the tray and freeze until required. Pack into a rigid container, cover and freeze.
High Quality Storage Life   3 months

Brown Bread Ice Cream

175g/6 oz fresh wholemeal
  bread (no crusts)
600ml/1 pint double cream
225g/8 oz sugar
60ml/4 tablespoons water

Cut the bread in slices and put it in a low oven 120°C/250°F/Gas ½ until dry. Break into coarse crumbs. Whip the cream and mix in 175g/6 oz sugar. Put the cream into a freezing tray, cover with foil and freeze for 1 hour. Melt the remaining sugar in the water and cool. Pour it on to the breadcrumbs. Mix the breadcrumbs in syrup into the cream mixture and put into one or two freezing trays. Freeze until firm, then pack into a rigid container for storage.
High Quality Storage Life   3 months

Chocolate Ice Cream

300ml/½ pint milk
2 egg yolks
125g/4 oz sugar
125g/4 oz plain chocolate
5ml/1 teaspoon instant
  coffee powder
150ml/¼ pint double
  cream

Bring the milk almost to boiling point. Beat the egg yolks and sugar until creamy, and pour on the milk, beating well. Return the mixture to the saucepan and stir over very low heat until the mixture forms a creamy custard. Put the chocolate and coffee powder into a bowl over hot water and heat until melted. Add this chocolate mixture to the custard and cool, stirring occasionally. Whip the cream to soft peaks and fold into the chocolate mixture. Put into a freezing tray and beat once half-way through a total freezing time of 3 hours.
High Quality Storage Life   3 months

Nut Ice Cream

175g/6 oz mixed nuts (eg walnuts, almonds and hazelnuts)
175g/6 oz caster sugar
a pinch of salt
600ml/1 pint double cream
2 eggs
5ml/1 teaspoon vanilla or coffee essence

Blanch the nuts in hot water and rub off the skins. Chop them fairly finely. Mix the sugar, salt and nuts and stir in the cream gradually. Put into the top of a double saucepan, or into a bowl over hot water and cook for 10 minutes. Remove from heat and gradually stir in the beaten eggs and vanilla or coffee essence. Cool and pour into a freezing tray. Freeze for 1 hour, then beat well and return to the freezer tray. Freeze for about 2 hours until firm. Scoop into a bowl or foil pudding basin and press down well. Cover with foil or a lid to store in the freezer.
High Quality Storage Life   3 months

Raspberry Honey Ice

450g/1 lb raspberries
150ml/¼ pint double cream
150g/5 oz plain yoghurt
150ml/10 tablespoons honey
30ml/2 tablespoons lemon juice
a pinch of salt
4 egg whites

Sieve the raspberries and add the purée to the cream, yoghurt, honey, lemon juice and salt. Put into a freezing tray and freeze until mushy. Whisk the egg whites to stiff peaks. Stir the frozen ice until smooth and soft, and fold in the egg whites. Continue freezing until firm. Pack into a rigid container for storage.
High Quality Storage Life   3 months

Raspberry Water Ice

125g/4 oz sugar
300ml/½ pint water
450g/1 lb raspberries

Put the sugar and water in a pan and boil for 5 minutes. Cool. Sieve the raspberries. Blend together with the syrup and freeze for 3 hours, whisking in a chilled bowl half-way through freezing. The ice will be improved if a stiffly whisked egg white is folded in after the ice has been whisked. Pack into a rigid container for storage.
High Quality Storage Life   1 month

Lemon Water Ice

225g/8 oz sugar
400ml/¾ pint water
2 lemons
1.25ml/¼ teaspoon
    ground ginger
salt

Combine the sugar and water in a saucepan, bring to the boil, and boil for 5 minutes. Grate the rind of 1 lemon and add the juice of both lemons, together with ginger and a pinch of salt. Gradually pour in the hot syrup until well blended. Cool and pour into a freezing tray, and freeze for 3 hours, stirring occasionally. Pack into a rigid container for storage.

High Quality Storage Life   1 month

Tangerine Ice

4 large tangerines
5ml/1 teaspoon gelatine
150ml/¼ pint water
75g/3 oz sugar
5ml/1 teaspoon grated
    lemon rind
15ml/1 tablespoon lemon
    juice
1 egg white

FOR SERVING
mint leaves or small green
    marzipan leaves

Remove the tops of the tangerines carefully so that they will form lids. Scoop out the flesh, saving all the juice. Wash the skins carefully and dry them. Soak the gelatine in a little of the water and boil the rest with the sugar for 5 minutes to a syrup. Stir the gelatine into the syrup and leave to cool. Add the grated lemon rind and juice, and all the juice of the tangerines. Whisk the egg white to stiff peaks and fold into the gelatine mixture. Put into a freezing tray and freeze for 3 hours, beating once half-way through freezing when the ice is mushy.

    Scoop the ice into the tangerine cases and put the lids on lightly. Put into the freezer for 1 hour before serving, and decorate with mint leaves or small green marzipan leaves. For longer storage, wrap tangerines in foil.

High Quality Storage Life   1 month

Orange Sorbet

10ml/2 teaspoons gelatine
300ml/½ pint water
175g/6 oz sugar
5ml/1 teaspoon grated
    lemon rind
5ml/1 teaspoon grated
    orange rind
300ml/½ pint orange juice
60ml/4 tablespoons lemon
    juice
2 egg whites

Soak the gelatine in a little of the water and boil the rest of the water and sugar for 10 minutes to a syrup. Stir the gelatine into the syrup and cool. Add the rinds and juices of the orange and lemon. Whisk the egg whites until stiff but not dry and fold into mixture. Freeze to a mush, beat once, then continue freezing, allowing 3 hours total freezing time. This ice will not go completely hard. Pack in rigid containers for storage.

High Quality Storage Life   1 month

Biscuit Tortoni

50g/2 oz toasted blanched
   almonds or macaroon
   crumbs
30ml/2 tablespoons water
65g/2½ oz caster sugar
30ml/2 tablespoons sherry
3 egg yolks
200ml/8 fl oz double cream

Grind the nuts if using. Put water and sugar in a small pan, bring to the boil and boil for 3 minutes. Put sherry and egg yolks into a bowl and gradually pour in hot syrup and blend well. Whip the cream and fold mixture into it; add the ground almonds or crumbs. Put in a freezing tray and freeze for 2 hours. Pack in rigid container for storage.
High Quality Storage Life   1 month

Marshmallow Tortoni

50g/2 oz glacé fruit
50g/2 oz nuts
30ml/2 tablespoons brandy
125g/4 oz marshmallows
400ml/¾ pint double
   cream
125g/4 oz sugar

Soak the chopped fruit and nuts in the brandy. Cut the marshmallows into very small pieces with wet scissors. Whip the cream to soft peaks and gradually whip in the sugar. Mix the fruit, nuts, brandy and marshmallows and fold into the whipped cream. Pour into a chilled mould and freeze for 3 hours. Cover and seal firmly to store.

To serve
Turn out on to chilled plate. Wrap in foil and freeze for 1 hour before serving.
High Quality Storage Life   1 month

Bombes

Melon Bombe
Line a mould with pistachio ice cream and freeze for 30 minutes. Fill with raspberry ice cream mixed with chocolate chips, and wrap for storage. This looks like a watermelon when cut in slices.

Raspberry Bombe
Line a mould with raspberry ice cream, freeze for 30 minutes and fill with vanilla ice cream.

Coffee Bombe
Line a mould with coffee ice cream and freeze for 30 minutes. Fill with vanilla ice cream flavoured with chopped maraschino cherries and syrup.

Three-flavoured Bombe
Line a mould with vanilla ice cream, freezing for 30 minutes.
Put in a lining of praline ice cream and freeze for 30 minutes.
Fill the centre with chocolate ice cream.

Tutti Frutti Bombe
Line a mould with strawberry ice cream and freeze for 30
minutes. Fill with lemon sorbet mixed with very well-drained
canned fruit cocktail and freeze till firm.

Raspberry-filled Bombe
Line a mould with vanilla or praline ice cream and freeze for
30 minutes. Fill with crushed raspberries beaten into whipped
cream and lightly sweetened.

Peach-filled Bombe
Line a mould with vanilla ice cream and freeze for 30 minutes.
Fill with whipped cream mixed with chopped drained canned
peaches flavoured with light rum.

To serve
Turn out on to chilled plate. Wrap in foil and freeze for 1 hour
before serving.
High Quality Storage Life   3 months

Ice Cream Layer Cake

1 round sponge cake
soft chocolate ice cream
soft strawberry ice cream
soft vanilla ice cream
sweetened whipped cream

Place the sponge cake in a deep spring-form tin. Put scoops of
chocolate ice cream on the sponge cake base and smooth with
a palette knife. Top with a layer of strawberry ice cream and
then a layer of vanilla ice cream (or use any other favourite
combination of flavours). Cover with foil and put in the freezer
until firm. Remove the spring-form sides of the tin and
decorate the cake with swirls of sweetened whipped cream.
Open freeze until the cream is firm and then put into a rigid
container for storage. If you do not wish to have the base of
your cake tin left in the freezer, use the spring-form sides of
the tin on a cake board base, ready for serving.
High Quality Storage Life   1 month

Iced Zabaglione

10ml/2 teaspoons gelatine
60ml/4 tablespoons hot
  water
6 egg yolks
125g/4 oz caster sugar
150ml/¼ pint sherry
60ml/4 tablespoons brandy
10ml/2 teaspoons vanilla
  essence
300ml/½ pint double
  cream
5 egg whites

Dissolve the gelatine in the hot water. Cool. Beat egg yolks and sugar until thick. Place in a basin over a pan of hot water, and add the sherry and brandy. Cook and stir until thick. Cool. Stir in the dissolved gelatine and the vanilla essence. Whip the cream and fold in carefully. Whisk the egg whites until stiff and add to the mixture. Pack in rigid container, cool until set, and freeze.

To serve
Remove from the freezer and allow to thaw whilst still covered. Stir lightly and spoon into individual serving dishes.
High Quality Storage Life 1 month

Meringue Bombe

6 large meringue shells
400ml/¾ pint double
  cream
4 pieces preserved ginger
30ml/2 tablespoons caster
  sugar
grated rind of 1 lemon
75ml/3 tablespoons kirsch

Break the meringue shells into small pieces. Whip the cream to soft peaks. Chop the ginger into small pieces. Fold the ginger, sugar, lemon rind, kirsch and broken meringue pieces into the cream. Put into a pudding basin or cake tin which has been lightly oiled, and smooth down the mixture. Cover with foil and freeze for 4 hours. Turn out of basin or tin and wrap in foil for storage.

To serve
Remove foil and put bombe on to a serving plate. Leave at room temperature for 10 minutes. This is delicious served with raspberries or strawberries or with a fruit sauce.
High Quality Storage Life 1 month

CAKES, BISCUITS AND BREADS

Chocolate Fudge Sandwich Cake

125g/4 oz margarine
50g/2 oz caster sugar
75g/3 oz golden syrup
2 eggs
150g/5 oz plain flour
50g/2 oz plain chocolate
2.5ml/½ teaspoon vanilla
  essence
2.5ml/½ teaspoon
  bicarbonate of soda
10ml/1 dessertspoon milk
chocolate icing

Cream together the margarine, sugar and syrup. Add the eggs one at a time, beating in a spoonful of sifted flour with each. Melt the chocolate in a bowl over hot water and add to the mixture with the vanilla essence. Fold in the remaining flour. Dissolve the soda in the milk, then add to the mixture. Divide between 2 greased and lined sandwich tins and bake at 190°C/375°F/Gas 5 for 25–30 minutes. Cool. Fill and ice with chocolate icing. Open freeze and wrap in foil or polythene to store.

To serve
Unwrap and thaw at room temperature for 3 hours.
High Quality Storage Life   4 months

One-Step Chocolate Cake

15ml/1 tablespoon cocoa
30ml/2 tablespoons milk
125g/4 oz soft margarine
150g/5 oz caster sugar
2 eggs
125g/4 oz self-raising flour

FOR SERVING
icing sugar or chocolate
  icing

Put all the ingredients into a bowl and blend with a wooden spoon or mixer until light and fluffy. Put into a greased round tin and bake at 180°C/350°F/Gas 4 for 40 minutes. Cool on a wire rack. Pack in polythene to freeze.

To serve
Unwrap and thaw at room temperature for 3 hours. Sprinkle with icing sugar or cover with chocolate icing. Serve as a cake, or as a pudding with whipped cream.
High Quality Storage Life   4 months

Uncooked Chocolate Cake

225g/8 oz Nice biscuit
  crumbs
125g/4 oz chopped
  walnuts
50g/2 oz glacé cherries
75g/3 oz sultanas
125g/4 oz chopped mixed
  peel
225g/8 oz plain chocolate
175g/6 oz butter
50g/2 oz caster sugar
2 eggs
60ml/4 tablespoons sherry
  or brandy

Mix the crumbs with the nuts, quartered cherries, sultanas and peel. Put the chocolate, butter, sugar and eggs into a bowl over warm water, heat and stir gently until the chocolate has melted and the mixture is smooth. Add the sherry or brandy and stir into the biscuit crumbs and fruit. When well blended, put into a greased loose-bottomed cake tin, and chill. Remove carefully from the tin and wrap in foil or polythene to freeze.

To serve
Thaw at room temperature for 3 hours and serve in small pieces as this cake is very rich.
High Quality Storage Life   4 months

Chocolate Truffle Cake

125g/4 oz margarine
25g/1 oz sugar
15ml/1 tablespoon golden
  syrup
25g/1 oz cocoa
225g/8 oz sweet biscuit
  crumbs
50g/2 oz plain chocolate

Cream the margarine and sugar and add the syrup and cocoa. Add the crumbs gradually to the mixture and stir well. Press down into a greased tin so that the mixture is about 1cm/½ inch thick. Melt the chocolate in a bowl over hot water and pour over the cake. Leave in a cool place to set, then mark into squares. Leave in the tin and wrap in foil or polythene to freeze.

To serve
Thaw at room temperature for 3 hours and cut in squares. This is a delicious cake and can also be used as a base for ice cream – it is particularly good with a topping of coffee ice cream.
High Quality Storage Life   4 months

Chocolate Roll (page 201)

Ring Doughnuts (page 213)

BELOW *Freezer Fudge* (page 217)

OPPOSITE TOP *Danish Pastry Pinwheels* (page 210)

OPPOSITE BELOW *Apricot Pastries* (page 208)

Eclairs (page 212)

Chocolate Roll

125g/4 oz self-raising flour
a pinch of salt
75g/3 oz butter or
   margarine
75g/3 oz caster sugar
2 eggs
2 drops vanilla essence

ICING
150g/5 oz butter
225g/8 oz icing sugar
225g/8 oz plain chocolate
15ml/1 tablespoon rum
50g/2 oz chopped nuts

Sift the flour and salt. Cream the fat and sugar until light and fluffy. Beat in the eggs one at a time with a little of the flour mixture, then stir in the remaining flour and essence. Spread evenly in a lined Swiss roll tin and bake at 220°C/425°F/Gas 7 for 10 minutes. Turn out on to a piece of sugared greaseproof paper. Trim off the edges and roll quickly with paper inside.

Make the icing by creaming the butter and icing sugar. Melt the chocolate in a bowl over hot water and work it into the butter mixture with the rum.

When the cake is cold, unroll carefully and spread half the icing on the surface. Roll up tightly and cover the cake with the remaining icing. Sprinkle with chopped nuts. Green pistachio nuts look particularly attractive. Open freeze and then pack in polythene or a rigid container to store.

To serve
Remove wrappings and thaw at room temperature for 3 hours. Serve as a cake in thin slices, or use for a pudding with rum-flavoured sweetened whipped cream.
High Quality Storage Life   2 months

Crumble Cake

125g/4 oz sugar
225g/8 oz plain flour
175g/6 oz margarine
10ml/2 teaspoons grated
   orange or lemon rind

Stir the sugar into the flour and rub in the fat until the mixture looks like fine breadcrumbs. Add the grated rind. Spread in a greased shallow tin and press down lightly. Bake at 160°C/325°F/Gas 3 for 30 minutes. Cool in the tin and cut in slices. Pack in a rigid container to freeze.

To serve
Thaw at room temperature for 3 hours. This cake is very good to serve with fruit or ice cream.
High Quality Storage Life   4 months

Farmhouse Apple Cake

450g/1 lb apples
6 cloves
sugar
125g/4 oz butter
125g/4 oz sugar
1 egg
225g/8 oz plain flour

Slice and cook the apples in very little water. Flavour with cloves and sweeten. Line a round foil container. Cream the butter and sugar until light and fluffy and beat in the egg. Stir in the flour until it looks like soft crumbs. Weigh off 175g/6 oz and put the remainder in the container and spread evenly. Cover the mixture with the cooked apple which must be well-drained. Cover the apple with the crumb mixture only around the edge to about 5cm/2 inches, leaving a circle in the middle. Cook at 180°C/350°F/Gas 4 for 45 minutes. Cool, cover and freeze.

To serve
Thaw at room temperature for 3 hours to serve cold with cream. Reheat at 180°C/350°F/Gas 4 for 35 minutes to serve hot.
High Quality Storage Life   4 months

Family Fruit Cake

225g/8 oz self-raising flour
1.25ml/¼ teaspoon salt
125g/4 oz butter
125g/4 oz soft brown
  sugar
125g/4 oz sultanas and
  raisins
50g/2 oz chopped mixed
  peel
grated rind of ½ lemon
1 egg
75ml/3 fl oz milk

Sift flour and salt and then rub in the butter until the mixture looks like fine breadcrumbs. Stir in sugar, dried fruit, peel and grated rind, and mix lightly with beaten egg and milk. Put into a greased and lined cake tin and bake at 180°C/350°F/Gas 4 for 1½ hours. Cool on a wire rack. Wrap in polythene to freeze.

To serve
Thaw in wrapping at room temperature for 3 hours.
High Quality Storage Life   4 months

Fruit Biscuit Cake

75g/3 oz sultanas
50g/2 oz raisins
50g/2 oz glacé cherries
50g/2 oz walnut halves
175g/6 oz sweet biscuit
  crumbs
1 egg
50g/2 oz butter
50g/2 oz brown sugar
5ml/1 teaspoon honey
5ml/1 teaspoon vanilla
  essence

Chop the sultanas, raisins, cherries and walnuts coarsely, and mix with the biscuit crumbs. Beat the egg and add butter and sugar. Bring to the boil, then remove from the heat. Add the honey and essence. Mix all the ingredients until the crumbs are damp. Press into a square tin lined with greased paper. Cover and freeze.

To serve
Thaw at room temperature for 3 hours and cut into squares.
High Quality Storage Life   4 months

Lardy Cakes

225g/8 oz flour
1.25ml/¼ teaspoon salt
1.25ml/¼ teaspoon mixed
  spices
8g/¼ oz fresh yeast or
  5ml/1 teaspoon dried
  yeast
150ml/¼ pint warm milk
50g/2 oz lard
50g/2 oz sugar
50g/2 oz dried fruit

Warm the flour, salt and spices. Blend the fresh yeast in the warm milk or reconstitute the dried yeast as directed on the packet. Add to the flour and mix to a soft dough. Beat well. Cover and stand on one side in a warm place until doubled in size. Roll out on a well floured surface to ½cm/¼ inch thickness. Spread on half the lard, sugar and fruit. Fold in three, turn to the left, and roll again. Repeat with the rest of the lard, sugar and fruit. Roll out to an oblong 2.5cm/1 inch thick. Place in a deep tin and leave in a lightly greased polythene bag till well risen. Score the top with a knife and brush with sugar and water. Bake at 230°C/450°F/Gas 8 for 30 minutes. Cool. Wrap in foil or polythene and freeze.

To serve
Thaw at room temperature for 3 hours.
High Quality Storage Life   1 month

Madeira Cake

250g/9 oz plain flour
5ml/1 teaspoon baking
  powder
a pinch of salt
175g/6 oz caster sugar
175g/6 oz butter
3 eggs
5ml/1 teaspoon grated
  orange rind
5ml/1 teaspoon grated
  lemon rind
milk or rum

Sift the flour with the baking powder and salt. Warm a mixing bowl and beater. Put the sugar and butter in the bowl and beat until white and fluffy. Add the eggs one at a time, beating well each time. Fold in the flour and orange and lemon rind. Add a little milk or rum. The mixture should shake easily from a spoon. Put in a lined cake tin and bake at 160°C/350°F/Gas 4 for 1 hour and 20 minutes. Cool on a wire rack and wrap in foil to freeze.

To serve
Thaw at room temperature for 3 hours.
High Quality Storage Life 4 months

Marmalade Cake

175g/6 oz butter
175g/6 oz caster sugar
3 eggs
275g/10 oz self-raising
  flour
45ml/3 tablespoons
  chunky marmalade
50g/2 oz chopped mixed
  peel
grated rind of 1 orange
75ml/3 fl oz water

Beat the butter and sugar together until light and creamy. Beat in the egg yolks, one at a time, then 15ml/1 tablespoon of the flour. Stir in the marmalade, peel, orange rind and water, and fold in the remaining flour. Whisk the egg whites to soft peaks and fold into the cake mixture. Turn into a greased and lined cake tin and bake at 180°C/350°F/Gas 4 for 1¼ hours. Cool on a wire rack and wrap in polythene to freeze.

To serve
Thaw in wrappings at room temperature for 3 hours.
High Quality Storage Life 4 months

Morning Coffee Cake

40g/1½ oz butter
125g/4 oz caster sugar
1 egg
150g/5 oz plain flour
5ml/1 teaspoon baking
  powder
a pinch of salt
65ml/2½ fl oz milk
1.25ml/¼ teaspoon lemon
  essence
2.5ml/½ teaspoon vanilla
  essence

Cream the butter and sugar and work in the egg. Add the flour sifted with the baking powder and salt alternately with the milk. Add the essences. Put into a greased rectangular tin and bake at 180°C/350°F/Gas 4 for 25 minutes. Cool, and cover with foil or put into a polythene bag to freeze.

Variations
1 Closely cover the surface of the cake mixture with stoned fresh plums, or cooked prunes. Sprinkle with 50g/2 oz sugar mixed with 5ml/1 teaspoon cinnamon, and bake.

2 Cover the surface with a thick layer of thinly sliced apples and sprinkle with 50g/2 oz mixed brown and white sugar and a pinch of cinnamon or a few chopped walnuts, and bake.

To serve
Reheat at 180°C/350°F/Gas 4 for 30 minutes, and serve warm cut into squares.
High Quality Storage Life   4 months

Orange Frost Cake

125g/4 oz butter
50g/2 oz caster sugar
30ml/2 tablespoons clear
  honey
grated rind of ½ orange
2 eggs
150g/5 oz self-raising flour
30ml/2 tablespoons orange
  juice

ICING
125g/4 oz butter
175g/6 oz icing sugar
15ml/1 tablespoon clear
  honey
15ml/1 tablespoon hot
  water
orange colouring

FOR SERVING
mimosa balls or
  crystallized orange slices

Cream the butter and sugar together until light and fluffy. Beat in the honey and orange rind and add eggs gradually. Fold in the flour and then add the orange juice and mix to a soft dropping consistency. Put into a greased and lined round sandwich tin. Bake at 190°C/375°F/Gas 5 for 25 minutes. Turn out and cool on a wire rack.

To make the icing, soften the butter and beat in the sifted icing sugar. Beat in the honey and water, and a few drops of orange colouring if liked. Beat until creamy and smooth and spread on the cake, making soft peaks with the back of a teaspoon. Open freeze and then wrap in foil or polythene to store.

To serve
Unwrap and thaw at room temperature for 3 hours. Decorate with mimosa balls or crystallized orange slices if liked.
High Quality Storage Life   4 months

Pineapple Upside-down Cake

1 medium pineapple
150g/5 oz butter
175g/6 oz brown sugar
50g/2 oz chopped mixed
  nuts
125g/4 oz caster sugar
1 egg
175g/6 oz plain flour
5ml/1 teaspoon baking
  powder
2.5ml/½ teaspoon salt
50ml/2 fl oz milk

Peel the pineapple and cut the flesh into rings. Melt 75g/3 oz butter and stir in the brown sugar until it melts. Pour this into a foil freezer container. Arrange the pineapple rings close together in the sugar and scatter with chopped nuts. Cream the remaining butter and sugar, beat in the egg, flour, baking powder and salt, and mix with the milk. Pour on to the pineapple and bake at 180°C/350°F/Gas 4 for 40 minutes. Cool, cover and freeze.

To serve
Heat at 180°C/350°F/Gas 4 for 35 minutes, turn out on to a hot plate and serve with cream.
High Quality Storage Life   2 months

Rich Cider Cake

300ml/½ pint cider
50g/2 oz dried apricots
50g/2 oz stoned dates
25g/1 oz stoned prunes
225g/8 oz butter
225g/8 oz dark soft brown
  sugar
3 eggs
275g/10 oz plain flour
salt
175g/6 oz currants
175g/6 oz sultanas
50g/2 oz raisins
50g/2 oz chopped peel
50g/2 oz chopped walnuts
50g/2 oz glacé cherries

TOPPING
150ml/¼ pint cider
50g/2 oz dried apricots
50g/2 oz glacé cherries
15g/½ oz sultanas
25g/1 oz walnut halves
15g/½ oz strips candied
  peel
40g/1½ oz Demerara
  sugar

Put the cider, chopped apricots, dates and prunes into a container, cover with a lid and soak overnight.

Cream the butter and sugar until light and fluffy, then beat in the eggs, one at a time. Add the sifted flour and salt with the currants, sultanas, raisins, peel, nuts and cherries, and fold lightly into the creamed mixture. Then fold in the soaked fruit and any remaining liquid. Transfer to a greased and lined cake tin, make a deep hollow in the centre and bake at 140°C/275°F/Gas 1 for 4 hours.

To make the topping, mix the cider, chopped apricots, cherries and sultanas overnight, and, when the cake goes into the oven, add the walnuts and peel. When the cake has cooked for 4 hours, drain the fruit for the topping, mix in the Demerara sugar and spread on top of the cake. Return to the oven for a further 30 minutes, then turn to 190°C/375°F/Gas 5 for 15 minutes. Lift out carefully and cool on a wire rack. Open freeze, then wrap in foil or polythene to store.

To serve
Thaw at room temperature for 3 hours.
High Quality Storage Life   2 months

Walnut Mocha Cake

125g/4 oz butter
225g/8 oz caster sugar
2 eggs
120ml/8 tablespoons milk
175g/6 oz flour
10ml/2 teaspoons baking
   powder
a pinch of salt
10ml/2 teaspoons vanilla
   essence
125g/4 oz walnuts

ICING
50g/2 oz butter
125g/4 oz icing sugar
25g/1 oz cocoa
strong black coffee

Cream the butter and sugar. Add the beaten yolks of the eggs and the milk. Sift the flour with baking powder and salt, and stir gradually into the egg mixture. Add the vanilla essence and the walnuts lightly broken up and tossed in flour. Fold in stiffly beaten egg whites, pour into a greased rectangular pan and bake at 180°C/350°F/Gas 4 for 40 minutes.

Make the icing by creaming together the butter, sugar and cocoa and softening the mixture with a little very strong coffee. Cover the cake and decorate with more walnuts if liked. Open freeze and wrap in foil or polythene to store.

To serve
Unwrap and thaw at room temperature for 3 hours.
High Quality Storage Life   2 months

Yoghurt Cake

125g/4 oz butter
175g/6 oz caster sugar
grated rind of 1 lemon
3 eggs
175g/6 oz self-raising flour
175g/6 oz natural yoghurt
chopped peel

FOR SERVING
lemon water icing

Cream the butter and sugar, add the lemon rind and beat well. Add the egg yolks one at a time and beat in. Add the sifted flour alternately with the yoghurt and stir in the peel. Whisk the egg whites until stiff and fold into the mixture. Spoon into a greased loaf tin and bake at 180°C/350°F/Gas 4 for 1 hour. Turn out on to a wire rack and cool. Wrap in foil or polythene and freeze.

To serve
Thaw at room temperature for 3 hours, and top with lemon water icing.
High Quality Storage Life   4 months

Apricot Pastries

350g/12 oz puff pastry
12 canned apricot halves
beaten egg
75g/3 oz apricot jam

Roll out the pastry into a large square. Divide into 14 squares. Put 12 pastry squares on to a baking sheet and place an apricot half in the centre of each. Cut the remaining squares into 24 strips and cross 2 strips over each apricot half. Brush the pastry with the beaten egg and bake at 220°C/425°F/Gas 7 for 20 minutes until the pastry is risen and crisp. Lift on to a wire rack and brush with hot melted jam. Cool and pack in a rigid container to freeze.

To serve
Thaw at room temperature for 1 hour, or reheat at 180°C/350°F/Gas 4 for 15 minutes.
High Quality Storage Life   2 months

Banbury Puffs

50g/2 oz butter
25g/1 oz stale cake crumbs
  or plain flour
1 egg yolk
30ml/2 tablespoons black
  treacle
125g/4 oz currants
25g/1 oz chopped mixed
  peel
2.5ml/½ teaspoon mixed
  spice
225g/8 oz puff pastry
egg white
caster sugar

Melt the butter in a pan, then add the cake crumbs or flour. Cook gently, stirring, for 3 minutes. Remove from the heat and beat in the egg yolk and treacle. Cool the mixture, then add the remaining ingredients apart from the pastry. Roll out the pastry thinly and cut into approximately 12 rounds with a 10cm/4 inch plain cutter. Divide the filling mixture equally between the rounds, moisten the edges of the pastry with water, then draw together so that the filling is completely covered. Turn each over with the join underneath – on to a lightly floured surface, and press with a rolling-pin into an oval. Transfer to baking trays, score tops into a diamond pattern (or make 3 diagonal slits in the top of each), then brush with lightly beaten egg white. Dust lightly with caster sugar, then leave in a cool place for 10 minutes. Bake at 220°C/425°F/Gas 7 for 15 to 20 minutes. Cool on a wire rack. Pack in polythene bags to freeze.

To serve
Thaw at room temperature for 3 hours.
High Quality Storage Life   1 month

Basic Scones

450g/1 lb plain white flour
5ml/1 teaspoon
    bicarbonate of soda
10ml/2 teaspoons cream of
    tartar
75g/3 oz butter
150ml/¼ pint milk

Sift together the flour, soda and cream of tartar, and rub in the butter until the mixture is like breadcrumbs. Mix with the milk to make a soft dough. Roll out and cut into circles, and place close together on a greased baking sheet. Bake at 230°C/450°F/Gas 8 for 12 minutes, then cool. Pack in polythene bags to freeze.

Variations

Fruit Scones
Add 40g/1½ oz sugar and 50g/2 oz dried fruit.

Cheese Scones
Add a pinch each of salt and pepper and 75g/3 oz grated cheese.

To serve
Thaw in wrappings at room temperature for 1 hour, or heat at 180°C/350°F/Gas 4 for 10 minutes with a covering of foil.
High Quality Storage Life 2 months

Tea Scones

225g/8 oz self-raising flour
1.25ml/¼ teaspoon salt
25g/1 oz sugar
25g/1 oz butter
125g/4 oz candied peel
150ml/¼ pint strong cold
    tea

Sift the flour, salt and sugar together in a mixing bowl. Rub in the butter, add the candied peel, then mix to a soft but manageable dough with the tea. Shape into a round on a greased and floured baking sheet. Mark into 8 triangles with a knife and bake at 190°C/375°F/Gas 5 until crisp and golden, about 20 minutes. Cool and wrap in foil or polythene to freeze.

To serve
Reheat at 180°C/350°F/Gas 4 for 20 minutes. Break into triangles and serve with butter.
High Quality Storage Life 2 months

209

Drop Scones

225g/8 oz plain flour
1.25ml/¼ teaspoon salt
2.5ml/½ teaspoon
  bicarbonate of soda
5ml/1 teaspoon cream of
  tartar
25g/1 oz sugar
1 egg
300ml/½ pint milk

Sift together the flour, salt, soda and cream of tartar. Stir in the sugar and mix to a batter with egg and milk. Cook in spoonfuls on a lightly greased griddle or frying pan. When bubbles appear on the surface, turn and cook other side. Cool in a cloth to keep soft. Pack in a rigid container with clingfilm between the layers, or pack in a polythene bag to freeze.

To serve
Thaw at room temperature for 1 hour and spread with butter.
High Quality Storage Life   2 months

Danish Pastry Pinwheels

225g/8 oz strong white
  flour
2.5ml/½ teaspoon salt
50g/2 oz sugar
15g/½ oz fresh yeast or
  8g/¼ oz dried yeast
150ml/¼ pint warm water
75g/3 oz butter
mixed dried fruit
beaten egg
water icing

Sift the flour and salt and mix in the sugar. Blend the fresh yeast in the warm water, or reconstitute the dried yeast as directed on the packet. Mix with the flour and sugar to a soft, slightly sticky dough, and leave to rise in a warm place until increased by one-third in volume. Form the butter into a rectangle and dust with flour. Flatten the dough with the hands and fold with the fat in the centre like a parcel. Roll and fold twice like puff pastry. Leave in a cold place for 20 minutes, then roll and fold twice more and leave for 20 minutes. Roll out to 1cm/½ inch thickness and sprinkle with dried fruit. Roll up like a Swiss roll and cut into 1cm/½ inch slices. Place on a baking sheet and brush with beaten egg. Bake at 190°C/375°F/Gas 5 for 30 minutes. Cool on a wire rack. The pastries may be frozen un-iced or with a light water icing. Pack in foil trays with a foil lid, or in boxes, and freeze.

To serve
Remove wrappings and thaw at room temperature for 1 hour.
High Quality Storage Life   2 months

Currant Buns

BATTER
125g/4 oz strong plain
  flour
5ml/1 teaspoon sugar
25g/1 oz fresh yeast or
  15g/½ oz dried yeast
150ml/¼ pint warm milk
150ml/¼ pint warm water
  less 60ml/4 tablespoons

DOUGH
50g/2 oz butter or
  margarine
350g/12 oz strong plain
  flour
50g/2 oz sugar
5ml/1 teaspoon salt
1 beaten egg
125g/4 oz currants

GLAZE
50g/2 oz sugar
60ml/4 tablespoons water

To make the batter, mix together the flour and sugar. Blend the fresh yeast in the warm milk and water, or reconstitute the dried yeast as directed on the packet. Blend with the flour and sugar and put to one side for 20–30 minutes until the batter froths.

Mix the dough ingredients, rubbing the fat into the flour with the sugar and salt, and mixing with the beaten egg and currants. Work in the frothy batter and mix to a dough which is soft and leaves the sides of the bowl clean. Knead for about 5 minutes on a lightly floured surface until smooth and not sticky. Put the dough into a lightly greased polythene bag, loosely tied and leave for about 1½ hours at room temperature until doubled in size.

Turn the dough on to a floured surface and flatten with the knuckles to knock out air bubbles. Knead to a firm dough and divide into 14 pieces. Shape into balls, working the dough until it is smooth. Put the buns well apart on a lightly floured baking sheet and flatten them slightly with the palm of the hand. Put inside a lightly greased polythene bag and leave to rise for about 30 minutes until the dough is springy. Remove the bag, and bake at 220°C/425°F/Gas 7 for 15–20 minutes until golden-brown.

Just before taking the buns from the oven, dissolve the sugar and water for the glaze. As soon as the buns are ready, put them on to a wire rack and brush liberally with the glaze. Leave until cool, pack into a polythene bag and freeze.

To serve
Thaw at room temperature for 1 hour, or reheat at 180°C/350°F/Gas 4 for 10 minutes.
High Quality Storage Life   4 months

211

Eclairs

150ml/¼ pint water
50g/2 oz lard
50g/2 oz plain flour
a pinch of salt
2 eggs

FOR SERVING
lightly sweetened whipped
   cream
chocolate or coffee glacé
   icing

Put the water and lard into a pan and bring to the boil. Tip in the flour and salt and draw the pan from the heat. Beat until smooth with a wooden spoon. Cook for 3 minutes, beating very thoroughly so that the mixture is smooth and is not sticking to the sides of the pan. Cool. Whisk the eggs together and add small quantities to the flour mixture. Beat well between each addition until the mixture is soft and firm but holds its shape – it may not be necessary to add all the egg. Pipe in finger-lengths on to baking sheets and bake at 220°C/425°F/Gas 7 for 30 minutes. Cool on a rack, making a small slit in each to allow any steam to escape. Pack in rigid containers to freeze.

To serve
Thaw at room temperature for 1 hour. Put éclairs on to a baking sheet. Heat at 180°C/350°F/Gas 4 for 5 minutes. Cool and fill with lightly sweetened whipped cream. Top with chocolate or coffee glacé icing.
High Quality Storage Life   1 month

Fruit and Nut Shortcake

60ml/4 tablespoons orange
   juice
125g/4 oz seedless raisins
125g/4 oz nut kernels
175g/6 oz plain flour
50g/2 oz caster sugar
125g/4 oz butter

FOR SERVING
caster sugar

Put the orange juice and raisins into a saucepan and bring slowly to the boil. Remove from the heat, mash lightly with a fork and stir in the coarsely chopped nuts. Sift the flour into a basin and stir in the sugar. Work in the butter until the mixture looks like breadcrumbs. Knead well and divide the dough into 2 pieces. Roll out into 2 rounds, one slightly larger than the other. Use the larger round to line a sandwich tin. Fill with the nut and raisin mixture and top with the second round of pastry. Seal the edges with a little water and mark with a fork. Prick all over with a fork. Bake at 180°C/350°F/Gas 4 for 45 minutes. Cool in the tin. Pack in polythene bags to freeze.

To serve
Thaw at room temperature for 3 hours and dust with sugar. Serve on its own or with sweetened whipped cream.
High Quality Storage Life   4 months

Nut Slices

350g/12 oz plain flour
125g/4 oz caster sugar
225g/8 oz butter

FILLING
150g/5 oz caster sugar
150ml/¼ pint single cream
150g/5 oz walnuts
15ml/1 tablespoon rum

FOR SERVING
caster sugar, icing sugar or
  water icing

Sift the flour into a basin and stir in the sugar. Work in the butter until the mixture looks like breadcrumbs. Knead well and divide the dough into 2 pieces. Roll out 1 piece carefully to line a square or rectangular tin.

Make the filling by heating the sugar until it melts and stirring in the cream, ground walnuts and rum. Leave to cool and then spread on to the pastry base.

Roll out the remaining pastry and cover the filling. Bake at 180°C/350°F/Gas 4 for 40 minutes. Cool and cut into pieces. Pack in a rigid container to freeze.

To serve
Thaw at room temperature for 3 hours. If liked, dust with caster sugar or icing sugar, or top with a little water icing.
High Quality Storage Life   2 months

Ring Doughnuts

225g/8 oz strong white
  flour
5ml/1 teaspoon salt
10ml/2 teaspoons sugar
15g/½ oz fresh yeast or
  8g/¼ oz dried yeast
150ml/¼ pint warm milk
15g/½ oz margarine

FOR SERVING
caster sugar

Sift the flour and salt and mix in the sugar. Blend the yeast in half the warm milk, or reconstitute the dried yeast as directed on the packet. Add the margarine to the remaining milk and cool until lukewarm. Mix the yeast liquid and milk and margarine into the flour, and knead well. Cover and leave in a warm place for 1 hour. Knead lightly and then roll out to 2.5cm/1 inch thick. Cut out 7.5cm/3 inch circles and then cut out centres with a 2.5cm/1 inch cutter. Roll out the cut-out centres and cut into extra rings as before. Put on baking trays and leave in a warm place for 20 minutes to rise. Fry 2 or 3 at a time in hot oil until golden-brown and drain very well on kitchen paper. Cool and pack in polythene bags to freeze.

To serve
Heat straight from the freezer at 200°C/400°F/Gas 6 for 8 minutes. Roll in caster sugar and serve at once.
High Quality Storage Life   1 month

Waffles

125g/4 oz self-raising flour
a pinch of salt
15ml/1 tablespoon caster
  sugar
1 egg
30ml/2 tablespoons melted
  butter
150ml/¼ pint milk

Mix the dry ingredients together in a bowl. Add the egg yolk, melted butter and milk, and beat well to a smooth batter. Whisk the egg white stiffly and fold into the batter.

Pour enough batter into a waffle iron to run over the surface. Do not overfill or the mixture will spill, and the waffle will not be able to rise properly. Close the iron over the mixture and leave to cook for 2–3 minutes, turning once. Waffles for freezing should not be over-brown. Leave to cool, and pack in foil or polythene to freeze.

To serve
Heat unthawed under a grill or in a hot oven. Serve with a choice of maple syrup (the traditional accompaniment), golden syrup or melted butter; or sandwich with layers of jam, whipped cream and redcurrant jelly, and dredge with icing sugar.
High Quality Storage Life 2 months

Walnut Brownies

175g/6 oz margarine
25g/1 oz cocoa
175g/6 oz caster sugar
2 eggs
50g/2 oz plain flour
50g/2 oz chopped walnuts

FOR SERVING
caster sugar or melted
  plain chocolate

Melt 50g/2 oz margarine and stir in the cocoa. Set aside to cool. Cream the remaining margarine with the sugar until soft and gradually beat in the eggs. Fold in the sifted flour and add the chopped walnuts and the cocoa mixture. Put into a greased and base-lined tin and bake at 180°C/350°F/Gas 4 for 45 minutes. Cool and turn out. Wrap in foil or polythene to freeze.

To serve
Thaw at room temperature for 3 hours and sprinkle with caster sugar, or cover with melted plain chocolate. Cut in squares to serve as a cake, or as a pudding with whipped cream or ice cream.
High Quality Storage Life 4 months

Coffee Kisses

175g/6 oz self-raising flour
a pinch of salt
75g/3 oz butter or
  margarine
50g/2 oz caster sugar
1 egg yolk
5ml/1 teaspoon coffee
  essence

ICING
50g/2 oz butter
75g/3 oz icing sugar
5ml/1 teaspoon coffee
  essence

Sift the flour and salt, rub in butter or margarine, and stir in the sugar. Mix to a stiff paste with the egg yolk and coffee essence. Shape into 24 small balls and put on a greased baking tray. Bake at 190°C/375°F/Gas 5 for 15 minutes. Cool on a rack.

Mix icing by gradually beating together the butter, icing sugar and coffee essence until soft and fluffy. Sandwich 'kisses' together in pairs with the icing. Pack in rigid container and freeze.

To serve
Thaw at room temperature for 1 hour, and dust with icing sugar.
High Quality Storage Life   2 months

Easter Biscuits

225g/8 oz plain flour
a pinch of salt
2.5ml/½ teaspoon mixed
  spice
75g/3 oz butter or
  margarine
75g/3 oz caster sugar
1 small beaten egg
75g/3 oz currants
milk

Sift the flour, salt and spice. Cream the fat and sugar until light and fluffy. Beat in a little egg and flour, then stir in the currants and remaining flour, adding a little more egg if necessary to make a firm paste. Roll out thinly, cut into large rounds and put on a greased tray. Prick with a fork, brush over with milk and sprinkle with caster sugar. Bake at 160°C/325°F/Gas 3 for 20 minutes. Cool on a rack. Pack in a rigid container and freeze.

To serve
Thaw at room temperature for 1 hour.
High Quality Storage Life   2 months

Marshmallow Biscuits

40g/1½ oz butter
225g/8 oz marshmallows
125g/4 oz plain chocolate
125g/4 oz rice krispies
    cereal

Put the butter into a bowl over hot water, or into the top of a double saucepan. Melt and stir in the marshmallows and broken chocolate. Stir until smooth and creamy. Put the cereal into a bowl and stir in the chocolate mixture. Put into a greased tin about 2.5cm/1 inch thick. Leave for about 1 hour until cold and firm. Cut into squares and pack in a rigid container to freeze.

To serve
Thaw at room temperature for 2 hours.
High Quality Storage Life   2 months

Hermits

125g/4 oz butter
175g/6 oz soft brown
    sugar
2 eggs
225g/8 oz plain flour
2.5ml/½ teaspoon salt
5ml/1 teaspoon baking
    powder
5ml/1 teaspoon ground
    cinnamon
1.25ml/¼ teaspoon
    ground cloves
1.25ml/¼ teaspoon
    ground nutmeg
275g/10 oz seedless raisins
75g/3 oz chopped nuts

Cream the butter and sugar, add eggs and beat until light and fluffy. Add all the other ingredients and mix well. Drop in spoonfuls on greased baking sheets. Bake at 180°C/350°F/Gas 4 for 10 minutes. Cool on a wire rack and pack in polythene bags to freeze.

To serve
Thaw at room temperature for 2 hours.
High Quality Storage Life   4 months

216

Waffles (page 214)

Currant Buns (page 211)
BELOW *Sugar Biscuits* (page 217)

Madeira Cake (page 204)

Brioches (page 218)

Sugar Biscuits

125g/4 oz butter
225g/8 oz caster sugar
1 egg
15ml/1 tablespoon milk
2.5ml/½ teaspoon vanilla
  essence
175g/6 oz plain flour
2.5ml/½ teaspoon baking
  powder
2.5ml/½ teaspoon salt
granulated or Demerara
  sugar

Cream the butter and work in the sugar, egg, milk and vanilla essence. Add the sifted flour, baking powder and salt and work into a firm dough. Roll out thinly and cut with a fluted cutter. Put on to greased baking sheets and bake at 190°C/375°F/Gas 5 for 10 minutes. Lift on to a wire rack, sprinkle with a little sugar and cool. Pack into rigid containers to freeze.

Variations
1 Use brown sugar instead of caster sugar; add 25g/1 oz chopped nuts if liked.

2 Add 25g/1 oz cocoa to basic biscuits; *or* flavour with 5ml/1 teaspoon ground ginger; *or* with 2.5ml/½ teaspoon lemon essence instead of vanilla.

To serve
Thaw at room temperature for 20 minutes.
High Quality Storage Life   2 months

Freezer Fudge

450g/1 lb granulated sugar
50g/2 oz butter
150ml/¼ pint evaporated
  milk
150ml/¼ pint water
2.5ml/½ teaspoon vanilla
  essence

Put the sugar, butter, evaporated milk and water into a thick saucepan and heat gently until the butter has melted and the sugar has dissolved. Bring to the boil and heat to 114°C/237°F*, stirring occasionally. Take off the heat, add the essence and beat until smooth and creamy. If liked, add some finely chopped nuts. Pour into a greased shallow tin and mark into squares when nearly set. When set, cut into squares and pack in small rigid containers to freeze.

* If you have no thermometer, test the fudge by dropping a little into a cup of cold water when it looks thick and creamy in the saucepan. If the drops in the water can be rolled together in the fingers to form a soft ball, the fudge has reached the correct temperature for beating.

To serve
Thaw for 2 hours at room temperature.
High Quality Storage Life   4 months

Banana Bread

50g/2 oz soft margarine
3 bananas
125g/4 oz caster sugar
1 egg
90ml/6 tablespoons milk
grated rind of 1 orange
50g/2 oz walnuts
275g/10 oz plain flour
5ml/1 teaspoon baking
    powder
1.25ml/¼ teaspoon
    bicarbonate of soda
2.5ml/½ teaspoon salt

Put the margarine into a bowl and add the bananas cut into small pieces. Mash thoroughly so that the bananas are completely broken up. Add all the remaining ingredients, chopping the walnuts finely. Beat well and put into a loaf tin, lined on the bottom with greaseproof paper. Bake at 180°C/350°F/Gas 4 for 1½ hours. Leave in the tin for 5 minutes, then turn out and cool on a wire rack. Pack in foil or polythene to freeze.

To serve
Thaw in wrappings at room temperature for 3 hours.
High Quality Storage Life   4 months

Brioches

225g/8 oz strong white
    flour
25g/1 oz fresh yeast or
    15g/½ oz dried yeast
30ml/2 tablespoons warm
    water
3 eggs
175g/6 oz melted butter
5ml/1 teaspoon salt
15g/½ oz sugar
milk

Put 50g/2 oz of the flour into a warm bowl. Blend the fresh yeast with the warm water, or reconstitute the dried yeast as directed on the packet. Mix with the flour until a ball of dough forms. Put the dough into a bowl of warm water and it will expand and form a sponge. Put the remaining flour into a bowl and beat in the eggs thoroughly. Add the butter, salt and sugar, and continue beating. Add the yeast sponge drained from the water and mix well. Cover the bowl with a damp cloth and leave in a warm place for 2 hours to rise.

Knead the dough well, cover the bowl and leave in a cool place overnight. Half fill castle pudding tins or fluted moulds with dough and top with smaller balls of dough. Leave in a warm place for 30 minutes. Brush with a little milk and bake at 230°C/450°F/Gas 8 for 15 minutes. Cool and pack in polythene bags to freeze.

To serve
Thaw at room temperature for 45 minutes to serve with butter.
High Quality Storage Life   6 weeks

Cheese Loaf

75g/3 oz soft margarine
225g/8 oz self-raising flour
5ml/1 teaspoon baking
  powder
5ml/1 teaspoon mustard
  powder
2.5ml/½ teaspoon salt
1.25ml/¼ teaspoon pepper
4 bacon rashers
1 egg
75g/3 oz Cheddar cheese
150ml/¼ pint milk

Put the margarine into a bowl with the flour, baking powder, mustard, salt and pepper. Chop the bacon and add to the bowl with the egg and cheese. Pour in the milk and beat together with a wooden spoon until well mixed. Put into a loaf tin, lined on the bottom with greaseproof paper. Bake at 190°C/375°F/Gas 5 for 45 minutes. Leave in the tin for 5 minutes, then turn out and cool on a wire rack. Pack in foil or polythene to freeze.

To serve
Thaw at room temperature for 3 hours and serve with salad or soup.
High Quality Storage Life   2 months

Croissants

150g/5 oz butter
150ml/¼ pint warm milk
5ml/1 teaspoon salt
22ml/1½ tablespoons
  sugar
25g/1 oz fresh yeast or
  15g/1 oz dried yeast
30ml/2 tablespoons warm
  water
350g/12 oz strong white
  flour
1 egg yolk beaten with a
  little milk

Put 25g/1 oz of the butter in bowl, pour on the warm milk and add the salt and sugar. Cool to lukewarm. Blend the fresh yeast with the warm water, or reconstitute the dried yeast as directed on the packet. Add to the butter mixture, then gradually add the flour to give a soft dough. Place the dough in a lightly greased polythene bag and leave for 2 hours. Knead dough, chill thoroughly, and roll into a rectangle. Spread the remaining butter lightly and evenly over the dough. Fold over dough to a rectangle and roll again. Chill, roll and fold twice more at intervals of 30 minutes. Roll dough out to 1cm/¼ inch thickness and cut into squares. Divide each square into 2 triangles, and roll each triangle up, starting at longest edge and rolling towards the point. Bend into crescent shapes, put on a floured baking sheet, brush with beaten egg and milk, and bake at 220°C/425°F/Gas 7 for 15 minutes. Cool. Pack into rigid containers to freeze.

To serve
Heat on baking sheet at 180°C/350°F/Gas 4 for 15 minutes.
High Quality Storage Life   6 weeks

Gingerbread Loaf

125g/4 oz self-raising flour
1.25ml/¼ teaspoon salt
5ml/1 teaspoon ground
  ginger
50g/2 oz soft brown sugar
25g/1 oz fine oatmeal
75g/3 oz lard
75g/3 oz golden syrup
5ml/1 teaspoon warm milk
1 egg

Sift the flour, salt and ginger into a bowl. Stir in the sugar and oatmeal. Put the lard and syrup into a saucepan and heat until the lard has melted. Add the milk. Mix into the dry ingredients and beat in the egg. Beat well and pour into a greased loaf tin. Bake at 160°C/325°F/Gas 3 for 1¼ hours. Leave on the tin for 5 minutes, then turn out and cool on a wire rack. Pack in foil or polythene to freeze.

To serve
Unwrap and thaw at room temperature for 3 hours. Serve in slices, with butter if liked.
High Quality Storage Life   1 month

Picnic Tea Loaf

450g/1 lb mixed dried fruit
225g/8 oz sugar
300ml/½ pint warm tea
1 egg
30ml/2 tablespoons
  marmalade
450g/1 lb self-raising flour

Soak fruit with sugar and tea overnight. Stir egg and marmalade into fruit and mix well with flour. Pour into 2 loaf tins and bake at 160°C/325°F/Gas 3 for 1¾ hours. Cool in tins for 15 minutes before turning out. Cool. Pack in polythene bags or foil and freeze.

To serve
Thaw at room temperature for 3 hours, then slice and butter.
High Quality Storage Life   4 months

Raisin and Walnut Bread

450g/1 lb plain flour
60ml/4 teaspoons baking
  powder
225g/8 oz sugar
a pinch of salt
150g/5 oz raisins
125g/4 oz chopped
  walnuts
2 eggs
300ml/½ pint milk
25g/1 oz melted fat

Mix together the flour, baking powder, sugar and salt, raisins and walnuts. In another bowl, beat lightly the eggs, milk and fat. Stir into the flour mixture and beat well. Pour into 2 greased and floured loaf tins and leave to stand for 30 minutes. Bake at 180°C/350°F/Gas 4 for 1 hour. Leave in the tins for 5 minutes, then turn out and cool on a wire rack. Wrap in foil or in polythene to freeze.

To serve
Thaw at room temperature for 3 hours and serve in slices, with or without butter.
High Quality Storage Life   2 months

Index

Page references to instructions on freezing individual ingredients or dishes are in **bold** type.